Level
3

AIM HIGH 에임하이

Active Curriculum for Successful Listening

LISTENING 리스닝

In-Depth Lab

We're
위아북스

AIM HIGH LISTENING • Level 3

지은이 In-Depth Lab ● **펴낸이** 전수용 · 조상현 ● **기획책임** 최상호 ● **펴낸곳** (주)위아북스 ● **등록번호** 제300-2007-164호
주소 서울특별시 종로구 인사동 194 홍익빌딩 4층 ● **전화** 02-725-9988 ● **팩스** 02-725-9863 ● **URL** www.wearebooks.co.kr
디자인 나인플럭스 ● **제작** 정민문화사 ● **출력** 우성 C&P

ISBN 978-89-93258-36-3 54740

Level
3

AIM HIGH 에임하이

Active Curriculum for Successful Listening

LISTENING 리스닝

In-Depth Lab

We're
위아북스

Prologue

청해 Listening Comprehension 란 내용을 듣고 이해하는 것을 말한다. 이는 단순히 영어를 얼마나 들을 수 있는가가 아니라 들은 내용을 얼마나 이해할 수 있는가를 뜻하는 것이다. 그러나 영어를 모국어로 하지 않는 사람들에게는 영어 자체가 잘 들리지 않는 경우가 많기 때문에 청해의 수준까지 도달하는 데에는 많은 어려움이 있다.

따라서 청취 실력을 향상시키기 위해서는 속도에 적응하는 것이 최우선 과제다. 빠른 속도로 지나가는 단어 하나하나를 들으려 하지 말고, 들리는 대로 덩어리째 듣고 이해할 수 있도록 많은 연습을 해야 한다. 듣는 것은 귀가 하지만 이해하는 것은 머리가 하는 일이므로, 영어의 빠른 속도에 적응하고 덩어리로 듣는 훈련과 동시에 들은 내용을 이해하는 훈련을 해야 한다.
이를 위해 본 교재에서는 청취한 내용을 머릿속에서 어떻게 정리해야 하는지 훈련시키는 Guided Listening 코너를 마련하였다. 이 코너에 포함된 Listening Notes를 이용해 들은 내용을 메모하면서 머릿속에 정리해라.

많은 교재들이 '들었는지 못 들었는지' 만 평가하는 문제들을 주로 다루고 있다. 하지만 실질적으로 청해 능력을 평가하기 위해 사용되는 문제의 형태는 좀 더 다양하다. 본 교재는 주제 및 목적 Main Idea/Purpose, 소재 Main Topic, 세부 정보 Detail, 기본 이해 Comprehension, 정보간의 관계 Relationship of Ideas, 세부 추론 Inference I, 전체 추론 Inference II, 화자의 입장 또는 목적 Stance/Function 등 8가지 문제 유형을 통해 청해 능력을 훈련하도록 구성하였다.

최근의 청취 시험들은 속도가 점점 빨라지고 있으며 내용도 길어지고 있다. 주제 또한 어려운 것들이 많아지는 추세이며 그 종류 또한 다양해지고 있다. 이러한 추세에 따라 본 교재에서는 다양한 주제의 대화 및 담화를 엄선하여 수록하였으며, 각종 시험의 청취 영역에 대비할 수 있도록 내용의 길이를 조절하였다.

청취 시험들이 변별력을 높이기 위해 시도 중인 것들 가운데 하나가 완벽한 이해를 요구하는 문제수를 늘리는 것이다. 세부 사항을 들었는지 묻는 문제보다는 내용을 완벽하게 이해했는가를 묻거나 전체를 이해했는지를 묻는 문제들이 늘고 있으며, 선택지들의 난이도 또한 높아지고 있다. 이에 대비하기 위해 본 교재에는 다양한 문제 유형은 물론 내용에 대한 완벽한 이해도를 묻는 문제들을 많이 수록하였다.

청취 훈련의 가장 기본은 '많이 듣는 것'이다. 따라서 듣고 문제를 푸는 데 그치지 않고 들은 내용을 충분히 반복 청취하여 완벽한 훈련이 될 수 있도록 각 section 뒤에 Dictation을 마련하였다. 본 교재의 모든 독자들이 영어의 속도에 완벽하게 적응하고 들리는 순서대로 덩어리째 이해할 수 있을 때까지 부단한 노력을 하기 바란다.

In-Depth Lab

Features

1 청취의 8가지 핵심 Question Types

토플, 텝스 등 각종 청취 테스트의 핵심적인 문제 유형을 면밀히 분석하여 세분하였다. 모든 유형의 청취 시험에 완벽하게 대비할 수 있도록 다양하고도 근본적인 listening skills들을 연습하도록 구성하였다.

▶ Main Idea/Purpose, Main Topic, Detail, Comprehension, Relationship of Ideas, Inference I, Inference II, Stance/Function

2 다양한 형태 및 주제에 대한 청취

여러 유형의 테스트에서 접할 수 있는 강의, 연구 결과, 방송, 연설 등의 다양한 담화문과, 일상생활에서 일어날 수 있는 실질적인 대화를 청취함으로써 다양한 청취 형태와 주제에 익숙해지도록 하였다.

3 소리로 익히는 청취 훈련

청취 훈련을 위해서는 눈으로 읽고 손으로 쓰는 훈련보다는 소리를 듣고 익히며 그 표현을 소리로 인식하고, 같은 뜻이나 비슷한 표현 또한 소리로 인식하는 것이 중요하다. 따라서 읽거나 쓰는 방식이 아닌, sound로 익히고 sound로 확인하는 다양한 청취 훈련을 하도록 구성하였다.

▶ 영어 설명을 듣고 해당 단어 쓰기
▶ 우리말 문장을 읽은 후 같은 뜻의 영어 문장을 듣고 찾기
▶ 세 덩어리의 영어를 듣고 하나의 완성된 영어 문장으로 만들기
▶ 영어 문장을 읽은 후 같은 뜻의 영어 문장을 듣고 찾기

4 Guided Listening 훈련

Listening Notes를 통해 청취하는 내용의 핵심 정보를 메모하는 것은 물론 내용의 전체적인 흐름을 머리로 이해하는 훈련이 되도록 하였다. 청취 지문의 전형적인 구조에 익숙해짐으로써 '예측 청취'를 가능케 하여 전반적인 청해 실력을 향상시킬 수 있다.

▶ Cause and Effect, Problem and Solution, Exemplifying, Classifying, Process or Sequence 등

Listening Skill Building **Question Types**

1 Main Idea/Purpose

전체적인 내용의 이해를 통해 직·간접적으로 드러난 대화의 목적 및 담화의 주제를 파악하는 능력

2 Main Topic

핵심어(key word) 및 대화와 담화에서 주로 이야기되고 있는 소재를 파악하는 능력

3 Detail

중요한 세부 정보에 대한 청취 능력

4 Comprehension

청취한 내용에 대한 이해 능력

5 Relationship of Ideas

언급된 정보들간의 관계 파악 능력

6 Inference I

세부적인 내용에 근거한 추론 능력

7 Inference II

전체 또는 다양한 정보에 근거한 추론 능력

8 Stance/Function

화자의 입장 및 목적 파악 능력

Topics

LEVEL

2

대화의 주제   총 56

의사전달	● ●	2
여행	● ● ● ● ● ●	6
계획/약속	● ● ● ● ● ● ● ●	8
교통	● ● ● ● ●	5
회사와 업무	● ● ● ● ● ●	6
쇼핑/상점/수리점	● ● ● ● ● ●	6
여가/취미생활	● ● ● ● ●	5
식사/식당	● ●	2
건강/병원/약국	● ● ● ●	4
학교	● ● ● ● ●	5
전화 통화	● ● ●	3
부동산 및 가정생활	● ● ● ●	4

담화의 주제   총 56

강의 및 조사 결과	● ● ● ● ● ● ● ● ● ● ● ● ● ● ● ● ● ● ● ●	20
연설	● ● ●	3
보도/방송	● ● ● ● ● ● ● ● ● ● ● ●	12
전화 메시지	●	1
안내 방송 및 공지 사항	● ● ● ● ● ●	6
광고	● ● ● ● ●	5
의견 제시 및 주장	● ● ● ● ●	5
기타	● ● ● ●	4

Topics

LEVEL 4

대화의 주제		총 48
의사전달	● ● ● ● ● ●	6
여행	● ● ● ●	4
계획/약속	● ● ● ●	4
교통	● ●	2
회사와 업무	● ● ● ●	4
쇼핑/상점/수리점	●	1
여가/취미생활	● ● ● ● ●	5
감정 표현	● ●	2
식사/식당	●	1
건강/병원/약국	● ● ● ● ●	5
인사/소개/칭찬/축하/감사	● ●	2
학교	● ● ● ● ●	5
전화 통화	●	1
부동산 및 가정생활	● ● ● ● ●	5
은행과 우체국	●	1

담화의 주제		총 64
강의 및 조사 결과	● ●	28
연설	● ● ● ● ● ● ●	7
보도/방송	● ● ● ● ● ● ● ● ● ● ● ● ● ● ●	15
전화 메시지	●	1
안내 방송 및 공지 사항	● ● ● ● ●	5
광고	● ●	2
의견 제시 및 주장	●	1
교육/소개 및 조언	● ● ● ● ●	5

How To Use This Book

VOCABULARY PREVIEW

몰라서 안 들릴 수 있는 어휘와 표현을 선행 학습함으로써 학습 효과를 높인다.

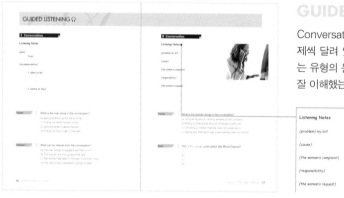

GUIDED LISTENING

Conversation 2개, Monologue 2개로 구성되었으며, 각 2문제씩 달려 있다. 하나의 Script를 들은 뒤 그 Chapter에 해당하는 유형의 문제 1과 추가적인 문제 2를 풀어 봄으로써 들은 것을 잘 이해했는지 확인한다. 선택지도 모두 영문으로 되어 있다.

Listening Notes

주어진 clues를 참고하여 들으면서 내용을 메모해 머릿속에 정리할 수 있도록 한다.

DICTATION GUIDED LISTENING

GUIDED LISTENING에 대한 받아쓰기 코너다. 듣기 어려운 단어, 연어, 중요한 표현 등이 빈칸으로 제시되어 들은 것을 재확인하며 학습할 수 있다. 본문의 문제를 그대로 보여 주기 때문에 2차 학습까지 용이하며 중요한 어휘도 학습할 수 있다.

PRACTICAL LISTENING

Chapter마다 10문제씩으로 구성되어 있다. 다양한 문제 유형을 풀어 볼 수 있으며, 그 Chapter에 해당하는 문제에는 유형이 제시되어 있다.

DICTATION PRACTICAL LISTENING

PRACTICAL LISTENING 10문제에 대한 받아쓰기 코너다. 듣기 어려운 단어, 연어, 중요한 표현 등이 빈칸으로 제시되어 들은 것을 다시 한 번 확인하며 학습할 수 있다. 본문의 문제를 그대로 보여 주기 때문에 2차 학습까지 용이하며 중요한 어휘도 학습할 수 있다. 선택지의 내용도 녹음하여 들려 줌으로써 자칫 놓치기 쉬운 부분까지 추가 학습이 가능하다.

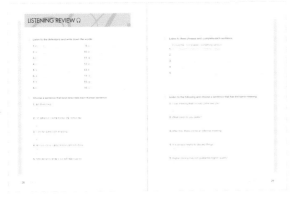

LISTENING REVIEW

소리로 익히는 훈련을 위한 테스트다. 4가지 방식의 훈련법으로 청취 연습을 할 수 있다.

A 영어 설명을 듣고 그에 해당하는 영단어를 써 보는 훈련이다.

B 영어 문장 2개를 들은 후 주어진 우리말과 같은 뜻의 문장을 찾는 훈련이다.

C 세 덩어리의 chunk를 듣고 하나의 완전한 문장이 되도록 배열한다.

D 영어 문장 2개를 들은 후 주어진 영어 문장과 같은 의미가 되는 문장을 찾는 훈련이다.

Contents

Prologue
Features
Listening Skill Building Question Types
Topics _ LEVEL 1~4
How To Use This Book

AIM HIGH

Active Curriculum for Successful Listening

LISTENING

CHAPTER 01

MAIN IDEA/ PURPOSE

VOCABULARY PREVIEW 🎧

Write down the meanings of the words.

01	fuel-efficient	13	custom-made	
02	soaring	14	cut down on	
03	commute	15	utility bill	
04	relocate	16	efficiency	
05	facilitate	17	coronary	
06	evaporate	18	hypertension	
07	liberation	19	charge	
08	notion	20	appliance	
09	prevalent	21	vegetation	
10	board of directors	22	carbon dioxide	
11	appreciably	23	shareholder	
12	hypnotic	24	undergo	

GUIDED LISTENING 🎧

1 Conversation

Listening Notes

New car

    Reason

Concern

    The man's plan

    The woman's sister

Purpose

1   What are the man and the woman doing in the conversation?

(a) comparing how energy efficient their cars are

(b) buying a car that uses less amount of gas

(c) talking about ways to overcome high gas price

(d) deciding the most energy efficient way to commute

Comprehension

2   Which is correct according to the conversation?

(a) A new car is expensive.

(b) The man will start using his bike.

(c) The woman's car is more fuel-efficient.

(d) People will replace their old cars.

2 Conversation

Listening Notes

Hotel

    (Reservation)

    (Stay)

    (Purpose of visiting)

    (Service) Would you like

Purpose

1   What is the man doing in the conversation?

    (a) looking for a good real estate agent

    (b) getting a room at a hotel

    (c) confirming a reservation for his grandma

    (d) finding a new apartment for his grandma

Inference II

2   What can be inferred from the conversation?

    (a)

    (b)

    (c)

    (d)

3 Monologue

Listening Notes

Effects of sun

    On human

    On food

    Water

Main Idea

1. What is the main idea of the lecture?

   (a) The water cycle depends on sunlight.

   (b) The sun is needed for farming

   (c) The sun is responsible for the formation of oceans.

   (d) The sun has major influence upon Earth.

Relationship of Ideas

2. What are the two things about the sun that the lecturer focuses on?

   (a) the role and the influences of sunlight

   (b) the kinds and strength of sunlight

   (c) the temperature and the rays of sunlight

   (d) the length and brightness of sunlight

4 Monologue

Listening Notes

(Widespread notion vs the fact)

(UNICEF report)

     Estimates

     It is sad to learn that

     Data from the U.K.

Due to

     The majority of these cases

Main Idea   1   What is the main point of the report?

    (a) Domestic violence is prevalent worldwide.

    (b) There is a lack of awareness among educated women.

    (c) UNICEF is planning to fight domestic violence.

    (d) The United Kingdom has the highest rate of domestic violence.

Comprehension   2   Which is correct according to the report?

    (a)

    (b)

    (c)

    (d)

1 Conversation

1 What are the man and the woman doing in the conversation?
 (a) comparing how energy efficient their cars are
 (b) buying a car that uses less amount of gas
 (c) talking about ways to overcome high gas price
 (d) deciding the most energy efficient way to commute

2 Which is correct according to the conversation?
 (a) A new car is expensive.
 (b) The man will start using his bike.
 (c) The woman's car is more fuel-efficient.
 (d) People will replace their old cars.

M You got a new car? It _____!

W Yeah, we badly needed a new one. Our old car needed so much gas; we _____ it.

M I can understand. My car is also old now. I should replace it _____ _____.

W Well... this car gets over 40 miles to the gallon. I'm glad we bought it. The soaring gas prices are hurting everyone.

M Actually, I'm _____, so that I can at least _____. I'm sure it would save me a lot of money!

W I agree. My sister has already started biking to work.

M That's a pretty good idea. I must suggest that to my brother. He doesn't live far from work.

---

hardly 거의 ~아닌 **(can) afford to** ~할 여유(형편)가 있다 **replace** 교체하다, 대체하다 **fuel-efficient** 연료 효율이 좋은 **to the gallon** 갤런당, 1갤런으로 **soaring** 치솟고 있는 **commute** 출퇴근하다, 통근하다 **at least** 조금이라도 **far from** ~에서 아주 먼

---

2 Conversation

1 What is the man doing in the conversation?
 (a) looking for a good real estate agent
 (b) getting a room at a hotel
 (c) confirming a reservation for his grandma
 (d) finding a new apartment for his grandma

2 What can be inferred from the conversation?
 (a) The man will leave the hotel soon.
 (b) The man will meet a real estate agent.
 (c) The woman can not confirm his reservation.
 (d) The woman has lived in this area for a long time.

W Good evening, sir. How may I help you?

M I have _____ for a single room. Could you please check?

W Under what name, sir?

M Steve Johnson. I reserved it a week ago.

W Oh yes, here it is. _____ will you be staying here, sir?

M Maybe a week or so. Actually, my grandma wants to move to another apartment and _____.

W Okay. Would you like to meet _____? I can arrange that for you.

M Well, I _____ that. Thank you.

---

reservation 예약 **real estate** 부동산 **agent** 대리인, 대리점 **arrange** 조정하다, 마련하다

---

3 Monologue

1   What is the main idea of the lecture?
(a) The water cycle depends on sunlight.
(b) The sun is needed for farming.
(c) The sun is responsible for the formation of oceans.
(d) The sun has major influence upon Earth.

2   What are the two things about the sun that the lecturer focuses on?
(a) the role and the influences of sunlight
(b) the kinds and strength of sunlight
(c) the temperature and the rays of sunlight
(d) the length and brightness of sunlight

M   The sun has a major role in regulating all forms of life found on Earth. Everything on Earth, directly or indirectly, _____ _____. Human activities such as walking, eating and working depend upon sunlight and are adjusted accordingly. Sunlight is _____. The sun directly affects the growth of vegetation by facilitating _____ from water and carbon dioxide. In fact, the very presence of water on Earth is largely due to the sun. _____, water from sources like lakes, rivers and oceans _____ to form clouds. These clouds cause rain, thus transporting the water back to Earth — a part of the Earth's "water cycle."

regulate 조절하다, 조정하다   directly or indirectly 직접적으로든 간접적으로든   adjust 조정하다, 순응하다   accordingly 그에 따라서   crop 작물   vegetation 식물, 초목   facilitate 촉진하다, 손쉽게 하다   sugar 당(糖)   carbon dioxide 이산화탄소   presence 존재   be due to ~ 때문이다   evaporate 증발하다   formation 형성

4 Monologue

1   What is the main point of the report?
(a) Domestic violence is prevalent worldwide.
(b) There is a lack of awareness among educated women.
(c) UNICEF is planning to fight domestic violence.
(d) The United Kingdom has the highest rate of domestic violence.

2   Which is correct according to the report?
(a) Women are the major victims of domestic violence.
(b) Women in developing countries experience more violence.
(c) Many cases of domestic violence are reported nowadays.
(d) 25% of women in the U.K. experience violence at home.

W   Today is the era of women's liberation. Although it is a widespread notion, it may be a totally false claim. Women all over the world still _____, reports UNICEF, which estimates that about 35% of women across the world experience some form of violence at home. It is sad to learn that even educated women fall into this group and, almost always, _____ _____. _____ _____ indicates that one out of every four women undergoes domestic violence during her lifetime. Due to social pressure and _____, the majority of these cases _____.

era 시대   liberation 해방, 평등   widespread 널리 보급되어 있는, 만연한   notion 개념   domestic 가정의   estimate 어림잡다, 추정하다   offender 가해자, 위반자   indicate 가리키다, 시사하다   undergo 경험하다, 견디다   unnoticed 주목되지 않는, 알아채지 않는   prevalent 널리 행해지는, 보급된

PRACTICAL LISTENING 🎧

1   Which is correct about the woman according to the conversation?

   (a) She is moving to New Hampshire this Friday.

   (b) She wants to attend another one of Sean's shows.

   (c) She will not be in the city on Saturday.

   (d) She is going away to buy something for Sean.

Main Idea

2   What is the speaker's main point in the talk?

   (a) A current plan has been thoroughly assessed.

   (b) Proposals for a new company site are not viable.

   (c) A company's construction project will succeed.

   (d) A company procedures are harming major cities.

3   Which is correct about Arab music in the talk?

   (a) It inspired music in Indonesia.

   (b) It relies heavily on external influences.

   (c) It has a rich and varied tradition.

   (d) It was brought from Southeast Asia.

4   What should a caller do if interested in the apartment?

   (a) to leave a number they can call during the day

   (b) to phone either Wendy or Todd directly

   (c) to visit at the address given in the message

   (d) to leave a message or call back later

Purpose

5   Why does the man call the woman in the conversation?

   (a) to complain about the food and the service

   (b) to complain about the bad taste of the food

   (c) to correct the order

   (d) to demand to see a restaurant's chef

6 Which is correct according to the announcement?

(a) Ties are optional for men.

(b) Business casual wear is permitted on Fridays.

(c) Women can choose between skirts and jeans.

(d) Employees must be dressed in company uniforms.

Purpose

7 Why does the woman want to see the man?

(a) to ask what the man has been doing

(b) to inquire about some furniture she likes

(c) to find out if the bicycle is fixed

(d) to ask about the price of a piece of furniture

8 What do the man and woman decide to do?

(a) to set up a more balanced schedule

(b) to cut back on spending

(c) to improve the efficiency of the heater

(d) to reduce the hours of painting classes

Main Idea

9 What is the speaker's main point in the talk?

(a) Coffee may be even healthier than people thought.

(b) Coffee must be reevaluated as a health drink.

(c) Coffee should not be linked to heart disease.

(d) Coffee has been wrongly considered as a health risk.

10 Which is correct according to the conversation?

(a)

(b)

(c)

(d)

1 Conversation

Which is correct about the woman according to the conversation?

(a) She is moving to New Hampshire this Friday.

(b) She wants to attend another one of Sean's shows.

(c) She will not be in the city on Saturday.

(d) She is going away to buy something for Sean.

W I won't be able to attend Sean's show this Sunday morning.

M Do you have any other plans that day?

W Well, _____ from Friday for a business meeting and it _____.
I'm not sure if I can come back by Sunday.

M Where's your meeting?

W In New Hampshire. It's _____.

M Oh, that's too far from here. I don't think you'll _____
_____. _____
him that.

W I hope he doesn't get disappointed.

M I'm sure he'll understand if you bring something for him when you get back.

W That's something I didn't think of. Thanks and I will definitely get something nice for him.

attend ~에 참석하다, 출석하다 **out of town** 도시를 떠나 **business meeting** 업무상 회의 **if** ~인지 아닌지 **away** 떨어져서, 떠나서 **far from** ~에서 멀리 **get back** 돌아오다 **definitely** 틀림없이

2 Monologue

What is the speaker's main point in the talk?

(a) A current plan has been thoroughly assessed.

(b) Proposals for a new company site are not viable.

(c) A company's construction project will succeed.

(d) A company's procedures are harming major cities.

M I'm sorry to inform you, the board of directors, that we have run into problems _____ our company headquarters from Boston to Philadelphia. _____
_____ in the housing and construction market, we anticipated low costs to build in Philadelphia. However, actual construction costs in that city have not only _____
_____, but actually increased over the last few months. Some board members have recommended moving to a new site in Boulder, Colorado. However, _____
_____ even faster than in Philadelphia and Boulder is far from where we do most of our business. My suggestion is that we give up the current plan for now and relocate when construction costs _____ on the East Coast.

board of directors 이사회 **relocation** 재배치, 이전 **headquarter** 본사, 본부 **nationwide** 전국적인 **downturn** (경기 등의) 침체, 하강 **current** 현재의 **appreciably** 분명히, 상당히 **East Coast** (미국의) 동해안, 대서양 연안 **viable** 실행가능한

3 Monologue

Which is correct about Arabian music in the talk?

(a) It inspired music in Indonesia.
(b) It relies heavily on external influences.
(c) It has a rich and varied tradition.
(d) It was brought from Southeast Asia.

W   Last week we discussed Indonesian music. In this week's class, I'll be talking about Arabian music. Traditional Arabian music _____ _____ are very unlike those found in the West. Westerners first listening to Arabian music often describe it as "hypnotic" for its lilting tones that almost _____ _____. Arabian music is what the famous "belly dancers" move to _____. Are you wondering why I've moved from Indonesia _____ _____? The reason is that Arabian musical traditions did impact Indonesia and Southeast Asia significantly. As Arabian traders and religious teachers came to Indonesia _____ _____, they brought both Islam and Arabian music.

tone 음색, 색조   hypnotic 최면의, 최면에 걸린   lilting (노래·목소리가) 경쾌한   sway (전후좌우로) 뒤흔들다. 요동시키다   tradition (전통) 양식, 형태

4 Monologue

What should a caller do if interested in the apartment?

(a) to leave a number they can call during the day
(b) to phone either Wendy or Todd directly
(c) to visit at the address given in the message
(d) to leave a message or call back later

W   Hello! This is 555-0783. Wendy and Todd _____ _____, or can't come to the phone. If you are calling about _____, please leave your name and number and we will call you back as soon as we can. _____ that we can use to contact you during the day. If you need _____, we are at 457 Andrews Avenue #913 in Groton City, across from the Templeton Movie Theater. If you want to know about the sports car for sale, it's been sold. If you _____, please leave a message. Thanks, and have a nice day.

for rent 임대용의, 세놓는   contact 연락(을 취함)   for sale 팔려고 내놓은

5 Conversation

Why does the man call the woman in the conversation?
(a) to complain about the food and the service
(b) to complain about the bad taste of the food
(c) to correct the order
(d) to demand to see a restaurant's chef

M   Excuse me, waitress.

W   Yes sir. Do you need anything?

M   I asked for _____, but this one is just soft-boiled.

W   Oh, I'm very sorry. I'll get you another one.

M   Okay, but please _____.

W   Sure, sir. This time _____. Is there anything else I can get you, sir?

M   Just get me a glass of water.

W   _____ and the hard-boiled egg.

M   Thank you, and _____.

ask for ~을 요구하다 hard-boiled egg 완숙으로 삶은 계란 soft-boiled 반숙한 chef 주방장, 요리사 mistake 잘못, 착오 make ~을 (…의 상태로)하다
quick 속히, 빨리(=quickly) complain about ~에 대해 불평(항의)하다 taste 맛 correct 고치다, 정정하다 demand to ~해달라고 요구하다

6 Monologue

Which is correct according to the announcement?
(a) Ties are optional for men.
(b) Business casual wear is permitted on Fridays.
(c) Women can choose between skirts and jeans.
(d) Employees must be dressed in company uniforms.

M   Before we break for lunch, I'd like to speak about the dress code at this employee orientation. Over the last few years, _____ in Canada _____. Now, while we do not _____, at Altius Inc. all employees _____. Men are asked to wear suits and ties, and women can choose between skirts or pantsuits. Every Friday, though, we _____.
However, jeans, T-shirts and torn or patched clothing are not allowed at any time. We expect you to look like professionals under all circumstances. You must remember that your image and appearance reflects the company to customers, suppliers and shareholders.

dress code 복장 규정 quiet a bit 상당히, 꽤 impose 강요하다 formally 공식적으로, 격식을 갖춰 pantsuit (여성용) 슬랙스와 재킷이 한 벌이 된 슈트
patched (헝겊 조각 등을) 덧댄 reflect 반영하다, 반사하다 supplier 공급업체 shareholder 주주

7 Conversation

Why does the woman want to see the man?
(a) to ask what the man has been doing
(b) to inquire about some furniture she likes
(c) to find out if the bicycle is fixed
(d) to ask about the price of a piece of furniture

M You wanted to see me?
W Yeah. _____?
M I've been in the garage looking for _____.
W So, are you done fixing it?
M I think so. Why?
W Nothing serious. I saw the chairs in the living room. I thought they are really nice and wanted to ask where you bought them.
M You know the shop Furniture Mart? The one on Pico Boulevard? _____.
W Did you have them custom-made?
M No, they _____ to look at the interior of our house, so that I'd get chairs _____.
W That's a really good service that they provided. Are they expensive?
M Not at all. They were very reasonable.
W Sounds good. I may also try getting my dining table from them.

garage 창고 boulevard 대로, 큰 길 custom-made 주문 제작의, 맞춤의 representative 판매 대리인, 세일즈맨 interior 내부, 실내도
provide 주다, 제공하다 reasonable 합리적인, 적당한, (가격이) 비싸지 않은 inquire about ~에 대해 문의하다 a piece of furniture 가구 한 점

8 Conversation

What do the man and woman decide to do?
(a) to set up a more balanced schedule
(b) to cut back on spending
(c) to improve the efficiency of the heater
(d) to reduce the hours of painting classes

W Honey, _____ this month.
M Are you sure? How did that happen?
W We paid extra this month for Susan's painting classes.
M Oh, that's right. We need to _____ _____.
W Yeah. Why don't we start _____?
M Good idea. So, let's not use the heater at night. We can use bigger blankets instead.
W We could also try to _____ to save money on telephone bills.
M Right. And we shouldn't eat out this month.
W Oh, should we _____ at the restaurant?
M Mmm, I really wanted to try that restaurant's food. Well, there is always next time.

go over (경비 등이 예산을) 초과하다 budget 예산, 경비, 생활비 extra 여분으로, 가외로, 부가적으로 cut down on ~의 소비를 줄이다, 절약하다
spending 소비, 지출 utility bill 공과금 (고지서) blanket 담요, 모포 make a call 전화를 걸다 set up ~을 세우다, 설치하다 efficiency 효율성

9 Monologue

What is the speaker's main point in the talk?
(a) Coffee may be even healthier than people thought.
(b) Coffee must be reevaluated as a health drink.
(c) Coffee should not be linked to heart disease.
(d) Coffee has been wrongly considered as a health risk.

W Let me now speak about the health issues related to coffee. _____ — ground coffee beans in hot water — coffee in recent years has become a "hot topic" of debate in the medical field. You may have heard that coffee is listed among risk factors for coronary heart disease, which include hypertension and high cholesterol levels. However, there is no direct link between drinking coffee and _____ _____. Clearly, _____ _____. In fact, drinking coffee has some positive health benefits. _____ that it _____ gall stones and kidney stones.

---

ground 빻은, 가루의 coronary 심장의 hypertension 고혈압 establish (사실 등을) 입증하다, 확증하다 | gall stone 담석 kidney stone 신장 결석

10 Conversation

Which is correct according to the conversation?
(a) The woman will exchange her microwave.
(b) The service center charges for pick up service.
(c) The man will take the woman to the service center.
(d) The woman needs an appliance repaired.

W My microwave seems to be broken. Do you know somebody who _____?
M You could try Michael's Service Center just down the street.
W Are they good?
M Well, I got my DVD player repaired by them. They did a good job and _____.
W Okay, _____?
M I'm not sure. You can call them and find out.
W How do I get the number?
M You know what? It is not that far and I might be available to take your microwave to the service center this afternoon.
W Will you do that for me? It is a little heavy for me to carry myself.
M _____.
W Can I cook something for you when you get back?
M _____.

---

microwave 전자레인지 broken 고장 난, 부러진 | repair 수리하다, 고치다 get+목+p.p. ~가…하게 하다, 시키다 fair 공평한, 정당한 exchange 교환하다, 교체하다 charge 비용을 청구하다 appliance 전기기구(제품)

A Listen to the definitions and write down the words.

1. soaring _____   9. d _____

2. c _____   10. i _____

3. f _____   11. s _____

4. e _____   12. i _____

5. n _____   13. e _____

6. p _____   14. u _____

7. d _____   15. a _____

8. a _____   16. h _____

B Choose a sentence that best describes each Korean sentence.

1. 돌아오면 뭐 좀 요리해 줄까?

(a) _____

(b) _____

2. 최근에 커피는 최대 논쟁 거리였습니다.

(a) _____

(b) _____

3. 분명히 말해 커피는 생각하는 것만큼 그렇게 나쁘지 않습니다.

(a) _____

(b) _____

4. 비용을 아끼기 위해서 전화를 덜 사용할 수 있어요.

(a) _____

(b) _____

5. 이번 달 예산을 초과했어요.

(a) _____

(b) _____

C   **Listen to three phrases and complete each sentence.**

in the garage / looking for some tools/ I've been

1. ➡ I've been in the garage looking for some tools. _____

2. _____

3. _____

4. _____

5. _____

D   **Listen to the following and choose a sentence that has the same meaning.**

1. The actual construction costs have failed to decrease.

    (a) _____

    (b) _____

2. I'll be out of town from Friday for a business meeting.

    (a) _____

    (b) _____

3. I don't think you'll get back in time for the show.

    (a) _____

    (b) _____

4. If you want to know about the sports car for sale, it's been sold.

    (a) _____

    (b) _____

5. All employees are expected to be dressed formally.

    (a) _____

    (b) _____

VOCABULARY PREVIEW 🎧

Write down the meanings of the words.

01	scorching	13	constitute
02	rash *n.*	14	blend *n.*
03	tolerate	15	consequence
04	utilization	16	imperative
05	candidate	17	audit *n.*
06	adhere to	18	composite
07	congress	19	skeleton
08	courtesy	20	evolve
09	offensive	21	deterioration
10	senator	22	confine
11	eligible	23	thriving
12	descent	24	penalize

GUIDED LISTENING 🎧

1 Conversation

Listening Notes

(Weather)

(What to do)

    (The woman)

        1.

        2. Sometimes

    (The man's opinion)

    (The man)

    (The woman's opinion)

Main Topic

1 What is this conversation about?

(a) preparing for unusual weather

(b) going swimming

(c) enjoying summer vacation

(d) avoiding summer heat

Detail

2 What is the woman's concern about the man staying home?

(a) the high energy cost

(b) skin rashes

(c) catching a cold

(d) drinking too much water

2 Conversation

Listening Notes

(Antonio)

> (The man's opinion)

> (The woman's opinion)

(Amanda)

> (The man's opinion)

> (The woman's opinion)

Main Topic

1 What is this conversation about?

(a) where to visit next time

(b) what to consider when electing

(c) which sporting event to attend

(d) who to support in the election

Stance

2 What can be inferred about the two speakers?

(a)

(b)

(c)

(d)

3 Monologue

Listening Notes

(Announcement)

    The launch of

    All are invited to

    (Cost)

(Basic principles)

    (Violating)

Main Topic

1 What is the announcement mainly about?

    (a) how to access the web board for a debate

    (b) who is eligible to use the web board

    (c) the basic courtesy rules for the web board

    (d) fees for using the web board

Detail

2 What would happen to a posting that is offensive?

    (a) The person who posted it will be fined.

    (b) The person will be kicked out of the board.

    (c) The posting will be removed without notice.

    (d) The posting will be reported to the police.

4 Monologue

Listening Notes

The population of the U.S.

(1st group)

(2nd group)

(3rd group)

Main Topic

1 What is the subject of the lecture?

(a) the history of blended American culture

(b) the diverse ethnic composition of the U.S. population

(c) immigration policies in the United States

(d) the proportion of Anglo-Scottish population in the American population

Comprehension

2 Which is correct according to the lecture?

(a)

(b)

(c)

(d)

1 Conversation

1 What is this conversation about?
(a) preparing for unusual weather
(b) going swimming
(c) enjoying summer vacation
(d) avoiding summer heat

2 What is the woman's concern about the man staying home?
(a) the high energy cost
(b) skin rashes
(c) catching a cold
(d) drinking too much water

M I've never seen such weather before!

W I know. I start sweating the moment I go out!

M Me too! I'd prefer to stay home rather than going out _____ _____. What do you do to keep cool?

W Well, I drink lots of juice to keep myself cool. Sometimes I also go swimming.

M _____; I get skin rashes from its chemicals. So generally, I sit at home _____.

W Doesn't _____ get so high that way?

M It does! _____. I can't tolerate hot weather.

W Let's hope the rest of the summer isn't too hot. I'm really looking forward to the cool fall and winter.

sweat 땀을 흘리다 the moment ~하자마자, 바로 그때 prefer to ~하는 것을 더 좋아하다 scorching 매우 뜨거운, 찌는 듯한 suit 적합하다 rash 발진, 뾰루지 with the air conditioner on 에어컨을 틀어 놓고 tolerate 견디다, 참다 look forward to ~을 학수고대하다

2 Conversation

1 What is this conversation about?
(a) where to visit next time
(b) what to consider when electing
(c) which sporting event to attend
(d) who to support in the election

2 What can be inferred about the two speakers?
(a) They both support the same candidate.
(b) They don't agree with each other.
(c) They don't like either of the candidates.
(d) They think it is not easy to pick one.

W Do you support Antonio?

M Yes. He's an intelligent politician — and has done so many things for society.

W You're correct, but that may not be enough to _____. He may not be able to handle the huge responsibility of leading a nation.

M I disagree. _____ and I'm sure he'll do well at a higher level as well. Well, who's your favorite?

W Amanda. She's _____ and is _____ in Congress.

M Well, she's been a good senator, but I feel she _____ _____.

W That's not true. When she speaks, everyone listens. Whatever she says, she does. I am sure she'll make a good leader.

M Let's see who gets elected: your candidate or mine!

support 지지하다, 후원하다 intelligent 지성이 있는, 지적인 prove 증명하다 worth 가치 mayor 시장 well-experienced 노련한, 경험이 많은 congress 의회, 국회 senator 상원의원 lack 결핍되다, 부족하다 conviction 확신 whatever ~하는 것은 무엇이든 candidate 후보자

3 Monologue

1 What is the announcement mainly about?
(a) how to access the web board for a debate
(b) who is eligible to use the web board
(c) the basic courtesy rules for the web board
(d) fees for using the web board

2 What would happen to a posting that is offensive?
(a) The person who posted it will be fined.
(b) The person will be kicked out of the board.
(c) The posting will be removed without notice.
(d) The posting will be reported to the police.

W We are delighted to announce the launch of a web board for our consumers. _____ , announce events, share important tips or discuss hot issues online. The services provided to visitors are free of charge. However, we request users to adhere to basic principles for making maximum utilization of the service. The web board _____ _____ and free expression of ideas; the participants are requested _____ to other visitors. If we _____ _____ of the board, we may immediately delete it _____ _____ . Postings should not be offensive, keeping in mind the large and diverse population we cater to.

launch 시작, 착수 board 게시판 consumer 소비자 post 게시하다, 알리다 share 공유하다 free of charge 무료인 adhere to ~을 지키다, 고수하다
principle 원칙, 원리 utilization 이용, 활용 debate 토론 participant 참여자, 참가자 violate 어기다, 침해하다 permission 허가, 허락
offensive 공격적인, 무례한 cater to ~의 요구에 응하다 access 접근하다, 들어오다 eligible 적격의, 자격이 있는 courtesy 예의

4 Monologue

1 What is the subject of the lecture?
(a) the history of blended American culture
(b) the diverse ethnic composition of the U.S. population
(c) immigration policies in the United States
(d) the proportion of the Anglo-Scottish population in the American population

2 Which is correct according to the lecture?
(a) The largest racial groups are German and French.
(b) White American is the largest racial group.
(c) Latin American population is the largest minority group.
(d) A majority of non-Native Americans are Europeans.

M The population of the United States is racially mixed in composition. There are _____ _____ and cultures. In today's class, we will look into the details of diversity in the American population and ____ _____ . Except for Native Americans, most of the American population _____ _____ . A majority of the non-Native Americans are Anglo-Scottish, Irish, French or Dutch. Some large groups also have their origins in Italy, Germany and Canada. There are also people from Africa, Eastern Europe, Asia, and Latin America _____ _____ . On the whole, the American population is diverse and has a blend of many ethnic groups.

racially 인종적으로 composition 구성 ethnic 인종의, 민족의 descent 혈통, 출신 detail 세부사항 diversity 다양성 constitute 구성하다
except for ~을 제외하면 emigrate 이주하다 majority 대부분, 대다수 Anglo-Scottish 앵글로 스코틀랜드 사람(의) Irish 아일랜드 사람(의)
Dutch 네덜란드 사람(의) on the whole 전체로 보아서, 대체로 proportion 비율 blend 혼합

PRACTICAL LISTENING 🎧

Main Topic **1** What is the news report mainly about?

  (a) complaints regarding safety in cargo trucks
  (b) the growing number of trucks that are not roadworthy
  (c) government action to make cargo trucks safe
  (d) measures taken by cargo companies to improve services

2 What will the man probably do in the afternoon?

  (a) go to a children's bookstore
  (b) take the woman shopping
  (c) work at the office
  (d) give his nephew a birthday party

3 Which is correct according to the lecture?

  (a) Conduction paths are engineered without composite fibers.
  (b) Aircraft skins are designed to conduct electricity.
  (c) Aircraft are frequently harmed by lightning strikes.
  (d) Lightning cannot damage fast-flying aircraft.

Main Topic **4** What is the topic of the conversation?

  (a) a band the man is listening to
  (b) an Internet site where music can be bought
  (c) how to find good music to listen to
  (d) recent trends in popular music

5 What can be implied from the lecture?

  (a) The T-Rex used to feed primarily on birds.
  (b) Wishbones were commonly seen in dinosaurs.
  (c) Reptiles do not have furcula bones.
  (d) Sue's skeleton proves an evolutionary link to reptiles.

6   What is the conversation mainly about?

(a) how long the man will be away from work

(b) why the man needs a day off

(c) where the man is going on his vacation

(d) which dentist is the best to see

7   What can be inferred from the lecture?

(a) Some exercises can be more beneficial for people at certain ages.

(b) Lifting weights helps in many types of health problems.

(c) Bone deterioration has largely become a concern for young women.

(d) Health experts are recommending various exercises to their members.

8   Which is correct about the man according to the conversation?

(a) He is selling an apartment to the woman.

(b) He is planning to show various apartments to the woman.

(c) He is working as a real estate agent.

(d) He is going to help the woman find a good house.

9   What is the news report mainly about?

(a) huge expenses incurred during divorce in India

(b) marriages in India that largely end in divorce

(c) corruption that has grown in Indian detective organizations

(d) private investigation agencies that are profiting from divorce in India

10   Why couldn't George come?

(a)

(b)

(c)

(d)

1 Monologue

What is the news report mainly about?
(a) complaints regarding safety in cargo trucks
(b) the growing number of trucks that are not roadworthy
(c) government action to make cargo trucks safe
(d) measures taken by cargo companies to improve services

W   The government has decided to _____ _____ into the cargo truck industry. This follows the high numbers of cargo trucks _____ _____ by state troopers, along with 200 major truck accidents this year alone. Since cargo trucks carry 75% of the goods in the United States, and truck accidents often _____ , it is imperative that they operate safely at all times. Officers from the Transportation Department will begin inspecting several major cargo truck companies starting next week. This will include mechanical and safety checks on the vehicles as well as audits of service records. Companies which are found to be _____ will be given 30 days to correct their problems or _____ _____ .

conduct 수행하다, 처리하다 extensive 넓은, 광대한 범위의 cargo truck 화물 트럭 random 무작위의 state trooper 주(州) 경찰관 goods 물자, 상품 consequence 결과, 결말 imperative 필요한, 꼭 해야 할 transportation department 교통부 audit 감사 service (교통 기관 등의) 운행, 편도

2 Conversation

What will the man probably do in the afternoon?
(a) go to a children's bookstore
(b) take the woman shopping
(c) work at the office
(d) give his nephew a birthday party

M   Sharon, I need your advice on something.
W   Sure. What is it?
M   The day after tomorrow is _____ . _____ for him?
W   Well, how old is he?
M   He's seven years old.
W   Do you know what he is interested in?
M   Well, his mom told me he likes reading, but I was thinking of getting him an MP3 player or some games. I'm not sure what _____ would like.
W   Why don't you get him _____ ? That will make his mom happy, too. You could find those in any bookshop.
M   That's a good idea. I'll have to ask my girlfriend to look for one since _____ until late.

advice 충고, 조언 the day after tomorrow 모레 nephew 조카 educational 교육의, 교육적인 look for ~을 찾다

3 Monologue

Which is correct according to the lecture?

(a) Conduction paths are engineered without composite fibers.

(b) Aircraft skins are designed to conduct electricity.

(c) Aircraft are frequently harmed by lightning strikes.

(d) Lightning cannot damage fast-flying aircraft.

W In this lecture we will discuss methods followed to _____ _____. Aircraft bodies are generally made of aluminum, which is _____ _____. Modern aircraft, however, tend to use _____. These kinds of materials _____ _____ devised to carry lightning currents. Since aircraft design ensures that there is no gap in conduction paths, a lightning current travels along the skin of the aircraft _____ _____ like the tail or wing tip.

aircraft 항공기 lightning 번개 conductor 전도체 composite 합성의 , 혼합의 exterior 외부, 표면 conductive 전도성의 fiber 섬유. 섬유질
devise 고안하다. 발명하다 carry (전기 등을) 통하게 하다. 흘리다 exit 나가다 extremity 끝, 말단 wing tip (비행기의) 날개 끝

4 Conversation

What is the topic of the conversation?

(a) a band the man is listening to

(b) an Internet site where music can be bought

(c) how to find good music to listen to

(d) recent trends in popular music

W You seem to _____. What are you listening to?

M Trance, a new pop music band.

W I haven't heard of them but this song sounds quite familiar.

M It's becoming very popular among music-lovers, _____ _____.

W Would you mind _____? It sounds good.

M Well, all their songs are.

W Then, I may buy that CD as well. Or, can I download them from any music site?

M I heard this site called "Melon" downloads MP3s _____ _____. You can _____ _____ if you become a member or something.

W That sounds good enough. Thanks a lot.

seem ~처럼 보이다, ~인 듯하다 in good spirits 기분이 좋은 familiar 잘 알려진. 익숙한, 낯익은 popular 인기 있는, 대중적인 among ~의 사이에
music-lovers 음악 애호가들 would you mind -ing ~해 주실래요? turn up 소리를 크게 하다 as well 게다가, ~도 reasonable 적절한, 적당한
recent 최근의, 새로운 trend 경향, 추세, 유행 popular music 대중음악

5 Monologue

What can be implied from the lecture?
(a) The T-rex used to feed primarily on birds.
(b) Wishbones were commonly seen in dinosaurs.
(c) Reptiles do not have furcula bones.
(d) Sue's skeleton proves an evolutionary link to reptiles.

W The largest and most _____ of a Tyrannosaurus Rex ever found belongs to "Sue," a dinosaur. Researchers are finding evidence from it to show that dinosaurs may be more closely _____.
_____ is a furcula or wishbone, typical of a bird's genital structure. No other T-Rex skeleton found previously has featured this wishbone. Sue's furcula, however, is _____ _____ that birds _____.

skeleton 해골, 골격 Tyrannosaurus Rex 티라노사우루스 렉스 (공룡의 한 종) belong to ~에 속하다 dinosaur 공룡 reptile 파충류 furcula (새 가슴의) 창사골(暢思骨) (=wishbone) genital 생식기의 previously 이전에 featured 특색으로 하는 evolve 진화하다

6 Conversation

What is the conversation mainly about?
(a) how long the man will be away from work
(b) why the man needs a day off
(c) where the man is going on his vacation
(d) which dentist is the best to see

M _____ some day this week.
W Not a problem. Are you _____? A vacation?
M Not exactly. I have to take my son to the dentist, Dr. Ibrahim, most likely.
W Does he have any problems?
M Yes, _____ for the last three days.
W Again?
M No. That was my first son, and this time it is my second.
W I see. Have you made an appointment already?
M Not yet. _____.
W You'd better make it now. The doctor _____ that day.
M Yeah. I will find out when I can get a day off and then I will call the dentist.

take a day off 하루 휴가를 얻다 vacation 휴가 not exactly 반드시 그렇지는 않다, 조금 틀리다 take 사람 to 사람을 ~로 데리고 가다 dentist 치과의사 complain of (고통·병의 상태를) 호소하다 toothache 치통 make an appointment 약속하다 day off 비번일, 휴일 away 부재중, 결석(결근)하여

7 Monologue

What can be inferred from the lecture?

(a) Some exercises can be more beneficial for people at certain ages.
(b) Lifting weights helps in many types of health problems.
(c) Bone deterioration has largely become a concern for young women.
(d) Health experts are recommending various exercises to their members.

M _____ is an increasing cause for concern among the elderly, especially women, with many patients having this complaint being confined to bed. Lindford University scientists recommend _____ _____ as being perhaps the ideal way _____. In the course of their study, _____ for the stress they placed on a bone. This helped them conclude that bone maintenance requires _____ _____ like lifting weights rather than exercises like jogging.

deterioration 악화, 노화   concern 관심, 염려   the elderly 중년 사람들   confine 감금하다   high-stress 고압박의   bone density 골밀도

8 Conversation

Which is correct about the man according to the conversation?

(a) He is selling an apartment to the woman.
(b) He is planning to show various apartments to the woman.
(c) He is working as a real estate agent.
(d) He is going to help the woman find a good house.

M Jeannie, I'm glad to see you!
W Hi, Steve. _____?
M I'm a real estate agent, and came here _____ _____. And you? Why are you here?
W I'm planning to buy an apartment. So I came here _____ _____.
M Okay. _____ a real estate agent?
W Yes, he should be here any moment.
M Okay, _____.
W Sure, I'll let you know. Thank you.

bring ~을 오게 하다, 가져오다   real estate agent 부동산 중개인   close 종결하다, 마치다, 체결하다   deal 거래, 흥정, 계약   have a look at ~을 한번 보다
any moment 어느 때라도, 언제든지, 당장이라도

9 Monologue

What is the news report mainly about?

(a) huge expenses incurred during divorce in India

(b) marriages in India that largely end in divorce

(c) corruption that has grown in Indian detective organizations

(d) private investigation agencies that are profiting from divorce in India

W   Moving on to other news, India's _____ is benefiting not just law firms but also _____

_____ . Divorce was traditionally rare in India, due to cultural and religious restrictions. Now, however, the country is experiencing one of the fastest-growing divorce rates in Asia. Detective agencies have thrived in this new situation, particularly since the common law system that India inherited from Britain _____

during divorce cases. Some detective agencies with the services of _____ , journalists and security personnel like bodyguards _____

_____ . It seems that suspicious spouses are undeterred by the fee charged for investigation, which can be the equivalent of USD 1,800.

divorce rate 이혼율 **thriving** 번성하는, 번영하는 **marital** 결혼의, 결혼 생활의, 부부의 **restriction** 규제, 속박 **detective agency** 탐정 사무소, 흥신소 **common law** 관습법, 불문율 **penalize** 유죄를 선고하다, 불리한 입장에 두다 **adulterous** 불륜의, 간통의 **spouse** 배우자 **case** 판례, 소송 사건 **undeterred** 저지되지 않은, 말리지 못한 **equivalent** 상응하는, 같은 가치의

10 Conversation

Why couldn't George come?

(a) He was touring.

(b) He was held up at the office.

(c) He had to go to see the woman's mom.

(d) He couldn't find someone to babysit.

W   Hi, Dad. Sorry, I'm late. _____ at the office.

M   It's alright. I'm glad to see you.

W   Me too. It's been so long since we met.

M   Yeah. Where's George? _____ ?

W   No, he's at home with the kids.

M   I was expecting him to come. It's been a long time _____

_____ .

W   Actually _____ , but this babysitter who was supposed to come _____ . And then we called my mom to see if she can take care of the kids, but she wasn't home.

M   I understand. I'll try to meet him sometime this week.

hold up 정지하다, 서다, ~을 방해하다, 막다, 지연시키다 **tour** 관광 여행하다, 느린 속도로 달리다 **expect** ~을 기대하다, 기다리다 **all set** 만반의 준비가 되어 **babysitter** 아이 봐주는 사람 **take care of** ~을 보살피다, 돌보다

LISTENING REVIEW 🎧

A Listen to the definitions and write down the words.

1. rash _____

2. t _____

3. m _____

4. c _____

5. a _____

6. c _____

7. c _____

8. c _____

9. e _____

10. d _____

11. i _____

12. a _____

13. m _____

14. t _____

15. s _____

16. e _____

B Choose a sentence that best describes each Korean sentence.

1. 서로 안 본 지가 꽤 됐구나.
   (a) _____
   (b) _____

2. 어머니한테 아이들을 봐 줄 수 있는지 여쭤 보았어요.
   (a) _____
   (b) _____

3. 이 나라는 가장 빠른 이혼 증가율을 보이고 있습니다.
   (a) _____
   (b) _____

4. 그는 3일 전부터 치통을 호소했어요.
   (a) _____
   (b) _____

5. 뼈를 유지하려면 고압박 활동이 요구된다.
   (a) _____
   (b) _____

C Listen to three phrases and complete each sentence.

   I will find out / a day off / when I can get
   1. ⇒ I will find out when I can get a day off.

   2. _____

   3. _____

   4. _____

   5. _____

D Listen to the following and choose a sentence that has the same meaning.

   1. Why don't you get him a good educational book?
      (a) _____
      (b) _____

   2. I'll have to ask my girlfriend to look for one.
      (a) _____
      (b) _____

   3. Companies found to be in violation of safety rules will be given 30 days.
      (a) _____
      (b) _____

   4. We will look into the details of diversity in the American population.
      (a) _____
      (b) _____

   5. We may immediately delete it without the poster's permission.
      (a) _____
      (b) _____

Write down the meanings of the words.

01	electrical circuit	13	flurry
02	undisputed	14	treacherous
03	disperse	15	bachelor
04	eliminate	16	intersperse
05	intensive	17	amnesia
06	witchcraft	18	discretion
07	spell *n.*	19	stroke
08	rationale	20	faint
09	reunion	21	sprain
10	sweep	22	reputation
11	virtually	23	conceive
12	postulate	24	tremendous

GUIDED LISTENING 🎧

1 Conversation

Listening Notes

Purpose of visiting

Problem

Solution

Detail 1 What does the woman want to do?

(a) to get a refund

(b) to have an item repaired

(c) to replace a toaster

(d) to buy a new toaster

Detail 2 What is the problem?

(a) It takes too long to toast bread.

(b) It burns bread.

(c) It doesn't toast bread well.

(d) It has no electrical circuits.

2 Conversation

Listening Notes

(Request)

    Can someone

      (Pick up)

      (How far)

      (Present time)

We would be able to

Detail   1   What time will the woman arrive at the Trade Globe Center?

    (a) 4:00

    (b) 3:45

    (c) 3:30

    (d) 3:50

Detail   2   Why does the woman want to arrive there earlier?

    (a)

    (b)

    (c)

    (d)

3 Monologue

Listening Notes

(Exercise)

    (Problem)

    (Feel guilty)

        and

        however,

Experts suggest

    For example,

    (Effect) These small activities

Detail

1 What do many people feel guilty about?

(a) not exercising at all throughout the week

(b) having busy schedules during the weekdays

(c) not taking time out for a little workout

(d) not exercising during the weekends

Comprehension

2 Which type of exercise is good for busy people?

(a) limited exercise on the weekend

(b) moderate exercise through the day

(c) intensive exercise every day

(d) light exercise in the office

4 Monologue

Listening Notes

(Yoruba)

  This group also

(Wild rabbit fur)

  (Belief)

Detail 1 How do the Yoruba use wild rabbit fur?

(a) They use it to put magic spells on others.

(b) They use it to acquire bigger houses.

(c) They use it to attack other tribes.

(d) They use it to protect their homes from fire.

Function 2 Why does the speaker mention wild rabbit fur?

(a)

(b)

(c)

(d)

1 Conversation

1 What does the woman want to do?
(a) to get a refund
(b) to have an item repaired
(c) to replace a toaster
(d) to buy a new toaster

2 What is the problem?
(a) It takes too long to toast bread.
(b) It burns bread.
(c) It doesn't toast bread well.
(d) It has no electrical circuits.

W Hi, where can I _____ ?

M Right here, ma'am. Do you _____ ?

W Yes. Here it is.

M Thank you. Is there _____ ?

W Yes, it _____ — even if you keep something inside it for half an hour.

M Oh, there might be some problem _____ _____. Do you want us to repair it and give it back to you?

W Yes, that would be nice. _____ ?

M Just ten to fifteen minutes. You can have a seat in the waiting room.

refund 환불, 반품 receipt 영수증 toast 굽다 electrical circuit 전기회로 have a seat 앉다 waiting room 대기실

2 Conversation

1 What time will the woman arrive at the Trade Globe Center?
(a) 4:00
(b) 3:45
(c) 3:30
(d) 3:50

2 Why does the woman want to arrive there earlier?
(a) She doesn't want to be late for the meeting.
(b) She has to prepare something before the meeting.
(c) She has to buy something for the meeting.
(d) She wants to eat something before the meeting.

(Telephone rings.)

M This is Orange Taxi. How may I help you?

W Can somebody _____ by the Trade Globe Center? I have a meeting there at 4 o'clock.

M What time do you _____ to pick you up, ma'am?

W In 15 minutes. It's _____ from here and it's already three o'clock. I want to get there a little earlier _____ before I go in.

M _____, ma'am?

W I'm here at 151 Fifth River Avenue.

M We can have a taxi there in half an hour, if you can wait until then.

W Okay, but don't take longer than half an hour.

pick ~ up ~를 데리러 오다 a twenty-minute drive 20분 운전 거리 grab 급히 잡다 cf. grab a sandwich 간단하게(빨리) 샌드위치를 먹다(사다)
half an hour 30분

1　What do many people feel guilty about?
(a) not exercising at all throughout the week
(b) having busy schedules during the weekdays
(c) not taking time out for a little workout
(d) not exercising during the weekends

2　Which type of exercise is good for busy people?
(a) limited exercise on the weekend
(b) moderate exercise through the day
(c) intensive exercise every day
(d) light exercise in the office

M　Exercise is important for our well-being. Although it is _____ _____, not many people are able to take time out for a little workout, due to their busy schedules. Many people _____ and try to exercise as much as possible on the weekends. However, this way of exercising is not a healthy option. Experts suggest that people who have busy weekdays should try to be physically active as much as possible _____ _____. For example, _____ _____. People can choose to walk short distances rather than to take cars. These small activities _____ may _____ on the weekends.

undisputed 의심할 여지없는, 당연한　workout 운동, 연습　due to ~ 때문에　as much as possible 가능한 한 많이　option 선택 사항　expert 전문가
disperse 흩뜨리다, 산재하다　eliminate 제거하다, 없애다　throughout the day 종일　limited 한정된, 제한된　intensive 강한, 강렬한

1　How do the Yoruba use wild rabbit fur?
(a) They use it to put magic spells on others.
(b) They use it to acquire bigger houses.
(c) They use it to attack other tribes.
(d) They use it to protect their homes from fire.

2　Why does the speaker mention wild rabbit fur?
(a) to show what the Yoruba people believed the most
(b) to illustrate the strong faith of the Yoruba in witchcraft
(c) to explain that it was the most common type of witchcraft
(d) to imply that wild rabbits were hunted the most

W　The Yoruba are a West African ethnic group and like many others, this group also _____. According to people from the Yoruba tribe, magic spells and other types of witchcraft can be used to harm others. Although there might be _____, the Yoruba people tend to believe it. According to their belief system, wild rabbit fur _____: the Yoruba believe it _____, if hung outside it. It is very common to find wild rabbit fur outside Yoruba houses. Some may _____ such witchcraft practices work or not, but the Yoruba people retain their belief that they do.

Yoruba 요루바족 (Guinea 지방에 사는 흑인)　ethnic 인종의, 민족의　witchcraft 마법, 주술　spell 주문　be used to ~하는 데에 사용되다　logical 논리적인
rationale 이론적 근거(설명), 원리　practice 관행　tend to ~하는 경향이 있다　fur 털　protect A from B A를 B로부터 보호하다　work 효과가 있다, 작용하다
retain 보류하다, 계속 실행하다, 잊지 않고 있다　acquire 얻다, 획득하다

1   What is the woman doing in the conversation?

(a) trying to find a jacket that she likes

(b) finding a sweatshirt whose price is either equal or lower

(c) getting a sweatshirt in exchange for a jacket

(d) getting a refund for the jacket she bought

2   What is the woman's concern?

(a) that she is not able to go to the school reunion party

(b) that she has to meet her high school friends

(c) that she has not changed a bit after high school

(d) that her old boyfriend will not remember her

3   Which of the following is correct according to the talk?

(a) Bottle-nose Dolphins have dwindled over the years.

(b) Some types of dolphins have learned to avoid tuna nets.

(c) Human beings are causing the destruction of dolphin habitats.

(d) Bottle-noses are no longer under the threat of extinction.

4   What does the woman want to know about?

(a) information on special packages available for families

(b) brochures for tours so that she can leave as early as she can

(c) inexpensive ways to tour around Egypt with her family members

(d) the minimum number of people for the tour and the schedule

5   What weather conditions can southern areas expect?

(a) clear and dry conditions

(b) showers and thunderstorms

(c) flurries and cloudy skies

(d) rainfall over four centimeters

6 Which is correct according to the conversation?

(a) The man is pretty satisfied with his single life.

(b) The woman has a problematic marriage.

(c) The woman has been married for the last five years.

(d) The man wants to get married at the earliest possible time.

Detail

7 Why are flashbacks mainly used according to the lecture?

(a) to interrupt a narrative that provides background

(b) to serve to raise an audience's expectations

(c) to help to present different perceptions in a narrative

(d) to show how characters evolve from the past

8 What is the main idea of the news report?

(a) New Zealand teachers have been given greater powers.

(b) Standards have dropped in New Zealand elementary schools.

(c) Changes are being adopted in elementary school testing.

(d) New Zealand schools offer greater flexibility to each student.

9 What are the man and woman mainly discussing?

(a) how the man's aunt had a stroke

(b) problems the man has had since falling down

(c) difficulties the man's aunt has had since a stroke

(d) how the man's aunt fell down while getting out of bed

10 What is the main topic of the lecture?

(a)

(b)

(c)

(d)

1 Conversation

What is the woman doing in the conversation?

(a) trying to find a jacket that she likes

(b) finding a sweatshirt whose price is either equal or lower

(c) getting a sweatshirt in exchange for a jacket

(d) getting a refund for the jacket she bought

M Good morning, ma'am. How may I help you?

W I'd like _____.

M Okay. Have a look at the sweatshirts available here.

W Do I have to _____ for the sweatshirt?

M Yes, _____ the jacket.

W Oh, okay. Do you also give refunds if I want?

M Yes, of course. But, _____, you will have to

_____.

W I think I put that in the pocket of the jacket. Would you look for it for me please?

M Sure. Wait a moment. Here it is. Now, have you found anything you would like to get?

W Yes, I have. Here it is.

ma'am 점원이 여자 손님을 부르는 말 | **exchange** (for) ~로 교환(교체)하다, 환전하다 **sweatshirt** 두껍고 헐거운 캐주얼 셔츠, 스웨트 셔츠
have a look at ~을 훑어보다, 한번 슬쩍 보다 **available** 이용할 수 있는, 유효한 **extra** 여분의, 추가의, 특별한 **price** 값을 매기다
refund 환불, 반환, ~을 갚다, 환불하다 **receipt** 영수증 **in exchange for** ~대신에, ~과 교환하여

2 Conversation

What is the woman's concern?

(a) that she is not able to go to the school reunion party

(b) that she has to meet her high school friends

(c) that she has not changed a bit after high school

(d) that her old boyfriend will not remember her

M Your friend told me that you're going to a party.

W Yes, _____.

M Great! I'm sure you're excited.

W Yes, because I'll be meeting _____.

M But will he recognize you? It's been more than ten years now.

W That's exactly what I'm worried about. I've changed a lot since high school and _____

_____.

M That is not bad.

W What do you mean?

M I mean _____ to him then. Go up to him and _____ if he does not recognize you.

W Yeah. That's not a bad idea.

M Well, good luck and I hope you have a good time there.

reunion 동창회, 재회 **sweetheart** 애인, 연인 **recognize** ~을 보고 알아보다, 분간하다, 인정하다 **concern** 걱정

3 Monologue

Which of the following is correct according to the talk?

(a) Bottle-nose Dolphins have dwindled over the years.
(b) Some types of dolphins have learned to avoid tuna nets.
(c) Human beings are causing the destruction of dolphin habitats.
(d) Bottle-noses are no longer under the threat of extinction.

M   It's a pleasure to announce that the Bottle-nose Dolphin has been _____. Our maritime research reveals that the dolphin population here has increased by 12% over the past 18 years in the animal's natural habitats. This has been despite the fact that large numbers of dolphins continue to be caught accidentally in tuna nets, especially "drag" nets _____ _____ out of the ocean in front of them. In spite of these challenges, _____ _____ that the Bottle-nose _____ _____. Some scientists postulate that the Bottle-nose, a highly intelligent creature, may even have learned _____.

Bottle-nose Dolphin 청백돌고래 the verge of ~의 직전, ~의 가장자리 extinction 멸종, 절멸 maritime 바다의, 해운상의 reveal 드러내다, 폭로하다
natural habitat 자연 서식지 drag net 저인망, 예인망, 후릿그물 sweep 쓸어내다, 쓸어버리다 virtually 사실상, 실제로
heartening 기운 나게 하는, 고무적인 (hearten v. 고무하다, 기운 나게 하다) prospect 가망, 기대, 예상 postulate 요구하다, 주장하다

4 Conversation

What does the woman want to know about?

(a) information on special packages available for families
(b) brochures for tours so that she can leave as early as she can
(c) inexpensive ways to tour around Egypt with her family members
(d) the minimum number of people for the tour and the schedule

W   Hi, I need information _____.
M   Okay, what would you like to know?
W   I saw your ad in the newspaper _____ _____ to Egypt.
M   Oh, the tours are so popular among many families.
W   What is the number of people required for the trip?
M   _____ for that two-week tour.
W   Oh I see. When does the tour start?
M   We leave the last Friday of the month.
W   Okay. I would like _____ for twelve members from my class for next month. Is twelve big enough?
M   Sure. Would you please _____?
W   Can I borrow a pen?

package 일괄상품, 소포, 포장한 상품 require ~을 필요로 하다 leave 떠나다 reserve 예약하다 fill in ~을 메우다, (서류에) 적어 넣다
detail 세부, 상세, 자세한 사항 form (문서의) 양식, 서식 brochure 팸플릿, 소책자 minimum 최소한의

5 Monologue

What weather conditions can southern areas expect?
(a) clear and dry conditions
(b) showers and thunderstorms
(c) flurries and cloudy skies
(d) rainfall over 4 centimeters

W Good morning, this is Nina with today's weather forecast. _____ _____, so get ready for _____.

You will do well to put on a warm coat and boots for the coming days. The colder weather will start today. Central areas of the state will _____ with a high of about 2 degrees Celsius in the afternoon. In the southern areas, _____ showers and thunderstorms with a high of 3 degrees. The south may also experience rain mixed with ice, which will create treacherous road conditions. The state _____ _____ and minus 8 degrees.

spell (날씨 등의) 계속되는 기간 | region 지역 | put on ~을 입다 | flurry 눈보라 | shower 소나기 | thunderstorm (강풍이 따르는) 뇌우 treacherous 위험한, 불안정한 | low 최저 기온

6 Conversation

Which is correct according to the conversation?
(a) The man is pretty satisfied with his single life.
(b) The woman has a problematic marriage.
(c) The woman has been married for the last five years.
(d) The man wants to get married at the earliest possible time.

M Now that you've been married for two years, what's _____ _____?

W Well, it's like a team of two people _____ _____.

M That's good. But how about giving space to each other?

W Certainly, that's important for personal growth.

M Yet not many people understand that, and _____ _____ because of that.

W That's not always correct. Is that the reason _____ _____?

M Yeah, and I'm quite happy _____.
At least I'm free to do whatever I want.

now that ~이므로, ~이기 때문에 | towards ~을 향하여 | space 공간, 우주, 장소, 거리, 간격 | personal 개인의, 사적인 | work well 잘 되어가다 stop 사람 from ~에게 …을 못하게 하다 | bachelor 미혼(독신) 남성 | problematic 문제가 있는 | get married 결혼하다

7 Monologue

Why are flashbacks mainly used according to the lecture?
(a) to interrupt a narrative that provides background
(b) to serve to raise an audience's expectations
(c) to help to present different perceptions in a narrative
(d) to show how characters evolve from the past

W   Now, I'm now going to speak about a common device used in cinema — the flashback. It is used _____ _____ by stopping briefly _____ _____. Flashbacks give filmmakers greater scope for narrating their stories. Apart from providing background, they produce multiple perspectives to events in the film and _____. Flashbacks can be interspersed throughout a film, or sometimes _____, such as when a main character with amnesia suddenly remembers who he is and how he became amnesiac. Sometimes a film _____ one long flashback: Mel Gibson's *The Patriot* is a good example.

flashback (영화 등에서의) 과거 장면으로의 순간적 전환 기법 narrative 이야기, 설명 | scope 기회, 배출구 perspective 견해, 관점
intersperse 흩뜨리다, 산재시키다 emerge 나타나다 amnesia 기억 상실 be composed of ~으로 구성되다 interrupt 방해하다 evolve 발전하다, 진화하다

8 Monologue

What is the main idea of the news report?
(a) New Zealand teachers have been given greater powers.
(b) Standards have dropped in New Zealand elementary schools.
(c) Changes are being adopted in elementary school testing.
(d) New Zealand schools offer greater flexibility to each student.

M   A pilot program _____ for a new elementary school testing system for kids in New Zealand. _____ _____ in this school level beginning next year. The government _____ and reduce pressure on children by placing greater importance _____ _____. Teachers under this new system will be able to judge which types of tests might be best for which types of classes or students. Teachers will also be able to decide the timing of tests, which could be given _____ _____ depending on class conditions. This would be an important move away from the standardization of the past.

pilot program (정규 프로그램 편성 전에) 시험용으로 제작된 견본용 프로그램 in progress 진행 중인 flexible 융통성 있는, 탄력적인
discretion 선택의 자유, (자유) 재량, 결정권 | move 조처, 수단 standardization 표준화

9 Conversation

What are the man and woman mainly discussing?

(a) how the man's aunt had a stroke

(b) problems the man has had since falling down

(c) difficulties the man's aunt has had since a stroke

(d) how the man's aunt fell down while getting out of bed

W How's your aunt doing?

M Well, she's not well after her stroke.

W Why? What's happened?

M She _____. She's not even able to go to the bathroom.

W Is she that bad?

M Yeah, the other day she tried getting out of bed, but _____ _____.

W Oh, _____. How's she managing now?

M _____ to look after her.

W That's good. I hope _____.

---

stroke 뇌졸중 **faint** 기절하다, 졸도하다 **get out of bed** 잠자리에서 일어나다 **the other day** 일전에, 며칠 전에 **fall down** 넘어지다, 쓰러지다 **sprain** ~을 삐다 | **ankle** 발목 | **manage** 이럭저럭 해나가다, 꾸려나가다 **appoint** 지명(임명)하다, 정하다 **nurse** 간호사, 간병인 | **look after** ~을 돌보다, 보살피다 | **get better** (병, 상황 등이) 좋아지다, 호전되다

---

10 Monologue

What is the main topic of the lecture?

(a) Brazil's changing growth patterns

(b) the significance of Brasilia as a capital city

(c) the unsuccessfully planned capital city of Brazil

(d) the way Brasilia made a comeback after failure

W You must have heard of Brasilia, the capital of Brazil, and its reputation as an example of poor urban planning. The city _____ _____ just over 50 years ago, but is often criticized. _____ that the growth of the city _____, but this growth has been almost entirely made up of civil servants who have been "forced" to move there. Brasilia is certainly not a human-friendly city. Even worse, the modern city _____ _____ of Brazil, which would have been necessary _____ to Brasilia. Instead, they prefer the exciting cultural attractions of coastal cities like Rio, where most of them remain.

---

reputation 명성, 평판 **urban planning** 도시 계획 **conceive** 생각하다, 계획하다 **tremendous** 굉장한, 거대한 **be made up of** ~으로 구성되다, 이루어지다 **civil servant** 공무원, 문관

LISTENING REVIEW 🎧

A   Listen to the definitions and write down the words.

1. reputation _____
2. c_____
3. f_____
4. s_____
5. a_____
6. d_____
7. p_____
8. e_____

9. s_____
10. b_____
11. t_____
12. r_____
13. e_____
14. p_____
15. p_____
16. r_____

B   Choose a sentence that best describes each Korean sentence.

1. 전기회로에 문제가 있는 것 같군요.
   (a) _____
   (b) _____

2. 저희가 수리해서 돌려 드릴까요?
   (a) _____
   (b) _____

3. 저를 태우러 와서 무역 세계 센터까지 데려다 줄 수 있나요?
   (a) _____
   (b) _____

4. 짧은 거리라면 차를 타고 가기보다는 걸어가는 것을 택할 수 있습니다.
   (a) _____
   (b) _____

5. 요루바족의 집 밖에서 야생 토끼털을 발견하는 것은 아주 흔한 일입니다.
   (a) _____
   (b) _____

C   Listen to three phrases and complete each sentence.

some time / to grab a sandwich / I can have

1. ➡ I can have some time to grab a sandwich.

2. _____

3. _____

4. _____

5. _____

D   Listen to the following and choose a sentence that has the same meaning.

1. Have you found anything you would like to get?
   - (a) _____
   - (b) _____

2. I'm so worried that he won't recognize me.
   - (a) _____
   - (b) _____

3. The dolphin population here has increased by 12% over the past 18 years.
   - (a) _____
   - (b) _____

4. What is the number of people required for the trip?
   - (a) _____
   - (b) _____

5. The south may also experience rain mixed with ice.
   - (a) _____
   - (b) _____

CHAPTER 04

COMPREHENSION

VOCABULARY PREVIEW 🎧

Write down the meanings of the words.

01	subordinate *n.*	13	immature
02	release	14	compliment
03	fraud	15	maintenance
04	pretext	16	laminated
05	in bondage	17	resistant
06	sanction	18	grease
07	measures	19	vapor
08	fairground	20	entry form
09	contestant	21	manure
10	fundraising	22	the former
11	revenue	23	stringent
12	doze	24	allege

GUIDED LISTENING 🎧

1 Conversation

Listening Notes

(Excited)

(When to join)

(Reason)

Comprehension 1 Which is correct according to the conversation?

(a) The woman is searching for a job in a marketing company.

(b) The man is switching to a new job.

(c) The man's boss has offered him a pay raise.

(d) The man is preparing a new worker to be his subordinate.

Detail 2 Why did he request to delay joining the company?

(a) He has a project going on.

(b) He wants to take time off.

(c) He has to train his subordinate.

(d) He has not talked to his boss.

2 Conversation

Listening Notes

Someone told the boss

(The man's thought)

I heard you

(Truth)

Comprehension 1 Which is correct according to the conversation?

(a) The man said something incorrect about the woman.

(b) The woman made her sister quit her job.

(c) The woman was planning to quit some time later.

(d) The man criticized the woman in front of the boss.

Detail 2 Why was the boss upset?

(a)

(b)

(c)

(d)

3 Monologue

Listening Notes

(Purpose of approaches & attempts)

   To end

(Attempt by Christian organizations):

   (Result)

      For instance

(Attempt by other groups and nations)

   (Result)

Comprehension

1 Which is correct according to the news report?

(a) Christian organizations purchase Sudanese slaves for labor.

(b) A Chinese company owns many slaves that it brings to China.

(c) Various attempts to end slavery have not been successful.

(d) Slave traders refuse to release slaves under any circumstances.

Detail

2 What do Christian organizations do to end slavery?

(a) They sell their property in exchange of their slaves.

(b) They fight against companies hiring many slaves.

(c) They persuade slave traders to free their slaves.

(d) They buy slaves from traders and free them.

4 Monologue

Listening Notes

(Announcement)

    (Award)

    (Requirements)
        1. (Age)

        2.

    (Others)

Comprehension

1   Which is correct according to the announcement?

(a) Anyone can just walk in and attend the contest on that day.

(b) Anyone in any age group can participate in the contest.

(c) Participants must bring necessary supplies to the contest.

(d) Contestants must provide personal information before the contest.

Main Topic

2   What is the announcement about?

(a)

(b)

(c)

(d)

1 Conversation

1 Which is correct according to the conversation?
   (a) The woman is searching for a job in a marketing company.
   (b) The man is switching to a new job.
   (c) The man's boss has offered him a pay raise.
   (d) The man is preparing a new worker to be his subordinate.

2 Why did he request to delay joining the company?
   (a) He has a project going on.
   (b) He wants to take time off.
   (c) He has to train his subordinate.
   (d) He has not talked to his boss.

M I'm excited. _____ from a marketing company!
W That's really good. So when are you joining them?
M Actually, they want me to join immediately. But _____
   _____.
W Do you have some work going on _____
   _____?
M Not exactly, but _____
   to my subordinate. I'll need some time to train her.
W Okay. Have you informed your boss that you're leaving?
M Yes. He wasn't very happy about it.
W Poor guy! He _____.

offer 제의, 제안 delay 연기하다, 늦추다 hand over 건네주다, 양도하다 subordinate 부하직원 dependent on ~에 의존하고 있는, 의지하는 switch 바꾸다, 교환하다 pay raise 월급 인상

2 Conversation

1 Which is correct according to the conversation?
   (a) The man said something incorrect about the woman.
   (b) The woman made her sister quit her job.
   (c) The woman was planning to quit some time later.
   (d) The man criticized the woman in front of the boss.

2 Why was the boss upset?
   (a) Because he thought the man told him a lie.
   (b) Because the man told him that he would quit.
   (c) Because he thought the woman was going to quit.
   (d) Because the woman gave him some wrong information.

M What happened? _____?
W You won't believe what happened! Someone told the boss that
   _____. Now, he's _____.
M Hey, it was me! But aren't you really quitting?
W No. Who told you I was?
M I heard you discussing that with your sister yesterday. Isn't it true?
W _____! It's my sister who is quitting her job, not me!
M I'm really sorry for this. I _____.
W Please tell the boss that, too!

quit 그만두다 misunderstand 잘못 생각하다, 오해하다 criticize 비난하다 in front of ~ 앞에서

3 Monologue

1 Which is correct according to the news report?

(a) Christian organizations purchase Sudanese slaves for labor.

(b) A Chinese company owns many slaves that it brings to China.

(c) Various attempts to end slavery have not been successful.

(d) Slave traders refuse to release slaves under any circumstances.

2 What do Christian organizations do to end slavery?

(a) They sell their property in exchange of their slaves.

(b) They fight against companies hiring many slaves.

(c) They persuade slave traders to free their slaves.

(d) They buy slaves from traders and free them.

M Many approaches _____ in Sudan. Some of the most recent attempts have been taken by Christian organizations. These organizations purchase hundreds of slaves from slave traders and then release them. The move was started in good faith; however, it has been learned that _____ _____ under the pretext of freeing slaves. For instance, some slave traders sell _____ _____ that are only _____ _____. Other groups or nations _____ _____ the Sudanese government to help free the slaves; sanctions were also put on a Chinese oil company that operated in Sudan. Despite the many measures taken, none of them have been effective enough in stopping the slave trade to date.

approach 접근, 해결 방법 slavery 노예제도 attempt 시도 release 풀어 주다. 석방하다 a great deal of 상당량의 fraud 사기, 기만
take place 발생하다. 일어나다 pretext 구실, 핑계 mass quantities of 대량의 in bondage 감금되어, 노예가 되어 sanction 재가, 인가, 제재, 처벌
despite ~에도 불구하고 measures 수단, 조치 to date 현재까지는 under any circumstances 어떠한 사정에서도

4 Monologue

1 Which is correct according to the announcement?

(a) Anyone can just walk in and attend the contest on that day.

(b) Anyone in any age group can participate in the contest.

(c) Participants must bring necessary supplies to the contest.

(d) Contestants must provide personal information before the contest.

2 What is the announcement about?

(a) a contest to get a free ticket to a TV program

(b) free coloring classes for children on TV

(c) art skills for children older than 4 years of age

(d) the grand opening of a bookstore

W An important announcement — the Happy Street _____ _____ will be held on Friday morning at the Wonder Center Fairgrounds. The event _____ Denver TV. The winners of the contest will be _____ _____ of a TV program as members of the audience! The recording is scheduled for Saturday, June 30th, at the Brown Center. Children interested in the contest _____. Contestants are required to fill out a contest registration form with personal details such as name, age, parents' names, address and contact number. All necessary supplies will be provided. Contestants _____.

announcement 안내방송, 발표, 공고 fairground 광장, 박람회장 co-sponsor 공동 후원하다 audience 관중 contestant 경쟁자, 경기 참가자
fill out 기입하다, 써넣다 registration form 등록 신청서 grand 거대한, 성대한

PRACTICAL LISTENING 🎧

Comprehension ▦

1 Which is correct according to the conversation?

(a) The man is going to have a meeting at the hotel.

(b) The woman will take the man's client to the hotel.

(c) The woman is going to take the man to the office.

(d) The man is going to arrive at the hotel after 4 o'clock.

2 What is the speaker's main point about fundraising?

(a) It needs to be run as if it were a business.

(b) Its primary aim is to raise money.

(c) Special skill is required to succeed at it.

(d) Corporate experience is essential for it.

3 What is the man's opinion of the movie?

(a) He did not like the action scenes.

(b) He found the story interesting.

(c) He thought it was saved by its good actors.

(d) He felt most of the actors weren't talented.

4 What is the man trying to do in the conversation?

(a) to help the woman practice dancing

(b) to compliment the woman on the performance

(c) to tell the woman where the curtain is

(d) to comfort the woman ahead of her performance

Comprehension ▦

5 Which is correct according to the radio program?

(a) Laminated surfaces need less maintenance.

(b) Kitchen walls must absorb moisture efficiently.

(c) Natural wood surfaces are ideal for kitchens.

(d) Mess is unavoidable while cooking.

6 What is the conversation mainly about?

(a) deciding on a restaurant to dine at

(b) how to arrange a meeting with the woman's cousin

(c) whether the cousin can join the dinner or not

(d) making an appointment for dinner

Comprehension

7 Which is correct according to the announcement?

(a) The festival is held every Sunday during the month of May.

(b) Purchases can be made from the festival's website.

(c) All shops offer gift certificates as prizes.

(d) Visitors can submit entry forms when leaving the Festival.

8 What is the talk mainly about?

(a) planning the layout of a classroom

(b) arranging activities for students

(c) making a classroom interesting

(d) choosing good course material

Comprehension

9 Which is correct according to the conversation?

(a) The man offered to buy manure for the woman.

(b) The woman bought a lot of seeds from a store.

(c) The woman bought garden pots before.

(d) The man is going to help the woman grow plants.

10 Which statement would Dr. Durant more likely agree with?

(a)

(b)

(c)

(d)

1 Conversation

Which is correct according to the conversation?

(a) The man is going to have a meeting at the hotel.

(b) The woman will take the man's client to the hotel.

(c) The woman is going to take the man to the office.

(d) The man is going to arrive at the hotel after 4 o'clock.

M Driver, get me downtown — quickly!

W Sure. _____, sir?

M Le Meridian Hotel on Silverstone Street. I will _____
_____ at 4:00. How long it will take?

W It won't take longer than 30 minutes from here if _____
_____.

M Sounds good. I believe it takes one hour by shuttle bus.

W Yeah, the shuttle takes longer than a taxi.

M Well, _____
after picking up my client. Do you think you can wait outside?

W If you don't take too long.

M I won't. And _____?

W Not more than $35, I would estimate.

downtown 번화가(중심지)에 **exactly** 정확히 **grab** (택시 따위를) 잡다 **not more than** ~보다 많지 않은, 많아야 **estimate** ~을 어림하다, 견적하다, 평가하다

2 Monologue

What is the speaker's main point about fundraising?

(a) It needs to be run as if it were a business.

(b) Its primary aim is to raise money.

(c) Special skill is required to succeed at it.

(d) Corporate experience is essential for it.

W I'd like to emphasize here that _____
_____ is very similar to running a company. Both demand the same planning, time and _____
_____. A company has a revenue or profit target, and a fundraising event sets a target of how much money it wants to raise. Thus, both require good leadership, and are chiefly concerned with making money. Both organizations must also _____,
staff and organizational techniques to meet their goals. So use the same strategies for fundraising as a business owner would and see how well you succeed. In particular, _____
_____ on a regular basis, so you can see how close to your financial goals you are as you would in a company.

fundraising 기금 모금 **planning** 계획, 기획 **financial** 재정의 **revenue** 수익, 세입
benchmarking 벤치마킹(자신의 제품이나 제조 방법의 향상을 위해 성공적인 또는 다른 회사와 비교하여 참고하는 것) **on a regular basis** 정기적으로

3 Conversation

What is the man's opinion of the movie?
(a) He did not like the action scenes.
(b) He found the story interesting.
(c) He thought it was saved by its good actors.
(d) He felt most of the actors weren't talented.

W Did you like the movie?

M It wasn't that bad.

W Really? Come on. I saw you _____ .

M You noticed that, huh? Well, _____

_____ .

W I guess _____ as

the storyline was quite weak.

M True, _____

_____ .

W The actors were immature _____ .

M Except for the actor who played the grandfather. He did very well.

W That's right. He was the only one who seemed to have any real

talent in the movie.

---

doze 꾸벅꾸벅 졸다 second half 후반전, 후반부 director 감독, 연출가 storyline 줄거리, 구상 illogical 비논리적인, 불합리한 unnecessary 불필요한
scene 장면 immature 미숙한, 미완성의 acting 연기 except for ~을 제외하고 play ~의 역을 맡다 talent 재주, 재능, 인재 save ~을 구하다, 구조하다, 지키다

---

4 Conversation

What is the man trying to do in the conversation?
(a) to help the woman practice dancing
(b) to compliment the woman on her performance
(c) to tell the woman where the curtain is
(d) to comfort the woman ahead of her performance

M Are you ready _____ ?

W Yes, but I'm nervous. I've never performed in front of an audience.

M You're an excellent dancer and _____

_____ .

W That's true, but _____ ?

M I'm sure that won't happen. Even if it did, _____

_____ , right?

W Yes. But still, _____ .

M Relax! Your performance will be excellent.

W I'm glad you're here to support me.

---

perform 연기하다, 공연하다 audience 청중, 관객 what if ~이라면 어찌 되는가? even if (비록) ~일지라도 cover up 감싸다, 숨기다
screw up 실수하여 엉망으로 만들다 performance 연기, 연주, 상연 compliment 칭찬하다 comfort 위로하다, 격려하다, 안심시키다

5 Monologue

Which is correct according to the radio program?
(a) Laminated surfaces need less maintenance.
(b) Kitchen walls must absorb moisture efficiently.
(c) Natural wood surfaces are ideal for kitchens.
(d) Mess is unavoidable while cooking.

W　The kitchen is where the most work is done in any household. Not only is it the place where we cook, it is also _____ _____. Tonight's program focuses on choosing _____ _____ so you can minimize the time that you have to spend there. The most important thing is _____ _____. You don't want kitchen surfaces that need intensive scrubbing. Remember that while natural wood looks great, it needs a lot of maintenance. _____ _____, however, doesn't. Also, make sure that your kitchen walls are _____, _____ from your cooking.

intensive 집중적인, 강한, 강렬한　maintenance 유지, 보수, 관리, 정비　surface 표면, 겉, 외부　laminated 코팅된　resistant 저항력이 있는, 저항하는
grease 기름, 유지　vapor 증기　moisture 습기, 수분, 물기

6 Conversation

What is the conversation mainly about?
(a) deciding on a restaurant to dine at
(b) how to arrange a meeting with the woman's cousin
(c) whether the cousin can join the dinner or not
(d) making an appointment for dinner

M　Would you like to have dinner with me tonight?
W　Um, I'll have to _____. I'm supposed to go out with her for dinner.
M　Oh, is she the one you were talking about before?
W　Right. She's here for a business meeting, so we thought _____ _____. You want to join?
M　If that is okay with your cousin, _____ _____.
W　Like I said, I will check with my cousin.
M　You do that. And _____, I can meet you tomorrow.
W　I'll let you know by 4 o'clock. Is that too late for you?
M　Not at all. If I can see you tonight, I'll pick you up at 8:00 p.m. then.

check with ~와 상담하다, ~에게 문의하다　cousin 사촌　business meeting 업무상 모임, 회의　catch up on 그동안 못했던 것을 하다
pick up ~을 데리러(태우러) 가다　decide on ~을 결정하다, ~로 정하다　dine 식사하다　arrange 준비하다, 주선하다

7 Monologue

Which is correct according to the announcement?

(a) The festival is held every Sunday during the month of May.

(b) Purchases can be made from the festival's website.

(c) All shops offer gift certificates as prizes.

(d) Visitors can submit entry forms when leaving the festival.

M You've been waiting for it all summer, and now it's here! _____ _____ Walcott Home and Garden Festival will be the best place to get quality goods at low prices from all over the province! This will be an event that you just won't want to miss. To take advantage of it, be at the Walcott Grounds on Sunday, _____ _____ This is your opportunity to buy or just look over quality items _____ _____. Visitors can also win _____ for furniture and garden supplies. Pick up your entry forms _____ _____, fill it out and hand it in at any of the exits.

annual 해마다의, 연간의 **province** 지역, (행정 구역으로서의) 주(州), 성(省), 현(縣), 도(道) **take advantage of** ~를 이용하다 **vendor** 행상인 **stall** 매장, 노점 **entry form** 참가신청서, 응모신청서 **participate** 참여하다, 참가하다 **hand in** ~을 제출하다 **exit** 출구 **gift certificate** 상품권 **submit** 제출하다

8 Monologue

What is the talk mainly about?

(a) planning the layout of a classroom

(b) arranging activities for students

(c) making a classroom interesting

(d) choosing good course material

W There's another important aspect of teaching. I'd like to discuss today, _____. This involves organizing the placement of desks, bookcases, file cabinets and so on. This does not involve just "making the room look nice." Classroom organization is in fact an important part of the entire learning experience and also _____ _____. Since your classroom indicates your style, _____ _____ a few personal touches like plants, art displays, colorful rugs or even cushions for the reading corner. _____, particularly young ones, to do their best in the class. At the same time, you need to make sure that students _____ so that they can work quickly and efficiently.

aspect 관점, 양상, 국면 **organization** 조직, 구성, 편성 **reflect** 반영하다, 나타내다 **indicate** 가리키다, 나타내다 **touch** 손길, 특색 **motivate** 자극하다, 동기를 주다 **have access to** ~에 접근할 수 있다, (자료 등을) 이용할 수 있다 **efficiently** 능률적으로 **layout** 배치

9 Conversation

Which is correct according to the conversation?

(a) The man offered to buy manure for the woman.

(b) The woman bought a lot of seeds from a store.

(c) The woman bought garden pots before.

(d) The man is going to help the woman grow plants.

M Where did you get these seeds? Are you trying to learn _____ _____?

W Well, my friend _____, I thought I _____ them.

M Have you ever done this before?

W Why do you think I have _____?

M What happened to plants you used to grow?

W Don't ask. _____. But this time I'll make sure that I do.

M Well, why don't you try putting some manure in the soil?

W That's a good idea. Where could I get it?

M In any home and garden store.

seed 씨앗 **gardening** 원예, 조경 가꾸기 **ought to** ~해야 하다 **grow** 기르다, 재배하다 (=garden) **pot** 단지, 항아리, 화분 **make sure** 확실히 ~하다 **try -ing** ~해보다, 시도하다 **manure** 비료, 거름 **soil** 흙, 토양 **buy + 목 + for** 사람 ~에게 …을 사주다 **plant** 식물

10 Monologue

Which statement would Dr. Durant more likely agree with?

(a) Most people decide to follow efficient diet programs.

(b) People are willing to pay for a diet if it is effective.

(c) Diet weight-loss regimens do not have long-lasting results.

(d) People should be persuaded to buy special diet programs.

W There are generally two types of books on weight loss in stores today: _____ and those concerning exercise. As we know, _____ _____. On today's show we will speak with Dr. Matt Durant, _____ and weight-loss industry in North America, and the books, videos and other programs that promote those diets. Dr. Durant alleges that most weight-loss regimens _____ _____ for quick weight reduction through dieting and _____. He argues that these programs are not really faster or better than regular exercise and healthy eating, both of which can be practiced by anybody with more sustained results.

weight loss 체중 감량 **concerning** ~에 관하여 **the former** 전자 (↔ the latter) **stringent** (규칙 등이) 엄격한, 강제적인 **allege** 주장하다, 진술하다 **regimen** (식사, 운동 등에 의한) 섭생, 처방 계획 **exploit** 착취하다, 부당하게 이용하다 **vast** 막대한 **sustained** 일관된, 지속적인 **persuade** 설득하다

A Listen to the definitions and write down the words.

1. subordinate _____

2. c _____

3. p _____

4. m _____

5. c _____

6. f _____

7. b _____

8. r _____

9. d _____

10. i _____

11. c _____

12. m _____

13. v _____

14. a _____

15. s _____

16. m _____

B Choose a sentence that best describes each Korean sentence.

1. 서점에는 체중 감량에 관해 일반적으로 두 가지 종류의 책들이 있습니다.

   (a) _____

   (b) _____

2. 그것들을 길러봐야 할 것 같았거든.

   (a) _____

   (b) _____

3. 이것은 책상, 책장, 파일함 등을 배치하는 것이 포함됩니다.

   (a) _____

   (b) _____

4. 밝은 색상은 학생들이 수업 중에 최선을 다할 수 있도록 해 줍니다.

   (a) _____

   (b) _____

5. 어느 집이나 가장 많은 집안일을 하는 곳이 바로 부엌입니다.

   (a) _____

   (b) _____

C   Listen to three phrases and complete each sentence.

go out / I'm supposed to / with her for dinner
1. ➡ I'm supposed to go out with her for dinner. _____

2. _____

3. _____

4. _____

5. _____

D   Listen to the following and choose a sentence that has the same meaning.

1. A fundraising leader sets a target of how much money it wants to raise.
   (a) _____
   (b) _____

2. Be certain to make use of benchmarking techniques on a regular basis.
   (a) _____
   (b) _____

3. You can see how close to your financial goals you are.
   (a) _____
   (b) _____

4. There wasn't much the director could do as the storyline was quite weak.
   (a) _____
   (b) _____

5. He was the only one who seemed to have any real talent in the movie.
   (a) _____
   (b) _____

RELATIONSHIP OF IDEAS

VOCABULARY PREVIEW 🎧

Write down the meanings of the words.

01	disaster	13	debris
02	death toll	14	spoil
03	attribute	15	ban *v.*
04	rebuke	16	phenomenon
05	vast	17	anonymously
06	deforestation	18	insulting
07	lessen	19	trait
08	momentum	20	encounter *n.*
09	dwelling	21	stimulus
10	aftermath	22	civility
11	destructive	23	discreet
12	landslide	24	proactive

GUIDED LISTENING 🎧

1 Conversation

Listening Notes

(Connecticut vs New York)

    (winter)

    (summer)

    (people)

Relationship of Ideas

1 What comparison do the speakers make between New York and Connecticut?

(a) working environment and condition

(b) climate and pace of life

(c) weather and prices of commodities

(d) temperature and personality

Comprehension

2 Which is correct about the man and woman?

(a) The man wants to return to New York.

(b) They both have been to New York.

(c) The woman thinks it is hotter in Connecticut.

(d) They both like Connecticut better.

2 Conversation

Listening Notes

(the Gordon Library)

    (location)

    (size)

(the City Library)

    (location)

    (size)

Relationship of Ideas

1 Which best explains the difference between the Gordon and City Library?

(a) One is neat but has less books; the other is messy but has more books.

(b) One is close but has old books; the other is far but has new books.

(c) One is near but has less books; the other is far but has more books.

(d) One is small but has more books; the other is big but has less books.

Comprehension

2 Which is correct according to the conversation?

(a)

(b)

(c)

(d)

3 Monologue

Listening Notes

(Problem)

(Result)

(expectation on condition)

      (reason) as there is a likelihood of

(opinions on the cause)

      (the Chinese government)

      (international organizations)

Relationship of Ideas

1 What comparison does the speaker make between the Chinese government and international organizations?

(a) what damages they think the flood had caused

(b) what measures they think are the best to prevent floods

(c) what they think are the causes for the flood

(d) how long the disaster would last this time

Comprehension

2 Which is correct about the current flooding in China?

(a) It is beneficial for areas which are usually dry.

(b) It has left hundreds of people dead.

(c) It has contributed to deforestation.

(d) It will lessen in a few days.

4 Monologue

Listening Notes

(Earthquakes)
> *the potential to cause*

(direct impact)
> *(result of the impact)*

(aftermath)
> *(land)*

> *(building)*

Relationship of Ideas | **1** How does the speaker categorize the effects of earthquakes?

(a) the first effects and the secondary effects

(b) the major effects and the minor effects

(c) the effects on humans and the environment

(d) the effects on the earth and the ocean

Inference II | **2** What can be inferred from the talk?

(a)

(b)

(c)

(d)

1 Conversation

1 What comparison do the speakers make between New York and Connecticut?
   (a) working environment and condition
   (b) climate and pace of life
   (c) weather and prices of commodities
   (d) temperature and personality

2 Which is correct about the man and woman?
   (a) The man wants to return to New York.
   (b) They both have been to New York.
   (c) The woman thinks it is hotter in Connecticut.
   (d) They both like Connecticut better.

M Hi, I'm Jeffrey Peterson.

W I'm Lillian Brook. Welcome to the Connecticut office. I guess you've _____ New York.

M Yes. I joined the office yesterday.

W _____?

M Well, _____. Winters are cold in New York, too. But it feels like it's much colder here.

W I think you're right. And summer is hot and humid throughout the state, but not as much as in New York, I guess.

M But things are calmer here. I mean, people are _____ _____.

W Right. I was in New York for one year. I couldn't believe ____ ____ _____.

transfer 옮기다, 전임시키다 humid 습한 relaxed 느긋한 fast-paced 속도가 빠른 commodity 일상용품

2 Conversation

1 Which best explains the difference between the Gordon and City Library?
   (a) One is neat but has less books; the other is messy but has more books.
   (b) One is close but has old books; the other is far but has new books.
   (c) One is near but has less books; the other is far but has more books.
   (d) One is small but has more books; the other is big but has less books.

2 Which is correct according to the conversation?
   (a) There is a library across from the coffee shop.
   (b) It is too far to walk to the City Library.
   (c) The woman is urgently looking for a library.
   (d) The man was heading for the department store.

W Excuse me. I'm new to this town. _____ _____?

M Sure. Which one are you looking for? There are a lot of public libraries here.

W I just need to get there _____.

M Okay. Just go straight from here and then _____ _____. You'll see a coffee shop there. There is a library on the same side as the coffee shop. It is the Gordon Library. It is a little small and they don't have many books there.

W Hmm, is there another library nearby?

M Actually, if you _____, you'll see the City Library right next to a department store. It's about a 30 minute walk, but there are more books and _____.

look for ~을 찾다 as fast as I can 될 수 있는 한 빨리 take a right 우회전하다 nearby 근처에

3 Monologue

1 What comparison does the speaker make between the Chinese government and international organizations?
   (a) what damages they think the flood had caused
   (b) what measures they think are the best to prevent floods
   (c) what they think are the causes for the flood
   (d) how long the disaster would last this time

2 Which is correct about the current flooding in China?
   (a) It is beneficial for areas which are usually dry.
   (b) It has left hundreds of people dead.
   (c) It has contributed to deforestation.
   (d) It will lessen in a few days.

W The Yangtze and Yellow Rivers are _____ _____. As a result, the northwest area of China, which is usually dry during these months, has been flooded. This is considered the worst natural disaster of the century, _____ _____ several hundred, with hundreds more still missing. The flood conditions are not expected to change for another week _____ _____ for the next few days. The Chinese government _____ _____, an unavoidable part of the natural cycle. However, international organizations have _____ _____ that may have contributed to the flooding.

overflow 넘쳐흐르다 bank 강둑 disaster 재해 death toll 사망(희생)자 수 likelihood 가능성 attribute ~의 탓으로 돌리다 rebuke 비난하다, 꾸짖다
vast 막대한, 광대한 deforestation 산림 벌채 beneficial 유익한, 이익이 되는 lessen 줄이다, 적게 하다

4 Monologue

1 How does the speaker categorize the effects of earthquakes?
   (a) the first effects and the secondary effects
   (b) the major effects and the minor effects
   (c) the effects on humans and the environment
   (d) the effects on the earth and the ocean

2 What can be inferred from the talk?
   (a) The amount of damage may increase as time passes.
   (b) Tidal waves generate earthquakes.
   (c) strong buildings may remain unaffected by earthquakes.
   (d) Landslides occur only in coastal areas.

W Earthquakes are a form of natural disaster that have the potential to cause damage _____. Earthquakes _____. Tidal waves can gain momentum and travel at very high speeds _____ _____. These waves may destroy human dwellings near coastal areas and also sweep away _____ _____. The aftermath of an earthquake is equally destructive. After an earthquake, an area may be hit hard by landslides and underwater slides, the consequences of which are horrific. Many people may become _____ _____ formed due to landslides and the collapse of buildings. Buildings and other structures weakened by earthquakes may collapse even weeks after an earthquake has occurred.

disaster 재해, 재난 potential 가능성, 잠재력 on a mass scale 대규모로 tidal wave 해일 momentum 운동량, 여세, 힘 dwelling 집, 거주
aftermath 여파, 영향 destructive 파괴적인 landslide 산사태 consequences 결과 debris 부스러기, 파편, 잔해 collapse 붕괴, 무너짐, 붕괴하다

1 What can be inferred from the conversation?

(a) The man will buy something similar to the woman's necklace.

(b) The woman usually shops at City Center Mall.

(c) The woman does not have much experience in buying jewelry.

(d) The woman is now turning 20.

Relationship of Ideas

2 What comparison do the speakers make between genetically modified and naturally-grown foods?

(a) the quality and nutrition

(b) the length of cultivation and diversity

(c) the convenience and health issue

(d) the cost and taste

Relationship of Ideas

3 Which best explains the relationship between stimuli and civility?

(a) Less stimuli cause better civility.

(b) More stimuli cause better civility.

(c) Better stimuli cause better civility.

(d) Worse stimuli cause worse civility.

4 What is implied about big businesses according to the news report?

(a) Their employees are given inadequate health facilities.

(b) Their workers are responsible for their own health care.

(c) Their aim is to avoid government interference.

(d) They spend generously on worker health insurance.

Relationship of Ideas

5 In what order, do the speakers explain the exhibition?

(a) from the most impressive thing to the least impressive thing

(b) from the first impression to the last impression

(c) from the exterior to the interior of the museum

(d) from the worst experience to the best experience

6   What is mainly being discussed about snails and slugs?

(a) what their shells are made of

(b) how they are different from each other

(c) why they are grouped together

(d) how their stomachs help them move

7   What does the lecture mainly focus on?

(a) Chekoya's system of writing the Cherokee language

(b) Chekoya's compilation of ancient Cherokee writing

(c) learning to speak and write Cherokee

(d) Chekoya's Cherokee language book

8   What are the speakers mainly talking about?

(a) the types of transportation that they prefer

(b) the benefits of traveling by trains

(c) the cost of a train and a plane

(d) how to avoid traffic congestion

Relationship of Ideas

9   What comparison does the speaker make between books and movies or plays?

(a) the price and the duration of enjoyment

(b) their cost and their convenience

(c) the benefits earned from reading or watching

(d) the amount of money that can be saved

10   What can be inferred from the conversation?

(a)

(b)

(c)

(d)

1 Conversation

What can be inferred from the conversation?

(a) The man will buy something similar to the woman's necklace.

(b) The woman usually shops at City Center Mall.

(c) The woman does not have much experience in buying jewelry.

(d) The woman is now turning 20.

M   _____ is very beautiful.

W   Thank you. I also like it.

M   _____?

W   Well, my friend gave it to me as a gift for my birthday. She got it from the Jewel House in City Center Mall.

M   Actually, _____. I'm sure _____.

W   In that case, I can _____ for your sister.

M   Thank you. My sister will be very happy.

pearl 진주   necklace 목걸이   wear 입고 있다, 몸에 걸치고 있다   jewel 보석, 액세서리   actually 실제로, 사실은   turn ~이 되다, ~로 변하다
in that case 그 경우에는, 그렇다면   similar 비슷한, 유사한   jewelry 보석류

2 Conversation

What comparison do the speakers make between genetically modified and naturally-grown foods?

(a) the quality and nutrition

(b) the length of cultivation and diversity

(c) the convenience and health issue

(d) the cost and taste

M   Are you aware that almost all foods are now _____ _____?

W   Yes, I know and I'm quite concerned about the consequences.

M   Well, _____, but I don't see any side effects.

W   They may not _____ for many years. Why can't we just _____?

M   Actually they spoil very easily, and you can't enjoy as many varieties with them.

W   At least _____ of genetically modified food, though.

M   I agree with you. We had better ban those foods.

genetically 유전학적으로, 유전적으로   modify 변경(수정)하다, 변화시키다   be concerned about ~에 대해 걱정하다   consequence 결과   side effect 부작용
evident 명백한, 분명한   naturally-grown 자연적으로 자란, 천연 재배된   spoil 상하다, 썩다   variety 변화, 다양성   ban 금지하다

3 Monologue

Which best explains the relationship between stimuli and civility?
(a) Less stimuli cause better civility.
(b) More stimuli cause better civility.
(c) Better stimuli cause better civility.
(d) Worse stimuli cause worse civility.

W Psychologists are taking interest in the new phenomenon of "flaming," where individuals _____ insulting messages on the Internet. This behavior is directed as much by individual personality traits as by the way the human brain is conditioned for interaction. _____ provide a wide range of stimuli like voice tone and facial expression, which guide human responses and serve to _____ _____. These are absent in online, _____. So when the brain doesn't receive such direct information, _____ _____.

psychologist 심리학자 **phenomenon** 현상 **flaming** 플레이밍(불특정 타인이나 무관심한 주제에 대하여 적대성을 표현하는 반사회적인 행동들로서 과거 오프라인에서는 경험하지 못한 소비자들의 새로운 행동들) **anonymously** 익명으로 **insulting** 모욕적인 **personality** 개성, 성격 **trait** 특징 **face-to-face** 정면으로 마주보는, 직접적인 **stimulus** 자극, 격려 (pl. stimuli) **civility** 정중함, 공손함 **text-only** 글자로만 **discreet** 분별 있는, 신중한

4 Monologue

What is implied about big businesses according to the news report?
(a) Their employees are given inadequate health facilities.
(b) Their workers are responsible for their own health care.
(c) Their aim is to avoid government interference.
(d) They spend generously on worker health insurance.

W Big businesses are beginning _____ the good health of their employees. _____ suggested by experts to reduce spending on future employee health problems. This trend is not just about the bottom line, according to health economist Robin Boon, but a move _____ _____. He says that if employees are not treated well, companies could _____ _____ and be forced to _____ _____. Big businesses would certainly not like this to happen.

pay attention to ~에 주의를 기울이다 **proactive** 전향적인, 미리 대책을 강구하는 **expert** 전문가 **comply with** ~에 따르다 **inadequate** 부적절한 **facilities** 편의시설 **interference** 간섭, 중재 **generously** 후하게, 관대하게

5 Conversation

In what order, do the speakers explain the exhibition?
(a) from the most impressive thing to the least impressive thing
(b) from the first impression to the last impression
(c) from the exterior to the interior of the museum
(d) from the worst experience to the best experience

M Did you like _____?

W Well, the paintings were excellent. How did you like it?

M When I first went in, I thought the place was really quiet and neat.

W Yes, it was. _____. It was really something.

M Right. But as more people came in, I _____ _____. And then, the museum became too crowded as more time passed.

W I know. The Art Hall at the City Center would have been _____ _____. The rooms in this museum are very small and can't even accommodate ten people.

M And with this crowd, it's too noisy.

W True. But it was surprising _____ _____. They were shaking hands with all the visitors who were leaving the exhibition.

M I thought that was very impressive, too.

art exhibition 미술전시회 | lighting 조명, 채광 | crowded 혼잡한, 붐비는, 만원인 | appropriate 적당한, 어울리는, 알맞은 | accommodate 수용하다, 숙박시키다 | crowd 군중, 관객, 많은 사람들 | impressive 인상적인 | exterior 외부, 외관 (↔ interior)

6 Monologue

What is mainly being discussed about snails and slugs?
(a) what their shells are made of
(b) how they are different from each other
(c) why they are grouped together
(d) how their stomachs help them move

M Let me now introduce you to gastropods. Gastropods are of two basic types, snails and slugs. Now, you might think the two _____ _____ since _____ and the slug has only a thin mantle. However, _____ _____ which puts them into the same family despite their external differences: in both creatures _____ _____. Actually, the term "gastropod" comes from this feature: it _____ "stomach feet."

gastropod 복족류(腹足類) (달팽이 따위) | snail 달팽이 | slug 민달팽이 | shell 껍질, 조가비 | mantle (연체동물의) 외투막(膜) | share 공유하다 | feature 특징 | family (생물) 과(科) | despite ~에도 불구하고 | external 외부의, 겉의 | digest 소화시키다 | term 용어, 어휘 | literally 글자 그대로 | stomach 위, 복부

7 Monologue

What does the lecture mainly focus on?
(a) Chekoya's system of writing the Cherokee language
(b) Chekoya's compilation of ancient Cherokee writing
(c) learning to speak and write Cherokee
(d) Chekoya's Cherokee language book

M Let me give you some information about the writing system in the Cherokee language, _____ chapter of our Cherokee language book. Most of _____ _____ to know that the written Cherokee language was developed rather recently. _____ _____ goes to Cherokee Indian warrior Chekoya. He began creating the 86 letters of the Cherokee alphabet in 1809. He used an English grammar book to access English symbols _____ in the Cherokee language. Chekoya's work _____, making it possible for people to read and write Cherokee for the first time.

credit 공로, 공적 | **warrior** 전사, 용사 | **adapt** 적합하게 하다 | **capture** 붙잡다, 손에 넣다 | **compilation** 편찬

8 Conversation

What are the speakers mainly talking about?
(a) the types of transportation that they prefer
(b) the benefits of traveling by trains
(c) the cost of a train and a plane
(d) how to avoid traffic congestion

M Oh, I feel so good traveling by train.
W Really? _____?
M One is that you don't have _____.
W You don't have that traveling by air. And it's faster.
M But _____. You have all the time to do whatever you want.
W That's true. But I just want to get there as fast as I can.
M Well, usually, airports are very far from cities and _____ _____. And _____ _____, too. And trains are less expensive than planes.
W I don't know. I still think _____.

specific 특별한, 분명한, 구체적인 **traffic congestion** 교통체증, 교통혼잡 **relaxing** 긴장을 풀어주는, 마음을 가라앉혀주는 **boarding** 탑승, 승선
expensive 비싼 **still** 아직도, 여전히

9 Monologue

What comparison does the speaker make between books and movies or plays?
(a) the price and the duration of enjoyment
(b) their cost and their convenience
(c) the benefits earned from reading or watching
(d) the amount of money that can be saved

W _____, when you seriously consider them. In Boston you'd have to pay 9 dollars for a movie. A first-run showing of a major play would cost 300 dollars while _____ or sports events cost about 150 dollars. Consider, however, that all these give only about 2-4 hours of entertainment. A good book, on the other hand, _____. A single large, interesting book can take anywhere from 2 weeks to a month to read. Moreover, you can lend it to friends, _____ _____. You can even sell it later, _____; things impossible to do with a movie or play. So, spending 25 dollars on a book seems pretty reasonable!

major 주요한, 일류의 **showing** (연극, 공연의) 상연 **front-row** 앞줄의, 앞좌석의 **entertainment** 오락, 여흥 **double** 두 배로 하다, 배로 늘리다 **triple** 세 배로 하다 **charity** 자선단체 **reasonable** 적당한, 비싸지 않은

10 Conversation

What can be inferred from the conversation?
(a) The man will go to Australia with the woman.
(b) The woman does not like Premier Travel.
(c) The man is looking for an inexpensive ticket.
(d) The woman works overseas.

W I heard you're _____ Australia. Have you reserved the tickets?

M No, _____, but all the travel agencies were too expensive.

W Why don't you try Premier Travel? They _____ _____.

M Are you sure? I've never heard of them.

W I always get my travel booked through them.

M Well, I'll check with them. Could you _____ _____?

W Sure, _____.

reserve 예약하다, 확보해 두다 **travel agency** 여행대리점, 여행사 **affordable** (가격 등이) 알맞은, 감당할 수 있는 **inexpensive** 값싼, 저렴한 **overseas** 해외에서, 외국으로

LISTENING REVIEW 🎧

A   Listen to the definitions and write down the words.

1. disaster _____
2. r _____
3. p _____
4. a _____
5. c _____
6. d _____
7. l _____
8. d _____

9. m _____
10. e _____
11. b _____
12. p _____
13. a _____
14. i _____
15. d _____
16. i _____

B   Choose a sentence that best describes each Korean sentence.

1. 그것은 친구가 생일 선물로 준 거에요.
   (a) _____
   (b) _____

2. 부작용들이 수년 동안 분명하게 드러나지 않을지도 몰라.
   (a) _____
   (b) _____

3. 직접적인 만남은 다양한 자극을 제공한다.
   (a) _____
   (b) _____

4. 글자로만 의사소통을 하는 온라인에서는 이런 것들이 결여되어 있다.
   (a) _____
   (b) _____

5. 이것은 전문가들이 제안한 전향적인 조치입니다.
   (a) _____
   (b) _____

C Listen to three phrases and complete each sentence.

could be forced / Companies / to comply with stricter guidelines
1. ➡ Companies could be forced to comply with stricter guidelines.
_____

2. _____

3. _____

4. _____

5. _____

D Listen to the following and choose a sentence that has the same meaning.

1. He used an English grammar book to access English symbols.
   (a) _____
   (b) _____

2. I still think we should have taken an airplane.
   (a) _____
   (b) _____

3. Consider that all these give only about 2-4 hours of entertainment.
   (a) _____
   (b) _____

4. You can lend it to friends, thereby doubling or tripling its enjoyment.
   (a) _____
   (b) _____

5. They offer many affordable packages.
   (a) _____
   (b) _____

CHAPTER 06

INFERENCE I

VOCABULARY PREVIEW 🎧

Write down the meanings of the words.

01	bridegroom	13	obligation
02	innate	14	legendary
03	portray	15	captivate
04	homebound	16	complication
05	exotic	17	avid
06	accompany	18	rub
07	frustration	19	remedy
08	abandon	20	restorative
09	detection	21	bizarre
10	upcoming	22	suspend
11	generate	23	inevitable
12	contractual	24	recession

GUIDED LISTENING 🎧

1 Conversation

Listening Notes

(problem of the man)

(solution from the woman)

(condition) remember to give them back

Inference I

1 What can be inferred about the woman?

(a) She is taking the same class as the man.

(b) She took chemistry last semester.

(c) She doesn't need her notes for a test.

(d) She doesn't want the man to borrow her notes.

Comprehension

2 Which is correct according to the conversation?

(a) The man had an illness.

(b) The woman wants her notes back today.

(c) The woman has recently passed a test.

(d) The man does not like chemistry.

2 Conversation

Listening Notes

(the woman's purpose of talk)

(the man's reason)

(the woman's order)

(the man's decision)

Inference I

1 What can be inferred about the man?

(a) He will not move his car until his friend comes.

(b) He is getting married today.

(c) He didn't see the no-parking sign before he parked.

(d) He got a ticket at the same place before.

Detail

2 What is the man's problem?

(a)

(b)

(c)

(d)

3 Monologue

Listening Notes

(innate talent)
       to be
       given
(Henry James)
       who
(childhood)
       never imagined
       (reason)
           1.
           2. He also suffered
(later)
       Gradually

Inference I

1 What can be inferred about Henry James?

(a) He didn't like his brother when he was young.

(b) He enjoyed staying home rather than going outside.

(c) He became recognized slowly over a long period of time.

(d) He wanted to study at Harvard University.

Comprehension

2 Which is correct according to the lecture?

(a) Some people are just born more talented.

(b) Henry James didn't receive proper education.

(c) Henry James spent a lot of time at home.

(d) People started to recognize him when he went to Harvard.

Listening Notes

(announcement)

    1. Hurry up, because

    2. you can get

    3 Don't delay, because

    4. For kids, we have

    5. With your membership you can

Inference I

1   What can be inferred about Shop Town?

    (a) They are providing discounts for limited time.

    (b) They ran out of most of their supplies.

    (c) They don't offer any discounts for non-members.

    (d) They are closing the store after this sale.

Detail

2   What is the maximum discount the members can get?

    (a)

    (b)

    (c)

    (d)

1 Conversation

1 What can be inferred about the woman?
   (a) She is taking the same class as the man.
   (b) She took chemistry last semester.
   (c) She doesn't need her notes for a test.
   (d) She doesn't want the man to borrow her notes.

2 Which is correct according to the conversation?
   (a) The man had an illness.
   (b) The woman wants her notes back today.
   (c) The woman has recently passed a test.
   (d) The man does not like chemistry.

W I heard that you were in the hospital for a week. What happened?

M Well, _____.

W Oh, how are you feeling now?

M Much better, but I'm more worried about the chemistry classes I missed.

W Don't worry. I'm sure you can _____. You can borrow my notes if you want.

M Really? Well, I'd be _____ if you lent them to me. Can I get them today?

W Sure, but remember to give them back next week. _____ _____.

M Okay, _____.

down with 병으로 누워 있는 chemistry class 화학 수업 miss 빠뜨리다, 빼먹다 catch up 따라잡다 borrow 빌리다, 차용하다
grateful 감사하고 있는, 고마워하는

2 Conversation

1 What can be inferred about the man?
   (a) He will not move his car until his friend comes.
   (b) He is getting married today.
   (c) He didn't see the no-parking sign before he parked.
   (d) He got a ticket at the same place before.

2 What is the man's problem?
   (a) His car won't work.
   (b) He is late for a wedding.
   (c) He doesn't know how to drive.
   (d) He failed to pay a ticket.

W This is a no-parking zone. _____.

M I didn't know that. Is it _____?

W It's on the board. Can't you read it?

M I'm sorry, but I have to park my car here. I'm waiting for a bridegroom.

W This is against traffic rules, so please _____.

M Well, I can't go without taking the bridegroom. We're already late for his wedding.

W _____. If you don't move on, I'll have _____.

M Okay, I'm going. I need to find another parking space, I guess.

no-parking zone 주차금지 구역 park 주차하다 bridegroom 신랑 drive off (차 따위가) 떠나버리다 write a ticket 교통 위반 딱지를 떼다

3 Monologue

1 What can be inferred about Henry James?
(a) He didn't like his brother when he was young.
(b) He enjoyed staying home rather than going outside.
(c) He became recognized slowly over a long period of time.
(d) He wanted to study at Harvard University.

2 Which is correct according to the lecture?
(a) Some people are just born more talented.
(b) Henry James didn't receive proper education.
(c) Henry James spent a lot of time at home.
(d) People started to recognize him when he went to Harvard.

W Everyone has _____ _____ and given enough room for growth. Henry James, the famous novelist who portrayed the upper class of American society, is the best example in this context. He might have never imagined that he could become _____ _____ of the 19th century. Henry James was always _____ _____ William James, who was more educated than him and was a professor of law at Harvard University. As a result, he was never recognized by others early in his life. He also _____, making him homebound most of the time. This gave him _____ _____. Gradually his works gained popularity and he gained recognition as a great writer.

innate 타고난, 선천적인 room 여지, 기회 novelist 소설가 portray 묘사하다 upper 상위의 context 문맥, 상황, 사정 count ~의 축에 들다, ~으로 간주하다 figure 인물 overshadow 그늘지게 하다, 어둡게 하다 suffer from ~으로 고생하다 homebound 집에 틀어박혀 있는 recognition 인지, 인정

4 Monologue

1 What can be inferred about Shop Town?
(a) They are providing discounts for limited time.
(b) They ran out of most of their supplies.
(c) They don't offer any discounts for non-members.
(d) They are closing the store after this sale.

2 What is the maximum discount the members can get?
(a) 60 %
(b) 80 %
(c) 75 %
(d) 70 %

M Good evening, ladies and gentlemen. Welcome to Shop Town! Hope you are having a good time _____ _____! Hurry up, because today is the last day of our Thanksgiving Day sale! Our prices have never been as attractive: you can _____, from clothing to footwear and from pots to exotic gift sets. Don't delay, because _____ _____. For kids, we have an exciting discount on a variety of toys, books and kids' wear. Attention, Shop Town Card Members! With your membership you can _____ _____ in addition to the already existing discounted prices.

Thanksgiving Day 추수감사절 attractive 매력적인, 마음을 끄는 footwear 신발류 pot 그릇 exotic 이국적인 delay 지체하다 run out 바닥이 나다 a variety of 다양한 extra 추가의

PRACTICAL LISTENING 𝒬

1 Which is correct according to the conversation?

(a) The man usually goes to the shopping mall.

(b) The woman has been to the shopping mall once.

(c) The woman and her friends are going to the mall.

(d) The man does not want to meet the woman's friends.

2 Which is correct about children with dyslexia according to the talk?

(a) They must be taught in special schools.

(b) They are students who learn differently.

(c) They need to stop engaging in crime.

(d) They tend to lag behind at school even with extra help.

Inference I

3 What can be inferred about the woman?

(a) She likes cooking some Italian food.

(b) She doesn't want the man to miss her food.

(c) She will wait until the man finishes the papers.

(d) She wants the man to finish his papers early.

4 What is the main topic of the conversation?

(a) what books the man reads while commuting

(b) the man's commute to work by subway

(c) how the man gets a seat on the subway

(d) the man's opinion about subway services

Inference I

5 What can be inferred about the speaker?

(a) The speaker has doubts about taking out loans.

(b) The speaker considers the terms of the contract unfair.

(c) The speaker objects to Olsons' high demands.

(d) The speaker is worried over the company's reduced revenues.

6 Which is correct according to the talk?

(a) His music company will re-launch his music.

(b) His style of music is no longer popular in Africa.

(c) His songs described Africa's traditional legends.

(d) His band made Swahili music known internationally.

7 Which is correct about hair loss according to the talk?

(a) Hair loss has increased since Ancient Egyptian times.

(b) Ancient Egyptian cosmetics were usually derived from laurels.

(c) Julius Caesar is believed to have used animal fat for hair-styling.

(d) Modern means to fight hair loss are no better than ancient ones.

Inference I   8 What can be inferred about the speakers?

(a) The woman thinks the pay is low.

(b) The man is irritated by the woman.

(c) The man is considering more pay for experienced workers.

(d) The woman doesn't like shopping.

9 What is the conversation mainly about?

(a) methods for improving productivity

(b) schedules for bonus payments

(c) the company's new policy and the reason behind it

(d) frustrations over the company's marketing strategies

Inference I 10 What can be inferred about CompuNext?

(a)

(b)

(c)

(d)

1 Conversation

Which is correct according to the conversation?

(a) The man usually goes to the shopping mall.

(b) The woman has been to the shopping mall once.

(c) The woman and her friends are going to the mall.

(d) The man does not want to meet the woman's friends.

W I heard that the new shopping mall is very big. _____

_____?

M No. How about you?

W No, _____. But I'm planning to go there this weekend.

M Would you mind _____? I need to do some shopping.

W Not at all, _____.

M Are you going along with them?

W Yeah, we've had this plan for the last two weeks.

either (부정문에서) ~도 또한 plan to ~할 작정이다 would you mind if ~해도 괜찮겠습니까? accompany ~와 동행하다, ~을 따라가다
do some shopping 쇼핑하다, 장보다 not at all 천만에, 그렇지 않다 provided 만약 ~라면 mind -ing ~을 싫어하다, 꺼리다 along with ~와 함께, 같이

2 Monologue

Which is correct about children with dyslexia according to the talk?

(a) They must be taught in special schools.

(b) They are students who learn differently.

(c) They need to stop engaging in crime.

(d) They tend to lag behind at school even with extra help.

W I'm going to start this talk on dyslexia by referring to dyslexic children and _____

_____. They typically _____

_____. In extreme cases, dyslexia can cause a child to eventually get into criminal trouble, as he or she abandons school for "street" activities. While early detection of dyslexia is one of the main ways to resolve it, another method is to get schools and teachers to _____

_____. It's important to remember that children with dyslexia are not people who can't or don't want to learn, they merely do so differently from others. Also, it's often the negative treatment they receive that turns them off of learning.

dyslexia 난독증 refer to ~을 언급하다 dyslexic 독서 장애의, 독서 장애자 hopelessness 가망 없음, 절망 frustration 좌절
blame A for B B에 대해 A를 비난하다 abandon 그만두다, 단념하다 detection 발견, 간파 resolve 해결하다 merely 단지, 다만 engage in ~에 가담하다
lag behind 뒤지다, 뒤떨어지다

3 Conversation

What can be inferred about the woman?
(a) She likes cooking some Italian food.
(b) She doesn't want the man to miss her food.
(c) She will wait until the man finishes the papers.
(d) She wants the man to finish his papers early.

(Telephone rings.)

W Hello, Sam. This is Lucy here.

M Hi Lucy. What's up?

W Well, _____. Would you like to _____?

M Thanks, Lucy. But I _____ _____. I can't come over now.

W Then let me bring it to your place.

M That'd be great. Are you sure it would be no problem?

W _____. I could walk it over. You could _____ _____ while we eat.

M Sounds like a plan! I'll be waiting for you.

prepare (요리 등을) 준비하다, 차리다 dish 접시, 요리 try out 시험하다 urgent 긴급한 paper 서류, 문서, (연구)논문, 보고서 take a break 잠시 휴식을 취하다 while ~하는 동안 wait for ~을 기다리다

4 Conversation

What is the main topic of the conversation?
(a) what books the man reads while commuting
(b) the man's commute to work by subway
(c) how the man gets a seat on the subway
(d) the man's opinion about subway services

W How do you _____?

M By subway. It saves a lot of time.

W I've found it _____. Do you always get a seat?

M Yes. I usually never have problems doing that. However, when I do, I have to stand for one and a half hours.

W One and half hours is quite long! What do you do during that time?

M I usually read books. _____.

W _____.

M Yeah, I've actually started loving the ride because _____ _____.

commute 통근하다, 통학하다 crowded 혼잡한, 붐비는 most of 대부분의 avid 열심인, 열광적인 kill time 시간을 보내다, 소일하다 ride (탈 것에) 타기, 타고 가기, 타고 있는 시간

5 Monologue

What can be inferred about the speaker?

(a) The speaker has doubts about taking out loans.

(b) The speaker considers the terms of the contract unfair.

(c) The speaker objects to Olsons' high demands.

(d) The speaker is worried over the company's reduced revenues.

M   I have a few concerns about our upcoming business deal with Olsons Inc. We need to rethink our position _____ _____ that company. Olsons is a great potential customer that may be able to generate millions of dollars worth of revenue each year for us. _____ _____. However, we also know that our company does not currently have _____ for them. We _____ to create enough goods to meet their demand. This means that we would need to borrow heavily in order to meet our contractual obligations with Olsons. There are _____, as you know, and I'm seriously worried about them.

upcoming 다가오는, 이번의 sign a contract 계약하다 potential 가능성이 있는, 잠재하는 generate 낳다, 생성하다 revenue 수익, 총수입 upside 위쪽, (가격 등의) 상승 경향 capital 자본, 자산 contractual 계약상의 obligation 의무, 책임 involved 포함된

6 Monologue

Which is correct according to the talk?

(a) His music company will re-launch his music.

(b) His style of music is no longer popular in Africa.

(c) His songs described Africa's traditional legends.

(d) His band made Swahili music known internationally.

M   Inkahta Music Company today announced _____ _____ Swahili singer Nelson Arutha, _____ _____. Arutha was the lead singer in the 1970s group "The African Tigers" which first introduced Swahili music to the world. The Swahili rhythms _____ around the world, from London to Beijing, and even _____ _____ of Swahili culture, history and language. Indeed, Swahili emerged as one of the few African languages that Westerners have at least _____ _____. Known for his gravelly voice, he was a popular figure among the old and young alike. Arutha was famed for going into the audience and encouraging people to dance, from kids to grandmothers. His death is said to be from complications due to lung disease.

legendary 전설적인 Swahili 스와힐리 사람 captivate ~의 마음을 사로잡다 breathe (생기 · 생명 · 영혼 따위를) 불어넣다 emerge 나타나다, 알려지다 passing 지나가는, 접하게 되는 gravelly 목소리가 귀에 거슬리는 figure 인물, 거물 complication 합병증 lung disease 폐질환

Which is correct about hair loss according to the talk?
(a) Hair loss has increased since Ancient Egyptian times.
(b) Ancient Egyptian cosmetics were usually derived from laurels.
(c) Julius Caesar is believed to have used animal fat for hair-styling.
(d) Modern means to fight hair loss are no better than ancient ones.

M   Cosmetics, as I have mentioned, date back to ancient Egypt. Cosmetics do not refer simply to items such as lipstick or coloring nor do they _____. Men have also been _____ of cosmetics to improve their appearance, in particular their hair. Since ancient times, _____ _____. The ancient Egyptians rubbed animal fat over their bald spots, in the hope that it would cause hair to re-grow. In ancient Rome, Julius Caesar wore his characteristic laurel wreath low in order to hide _____. No doubt these sound silly to us today, but modern remedies ranging from hair restorative lotions to toupees are _____ _____.

cosmetics 화장품 have to do with ~와 관련이 있다 avid 탐내는, 갈망하는 appearance 외모, 모양 hair loss 탈모 rub 바르다, 문지르다 fat 지방 laurel wreath 월계관 in order to ~하기 위해서 recede 물러나다, 멀어지다 remedy 치료, 치료법 restorative 회복시키는, 강장제의 toupee (남자용) 부분 가발 bizarre 괴상한, 이상한

What can be inferred about the speakers?
(a) The woman thinks the pay is low.
(b) The man is irritated by the woman.
(c) The man is considering more pay for experienced workers.
(d) The woman doesn't like shopping.

(Telephone rings.)

M   Hello, this is Steven from Trix Supermarket.

W   Hi, I saw _____. I need some more details about it.

M   Okay, what would you like to know?

W   Well, what's the salary for this job?

M   _____ would be the starting pay.

W   Are you sure? Is there _____ _____?

M   Well, it's _____ for everybody _____ _____.

job advertisement 구인 광고 details 상세한 설명 minimum wage 최저 임금 starting pay 초봉 extra 추가의, 여분의, 특별한, 별도의 experienced 경험이 있는 applicant 지원자, 신청자 standard 표준의, 기준이 되는 rate 요금, 임금 irritate ~을 짜증나게 하다, 화나게 하다

9 Conversation

What is the conversation mainly about?
(a) methods for improving productivity
(b) schedules for bonus payments
(c) the company's new policy and the reason behind it
(d) frustrations over the company's marketing strategies

M There's _____ that our bonuses have been _____.

W Yeah, I've heard that. _____.

M Why do you say so?

W The market is experiencing _____ and every company has to take measures to cut expenses and maintain stability.

M Aren't there other ways of doing that?

W Yes, there are. Our benefits could be reduced, working hours increased or employees told to leave.

M I do understand. _____. Even so, suspending the bonuses is very unfair.

rumor 소문 temporarily 일시적으로 suspend 미루다, 일시 정지하다 inevitable 피할 수 없는, 당연한 recession 불황, 경기침체
take measures 조치를 취하다 expense 비용, 지출 maintain 유지하다, 지속하다 stability 안정(성) benefit 수당, 보조금 employee 종업원, 직원
even so 그렇다 하더라도 unfair 불공평한, 부당한 strategy 전략 overcome 이겨내다, 극복하다 downturn 하강, 침체 frustration 좌절, 실망, 불만

10 Monologue

What can be inferred about CompuNext?
(a) It has experienced decreased sales recently.
(b) It is the most leading company in the market.
(c) Its products have not attracted young people.
(d) It has been customizing its products.

M Good morning. We're meeting today to discuss CompuNext's _____. Up to now, _____ _____ for older professionals, the kinds of people we see _____ in cafes or in parks. I believe that we must _____ _____. We can do that by making it possible for our users to express their individuality. In short, we need to provide more customization features. This should be our key strategy to attract young buyers _____ _____, both male and female, if we are to increase our market share.

product line 제품군, 제품 라인 share 시장 점유율 shift 옮기다, 바꾸다 customization 주문에 응하여 만듦, 고객 취미에 맞게 설정함 attract ~의 마음을 끌다

LISTENING REVIEW 🎧

A   Listen to the definitions and write down the words.

1. strategy

9. b

2. a

10. r

3. r

11. g

4. i

12. o

5. r

13. c

6. s

14. a

7. r

15. u

8. r

16. a

B   Choose a sentence that best describes each Korean sentence.

1. 모든 사람은 인정받아야 할 타고난 재능이 있다.
   (a)
   (b)

2. 이것이 그의 모든 에너지를 글쓰기에 몰두할 수 있는 기회를 주었다.
   (a)
   (b)

3. 점차적으로 그의 작품은 인기를 얻게 되었고, 그는 인정을 받게 되었습니다.
   (a)
   (b)

4. 기존의 할인가에서 15% 추가 할인을 받으실 수 있습니다.
   (a)
   (b)

5. 전혀요. 내 친구들과 만나는 게 싫지 않다면요.
   (a)
   (b)

C Listen to three phrases and complete each sentence.

who can't learn / are not people / Children with dyslexia
1. ➡ Children with dyslexia are not people who can't learn.

2. _____

3. _____

4. _____

5. _____

D Listen to the following and choose a sentence that has the same meaning.

1. Olsons is a great potential customer that may be able to generate millions of dollars.
  (a) _____
  (b) _____

2. Our company does not currently have enough capital to complete major orders.
  (a) _____
  (b) _____

3. He was a popular figure among the old and young alike.
  (a) _____
  (b) _____

4. Men have also been avid users of cosmetics to improve their appearance.
  (a) _____
  (b) _____

5. Is there anything extra for experienced applicants?
  (a) _____
  (b) _____

CHAPTER 07

INFERENCE II

VOCABULARY PREVIEW 🎧

Write down the meanings of the words.

01	donate	13	incoherent
02	take ~ for granted	14	antibody
03	agenda	15	toxic
04	significant	16	infectious
05	revise	17	uptight
06	threat	18	primitive
07	controversial	19	wondrous
08	cite	20	sophisticated
09	detrimental	21	skeptical
10	revive	22	progressive
11	hustle and bustle	23	innate
12	incapacitate	24	emergence

GUIDED LISTENING 🎧

1 Conversation

Listening Notes

(problem)

    (the man thought)

    (Jane thought)

(the woman's suggestion)

Inference II

1 What can be inferred from the conversation?

    (a) Amy will now call Jane to explain what happened.

    (b) Jane totally forgot her appointment with the man.

    (c) The man is much angrier than Amy and Jane.

    (d) The man and Jane misunderstood each other.

Main Topic

2 What are the man and woman talking about?

    (a) where to meet Amy next time

    (b) a problem the man will have with Amy

    (c) how to make an appointment

    (d) why the appointment fell through

2 Conversation

Listening Notes

(Mr. Barkley)

     (donated to)

     (has been supporting)

(reason)

(the woman's thought)

Inference II

1 Which best describes the lesson learned?

(a) Don't expect money from others.

(b) Don't trust anyone unconditionally.

(c) Don't take anything for granted.

(d) Don't accept gifts without knowing.

Comprehension

2 Which is correct about Mr. Barkley?

(a)

(b)

(c)

(d)

3 Monologue

Listening Notes

(agenda)

    is to

(survey)

    indicates that

    Another significant finding

(conclusion)

    Therefore, I strongly feel that

        • *(focus)*

        • *this can be done*

Inference II

1 What can be inferred from the talk?

    (a) The previous marketing plan targeted a broader age range.

    (b) Their marketing plan for their cola product has failed.

    (c) Less teen consumers like cola drinks nowadays.

    (d) Women over 35 years of age drink lighter drinks.

Main Topic

2 What is mainly being discussed?

    (a) new products to promote

    (b) new consumers to target

    (c) adjusting the age group to focus on

    (d) problems with their products

4 Monologue

Listening Notes

(Use of threat in foreign policy)

(definition)

(consequence)

　　The threatened country tends to

　　(example)

Inference II

1　What can be inferred from the lecture?

(a) Germany is still threatened by Britain and France.

(b) World War II is to blame for much change in foreign policies.

(c) Threatening with military force may create resistance.

(d) Peace is more desirable than war.

Detail

2　Which country is mentioned as an example of a "target country"?

(a)

(b)

(c)

(d)

1 Conversation

1 What can be inferred from the conversation?
(a) Amy will now call Jane to explain what happened.
(b) Jane totally forgot her appointment with the man.
(c) The man is much angrier than Amy and Jane.
(d) The man and Jane misunderstood each other.

2 What are the man and woman talking about?
(a) where to meet Amy next time
(b) a problem the man will have with Amy
(c) how to make an appointment
(d) why the appointment fell through

M Amy, what's the problem with Jane? You know what she did yesterday?

W I guess _____ somewhere, right?

M Yeah, but Jane didn't show up! I waited there _____ _____ for her.

W Are you sure? She told me _____ for more than an hour at Lee's cafe.

M Is she crazy? We were supposed to meet at Presto's.

W That means you both waited for each other _____ _____. Have you spoken to Jane since then?

M No. _____ .

W You can use my phone if you want.

be supposed to ~하기로 되어 있다 **show up** 나타나다, 나오다 **since then** 그때 이후로 **clear ~ up** (문제·의심 따위를) 풀다, 해결하다
fall through 수포로 돌아가다, 실패하다

2 Conversation

1 Which best describes the lesson learned?
(a) Don't expect money from others.
(b) Don't trust anyone unconditionally.
(c) Don't take anything for granted.
(d) Don't accept gifts without knowing.

2 Which is correct about Mr. Barkley?
(a) He didn't want to donate to Nevada University.
(b) He had donated to New Castle for many years.
(c) He is not financially sound this year.
(d) He was asked for a donation by New Castle.

M I heard the dean say that Mr. Barkley donated one million dollars to New Castle University instead of us here at Nevada University.

W Are you sure? Mr. Barkley _____ Nevada University for a long time.

M Yes, everybody at Nevada University was surprised _____ _____ .

W But _____ ? He always really loved Nevada University.

M That's right. I guess we were overconfident about ourselves. We never imagined _____ .

W Why do you say so?

M Actually, New Castle University asked him for donations, and we didn't. I guess we thought he'd always donate to us even if we didn't ask.

W It is a lesson for us but we _____ !

donate 기부하다 **support** 후원하다, 지지하다 **overconfident** 자신만만한, 자부심이 강한 **even if** ~할지라도 **take ~ for granted** ~을 당연하게 생각하다

3 Monologue

1 What can be inferred from the talk?
   (a) The previous marketing plan targeted a broader age range.
   (b) Their marketing plan for their cola product has failed.
   (c) Less teen consumers like cola drinks nowadays.
   (d) Women over 35 years of age drink lighter drinks.

2 What is mainly being discussed?
   (a) new products to promote
   (b) new consumers to target
   (c) adjusting the age group to focus on
   (d) problems with their products

M   The agenda of today's meeting is to modify our marketing plan _____. A survey conducted by our consumer research department indicates that teenagers _____ are the biggest drinkers of our cola. Another significant finding is that women over 35 years of age seldom drink our product. Therefore, I strongly feel that _____. We should _____ our product and this can be done if we advertise our cola on the Internet and television. The advertisements must also cover schools and cafes, as these are _____ by this group.

agenda 안건 modify 수정하다 in light of ~에 비추어 consumer 소비자 indicate 표시하다, 지시하다 significant 중대한, 의미 있는 finding 발견, 조사 결과 seldom 거의 ~하지 않다 revise 개정하다, 수정하다 strategy 전략 focus on ~에 집중하다, 초점을 맞추다 advertise 광고하다 frequently 자주, 빈번하게

4 Monologue

1 What can be inferred from the lecture?
   (a) Germany is still threatened by Britain and France.
   (b) World War II is to blame for much change in foreign policies.
   (c) Threatening with military force may create resistance.
   (d) Peace is more desirable than war.

2 Which country is mentioned as an example of a "target country"?
   (a) France
   (b) England
   (c) Germany
   (d) The United States

W   _____ has been controversial from ancient days. Today, we will discuss its significance in relationships among countries. Many examples can be cited from history which describe the detrimental consequences of threatening a country with military force or using military force on a country. We use the term "target country" for one which is being threatened by another. Threats are likely to make the target country _____, which may compel it to react with force itself. _____ tends to increase its military and _____ and _____. Let's take a look at Germany prior to World War II. Germany revived its military force to counter Britain and France's threats in the late 1930s.

threat 위협 controversial 논쟁의, 논란의 대상이 되는 significance 심각성, 중대성 cite 인용하다 detrimental 유해한, 해가 되는 threaten 위협하다 military force 군세, 병력, 무력 compel ~ to ~로 하여금 …하지 않을 수 없게 하다, 강제로 시키다 tend to ~하는 경향이 있다 prior to ~이전의 revive 부활시키다, 소생시키다 resistance 저항 desirable 바람직한

PRACTICAL LISTENING 🎧

Inference II

1 What can be inferred from the conversation?

(a) Both the woman and George are interested in each other.

(b) The man and the woman will meet George together.

(c) They are not interested in having a blind date.

(d) The man wants to go out with the woman.

2 Which is correct about the contest according to the advertisement?

(a) Two prizes will be given.

(b) It offers a prize of an eight-day luxury stay.

(c) Shoppers can submit only one entry each.

(d) Shoppers can win gifts worth over 100 dollars.

3 Why didn't the man go to the party?

(a) He had to go to the hospital.

(b) He became sick on the way to the party.

(c) He was not informed of the party.

(d) He wants to meet the woman alone.

Inference II

4 What can be inferred from the lecture?

(a) Several benefits are associated with fever.

(b) It is risky to leave a fever untreated.

(c) A fever should not be the target of treatment.

(d) A fever is frightening to ordinary people.

5 What are the man and woman mainly talking about?

(a) countries the woman has visited

(b) vacations with parents

(c) places they want to visit for their vacation

(d) difficulties to face while traveling

6 Which is correct about the man?

(a) The man is not prepared for the presentation.

(b) The man has lost his keys many times.

(c) The man is nervous about the presentation.

(d) The man found the keys on the dresser.

Inference II

7 What can be inferred from the conversation?

(a) The man is worried about the woman looking after his pet.

(b) This is the second time the woman has looked after her aunt's cat.

(c) Cats cause more health problems than dogs for many people.

(d) They have known each other for many years.

8 Which is correct according to the lecture?

(a) All humans once spoke a single language.

(b) Ancient myths are usually based on truth.

(c) Myth-making has long been a part of human culture.

(d) Diverse primitive societies have often invented similar myths.

Inference II

9 What can be inferred from the lecture?

(a) Shakespeare's progressive vision contributed to feminism.

(b) Shakespeare was cynical about women in power.

(c) Shakespeare's heroines succeeded because of innate strength.

(d) Shakespeare was critically aware of discrimination against women.

10 Which is correct according to the lecture?

(a)

(b)

(c)

(d)

1 Conversation

What can be inferred from the conversation?
(a) Both the woman and George are interested in each other.
(b) The man and the woman will meet George together.
(c) They are not interested in having a blind date.
(d) The man wants to go out with the woman.

M So, Jennie, how did you like the food here?

W I liked it very much. I think I want to bring my friends here next time.

M By the way, _____?

W _____? Well, I don't know. I mean I don't really like it. Why do you ask?

M My cousin, George, is coming home from Paris for his vacation.

W And you want me to go on a date with him?

M Yes. You _____ the other day, right? You told me he is cute.

W Yeah, but I'm not sure if he would like to see me.

M He knows that we are meeting today and he wanted me _____ _____.

W Well, how does he know about me?

M _____ and he saw you there.

blind date 소개팅 go on a date with ~와 데이트하다 cute 귀여운 go out with ~와 사귀다

2 Monologue

Which is correct about the contest according to the advertisement?
(a) Two prizes will be given.
(b) It offers a prize of an eight-day luxury stay.
(c) Shoppers can submit only one entry each.
(d) Shoppers can win gifts worth over 100 dollars.

M Are you tired of _____ of city life? Here's your chance to get away! _____ _____ at the Paradiso Island Resort in the Bahamas! Purchase _____ at a Top Mart store and you automatically enter our contest for an all-expenses-paid vacation for two, worth over $10,000. This includes your stay for seven nights and eight days at the Resort's _____ _____, with a personal assistant, a driver, and an 80-foot yacht at your service. Live like royalty during your vacation, having all your personal needs attended to. Don't miss this opportunity of a lifetime: enter the contest at any Top Mart store right away! _____?

hustle and bustle 혼잡, 북새통 luxury 호화로운, 사치스러운 automatically 자동적으로 all-expenses-paid 모든 경비가 지급되는
presidential suite (대통령, 귀빈 등이 묵는) 특별실, 귀빈실 royalty 왕족, 왕위 attend to (맡은 일 등을) 챙기다 lifetime 일생, 일생의

3 Conversation

Why didn't the man go to the party?
(a) He had to go to the hospital.
(b) He became sick on the way to the party.
(c) He was not informed of the party.
(d) He wants to meet the woman alone.

W Why didn't you _____ last night? I'm sure I told you about the party we were having.

M Actually _____, but _____ _____ from the hospital.

W What happened? Anything serious?

M Yes, there was an emergency. A person needed _____ _____.

W Oh, that's too bad. At least you could have informed me about that, though.

M Yes, I meant to, but I became very caught up in the situation. I'll _____ some other time.

W Okay, I'll look forward to that.

---

turn up 나타나다 on one's way to ~에 가는 길에 emergency 비상, 긴급 사태 immediate 즉시의, 즉각적인 at least 적어도, 최소한 though 그러나, 하지만 mean to ~을 의도하다, 할 작정이다 be caught up in ~에 휩싸려 들다, 열중하다, 몰두하다 make ~up (손해 등을) 보상하다 look forward to ~을 기대하다

4 Monologue

What can be inferred from the lecture?
(a) Several benefits are associated with fever.
(b) It is risky to leave a fever untreated.
(c) A fever should not be the target of treatment.
(d) A fever is frightening to ordinary people.

M A fever may look quite frightening to ordinary people. This is especially so in the cases of extreme fever, where a patient may be truly incapacitated, _____.
As medical students you need to remember that fever is not so much an illness as a symptom of one. It is generally the result of a sickness and is _____
working hard to produce _____
_____. A fever works with antibiotics _____. In other words, fever is the body's way of trying to fight sickness and it is therefore _____.

---

fever 열, 열병 frightening 겁나게 하는 extreme 극단적인 incapacitate 무능력하게 하다 incoherent 조리가 없는, 횡설수설하는
defense mechanism 방위 기제 antibody 항체, 항독소 get rid of ~을 제거하다 toxic 독성의 infectious 전염성의, 전염병의

5 Conversation

What are the man and woman mainly talking about?

(a) countries the woman has visited
(b) vacations with parents
(c) places they want to visit for their vacation
(d) difficulties to face while traveling

M Sharon, I heard you've traveled a lot. Is that true?

W Yeah, _____.

M _____! Have you been to Malaysia?

W Yes, I've been there once with my parents.

M Mmm, what about Indonesia?

W Oh, it is a beautiful country. _____

_____ sometime.

M One of my friends lives there and _____

_____ whenever I talk to him. What about

Mauritius? Have you been there?

W Well, no, but we're planning to go there this summer.

M I heard that's _____.

W Yes, it's famous for its beaches.

have been to ~에 가 본 적이 있다 **definitely** 확실히, 틀림없이 **be famous for** ~로 유명하다 **face** ~에 직면하다, ~의 쪽을 향하다

6 Conversation

Which is correct about the man?

(a) The man is not prepared for the presentation.
(b) The man has lost his keys many times.
(c) The man is nervous about the presentation.
(d) The man found the keys on the dresser.

M Rose, _____. Have you seen them?

W No, dear. Have you looked on the dresser?

M Yeah, but they aren't there. I even searched for them in my bag.

W _____?

M No. I'll look.

W Are they there? You might have left them while you were _____

_____.

M You're right. The keys are right here.

W Honey, you should _____. This is not the

fist time that you're giving a presentation. You should be more

confident in yourself.

M I don't know. _____ before any

presentation.

dear 친애하는 사람, 애인, 연인, (주로 부르는 말로) 여보 **dresser** 화장대, 옷장 **search for** ~을 찾다 **drawer** 서랍 **might have p.p.** ~했을지도 모른다 **bill** 계산서, 지폐, 법안 **calm down** 침착하다, 진정하다 **confident** 자신이 있는, 확신하는 **can't help -ing** 어쩔 수 없이 ~하다 **uptight** 초조한, 불안한

7 Conversation

What can be inferred from the conversation?

(a) The man is worried about the woman looking after his pet.

(b) This is the second time the woman has looked after her aunt's cat.

(c) Cats cause more health problems than dogs for many people.

(d) They have known each other for many years.

(Telephone rings.)

M Hi, Jenny. This is Tom here.

W Hi, Tom. How are you?

M Well, I'm good. _____.
When did you get a cat?

W That's my aunt's. _____, so I'm looking after him.

M But didn't you tell me that _____?
Or was it dogs?

W Cats. Yeah, _____.

M I remember when we were in college you had to look after someone's cat and you had to go to the hospital for a few days.

W Exactly. But after I graduated, for some reason, _____
_____.

M Good for you. I hope you're having a good time with him.

look after ~을 돌보다, 보살피다 allergic to ~에 대해 알레르기가 있는, ~을 몹시 싫어하는 used to 이전에는 ~이었다 get along with ~와 잘 지내다

8 Monologue

Which is correct according to the lecture?

(a) All humans once spoke a single language.

(b) Ancient myths are usually based on truth.

(c) Myth-making has long been a part of human culture.

(d) Diverse primitive societies have often invented similar myths.

W As I said last class, _____
of either history or science that could help them understand their world. They also _____
_____ that they could use to comprehend the physical and biological phenomena that they observed — from the birth of a baby _____, the flow of a river or the rise of the sun. So they created myths to explain the things that they could not understand. For example, the Biblical story of Babel is _____
_____ in the world. All human societies, right _____,
have displayed this tendency to create wondrous stories for real-world events beyond their understanding.

reasoning 추리, 이론 logic 논리, 논법 phenomenon 현상 (pl. phenomena) observe 관찰하다, 목격하다 myth 신화 Biblical 성서의, 성서에 나오는
primitive 원시의, 미개발의 tendency 경향, 추세 wondrous 불가사의한, 놀랄 만한

9 Monologue

What can be inferred from the lecture?

(a) Shakespeare's progressive vision contributed to feminism.

(b) Shakespeare was cynical about women in power.

(c) Shakespeare's heroines succeed because of innate strength.

(d) Shakespeare was critically aware of discrimination against women.

W Today I'll be talking about the heroines in Shakespeare's plays. Although women's rights were _____, Shakespeare depicted women's issues with great insight. His heroines showed _____, and were not simply "weak women" needing protection from men. He showed his heroines _____ established by sexism for instance, one of his heroines had to _____ _____ so that men would take her seriously. Other women, such as those in *King Lear*, devised sophisticated social and political strategies. It could even be argued that he was _____ of the sexist social values of his time.

heroine 여주인공 unheard 알아주지 않는, 귀담아 들어 주지 않는 insight 통찰력 protection 보호 cope against ~에 맞서 대처하다 sexism 성차별(주의) disguise 가면, 가장복 devise 궁리하다, 고안하다 sophisticated 기교적인, 세련된 strategy 전략 intensely 강렬하게, 심하게 skeptical 회의적인 sexist 성차별주의자(의) progressive 진보적인 innate 타고난 discrimination 차별, 구별

10 Monologue

Which is correct according to the lecture?

(a) Ancient philosophy reinforced the doctrines of superstitious thought.

(b) Abstract thinking was first introduced by the Pythagoreans.

(c) Philosophy emerged in ancient cultures around the world in 600 B.C.

(d) Some philosophers saw mathematical relationships reflected in reality.

W I'd like to introduce you to Western philosophy by going back to the 6th century B.C. This saw _____ _____ relating to the ultimate nature of the world and human life. This significant move from _____ _____ characterizes ancient Greek philosophy. Prior to that time, most people felt that "gods" or other supernatural forces were at work in all the things around them. The idea that nature could be logically explained was _____ _____, led by a group of what were then radical thinkers. Such a group of men were the Pythagoreans. They followed Pythagoras's view that all features of the world reflected _____. They also believed that human life should _____ as well.

emergence 출현, 발생 abstract 추상적인 ultimate 근원적인, 최고의 nature 자연, 자연 현상(법칙) superstition 미신 explanation 해설, 설명 prior to ~에 앞서, ~보다 전에 radical 급진적인 departure (방침 등의) 새 발전, 출발, 떠남 thinker 사상가 Pythagoreans 피타고라스 학설 신봉자 mathematic 수학적인 ratio 비, 비율 discernible 보고 알 수 있는, 식별할 수 있는 adhere to ~를 견지하다, ~을 신봉하다

LISTENING REVIEW 🎧

A Listen to the definitions and write down the words.

1. sophisticated

2. d

3. d

4. t

5. p

6. a

7. u

8. i

9. i

10. e

11. d

12. a

13. s

14. a

15. s

16. i

B Choose a sentence that best describes each Korean sentence.

1. 너희 둘이서 어딘가에서 만나기로 했었던 것 같은데.

   (a)

   (b)

2. 당신이 그녀를 Lee's 카페에서 한 시간 이상 기다리게 만들었다.

   (a)

   (b)

3. Nevada 대학의 모든 사람들이 그가 한 일을 듣고서 놀라워했어요.

   (a)

   (b)

4. 우리가 요청하지 않아도 그는 언제나 우리에게 기부할 거라고 생각했어요.

   (a)

   (b)

5. 우리는 10대들이 우리 제품에 대해 알게 하는 데에 집중해야 한다.

   (a)

   (b)

C Listen to three phrases and complete each sentence.

threats are likely / fearful / to make the target country

1. ➡ Threats are likely to make the target country fearful.

2. _____

3. _____

4. _____

5. _____

D Listen to the following and choose a sentence that has the same meaning.

1. Fever is the body's way of trying to fight sickness.
   (a) _____
   (b) _____

2. You might have left them while you were taking out some bills.
   (a) _____
   (b) _____

3. I can't help being uptight before any presentation.
   (a) _____
   (b) _____

4. Didn't you tell me that you're allergic to cats?
   (a) _____
   (b) _____

5. They created myths to explain the things that they could not understand.
   (a) _____
   (b) _____

CHAPTER 08

STANCE/ FUNCTION

VOCABULARY PREVIEW 🎧

Write down the meanings of the words.

01	resign	13	intervention
02	dean	14	excuse
03	overhear	15	genuine
04	qualified	16	aggravate
05	disciplinary	17	mitigate
06	liable	18	severity
07	obesity	19	binding
08	resort to	20	be in jeopardy
09	shed	21	strike
10	lean	22	demolish
11	prevalent	23	be doomed to
12	in this respect	24	prevailing

GUIDED LISTENING 𝛀

1 Conversation

Listening Notes

(news)

(reason)
      the board members

(the speakers' thought)

Stance

1 Which best describes the speakers' feeling?

(a) They are worrying about upcoming exams.

(b) They are distrustful of the board members.

(c) They are concerned about a professor's resignation.

(d) They are optimistic about the next administration.

Detail

2 Why was Professor Stanley fired?

(a) He administered the school as he liked and ignored others.

(b) The board members didn't like the way he administered.

(c) The board members have found a better qualified person.

(d) He was neglecting his work while he was administering.

2 Conversation

Listening Notes

(the woman's request)

(the man's opinion)

(the woman's opinion)

Stance

1 What can be inferred about the man?

(a) He thinks that the company can fix it in no time.

(b) He thinks he will have to exchange it with a new one.

(c) He feels that the woman will have to pay for a new CD.

(d) He is not sure if the company is liable for its replacement.

Detail

2 Why isn't the CD playing?

(a)

(b)

(c)

(d)

3 Monologue

Listening Notes

(statistics)

　　reveal that

　　　　(Most obese Americans)

　　　　　resort to

　　　　　(result)

　　　　(dieting)

　　　　　has become

　　　　　(result)

Function

1 Why does the speaker mention the pounds comparison?

(a) to emphasize that many Americans are fatter now

(b) to show how much weight Americans should lose

(c) to illustrate that their lifestyle has changed a lot

(d) to imply that the average American will gain more weight

Comprehension

2 Which is correct according to the talk?

(a) Most Americans are on diets.

(b) Almost one third of American adults are overweight.

(c) American children gained 6 pounds last year.

(d) Dieting is helpful to lose weight.

4 Monologue

Listening Notes

(views)

> *about*
> *there is no indication that*
> *(reason) largely due to*

(Capitalism)

> *is responsible for*
> *It also gives*
> *The growing global economy*

(the speaker's opinion)

Stance   1   What can be inferred about the speaker?

(a) He is concerned about government intervention.

(b) He is doubtful of the indication of income gap.

(c) He is negative about the current capitalism.

(d) He is positive about the global economy.

Main Idea   2   Which best explains the speaker's opinion?

(a)

(b)

(c)

(d)

1 Conversation

1 Which best describes the speakers' feeling?
   (a) They are worrying about upcoming exams.
   (b) They are distrustful of the board members.
   (c) They are concerned about a professor's resignation.
   (d) They are optimistic about the next administration.

2 Why was Professor Stanley fired?
   (a) He administered the school as he liked and ignored others.
   (b) The board members didn't like the way he administered.
   (c) The board members have found a better qualified person.
   (d) He was neglecting his work while he was administering.

M Is it true that Professor Stanley _____ _____ as dean of the university?

W I guess so. But _____.

M What?

W Well, I believe he's been fired. I overheard some professors discussing it.

M That can't be true. How could someone as qualified as him be fired?

W Actually, the board members didn't like _____ _____. And you know that Professor Stanley _____ _____ and their _____. So, ultimately he lost his job.

M That's really a loss for the school. He was a good administrator.

W Yeah, I agree.

resign 사임하다, 사직하다 **post** 지위, 직장 **dean** 학장 **be fired** 해고되다 **overhear** 어쩌다 듣게 되다, 엿듣다 **qualified** 자격 있는, 실력 있는 **board** 위원회 **administration** 행정, 관리 **method** 수단, 방법 **pay attention to** ~에 주의하다 **disciplinary** 규율의, 징계의 **ultimately** 결국, 마침내 **upcoming** 다가오고 있는 **be concerned about** ~에 대해 걱정하다 **resignation** 사직, 사임

2 Conversation

1 What can be inferred about the man?
   (a) He thinks that the company can fix it in no time.
   (b) He thinks he will have to exchange it with a new one.
   (c) He feels that the woman will have to pay for a new CD.
   (d) He is not sure if the company is liable for its replacement.

2 Why isn't the CD playing?
   (a) Because the woman put it into a wrong player.
   (b) Because the woman accidentally let it fall.
   (c) Because the woman has torn its cover by mistake.
   (d) Because the woman bent it to pull it out.

W Excuse me, I _____ this CD here.

M I see...

W _____?

M Is there any problem with it?

W Actually my friend bought this for me. I _____ _____ and now it's not playing.

M So the CD was _____, right?

W But I haven't used it even once. I _____ _____.

M Well, I will have to talk to my manager about this.

purchase 구입하다 **exchange** 교환하다 **by mistake** 실수로 **liable** 책임을 져야 할 **replacement** 교환, 대치

3 Monologue

1 Why does the speaker mention the pounds comparison?
   (a) to emphasize that many Americans are fatter now
   (b) to show how much weight Americans should lose
   (c) to illustrate that their lifestyle has changed a lot
   (d) to imply that the average American will gain more weight

2 Which is correct according to the talk?
   (a) Most Americans are on diets.
   (b) Almost one third of American adults are overweight.
   (c) American children gained 6 pounds last year.
   (d) Dieting is helpful to lose weight.

M _____ is a serious problem in America. _____ that roughly 33 percent of American adults between the ages of 25 and 74 are overweight. _____ resort to dieting to shed extra pounds from their bodies; however, that rarely works. Despite that, dieting has become so common that nearly half of American women and _____ are on diets, estimates a study. Yet, because dieting rarely works, Americans are _____. Today, on average, Americans are six pounds heavier than they were in 1960.

obesity 비만 statistics 통계 reveal 드러내다, 나타내다 roughly 대략 overweight 과체중의 obese 살찐, 뚱뚱한 resort to ~에 의지하다, 도움을 청하다 shed 벗어 버리다, 없애다 rarely 거의 ~가 아닌 despite ~에도 불구하고 estimate 추정하다, 어림잡다 work 효과가 있다 lean 여윈, 마른

4 Monologue

1 What can be inferred about the speaker?
   (a) He is concerned about government intervention.
   (b) He is doubtful of the indication of income gap.
   (c) He is negative about the current capitalism.
   (d) He is positive about the global economy.

2 Which best explains the speaker's opinion?
   (a) Globalization has a positive impact on underdeveloped countries.
   (b) Government must not intervene in the market.
   (c) Capitalism should be changed for a better system.
   (d) Income inequality only exists in capitalist societies.

M I am going to put forward my views about the income gap prevalent in our society. There is a large gap between the incomes of the upper and the lower classes, and there is no indication that this gap may be narrowed. _____ is largely due to capitalism, _____ _____. Capitalism is responsible _____ with each growing year. It also _____ where everybody wants to succeed. The growing global economy has done nothing favorable in this respect. We have to rethink whether the "economic freedom" of capitalism might be better replaced by more _____.

put forward 제안하다, 제출하다 view 의견, 관점 income gap 소득 격차 prevalent 널리 보급된, 만연한 indication 징조, 징후 inequality 불평등 capitalism 자본주의 give rise to ~을 일으키다, 생기게 하다 competition 경쟁 favorable 호의적인, 적절한 in this respect 이 점에서 intervention 간섭, 중재 underdeveloped country 재개발국, 후진국

PRACTICAL LISTENING 🎧

Stance

1 Which of the following best describes the man's feeling?

(a) satisfied

(b) sad

(c) worried

(d) disappointed

2 Which is correct about osteoarthritis according to the lecture?

(a) It is primarily caused by obesity.

(b) Its effects cannot be minimized.

(c) It can be prevented only by regular exercise.

(d) It is common among people over 40.

Function

3 Why does the man mention Susan's computer?

(a) to tell the woman to take the computer to the service center

(b) to explain that the man has fixed her computer

(c) to suggest the woman buy another computer

(d) to imply that the problem is not very serious

4 Which is correct according to the conversation?

(a) The woman will be late for an appointment.

(b) The man has a date with someone at 4:00 p.m.

(c) The woman forgot the location of Middleton Avenue.

(d) The man wants to accompany the woman.

Function

5 Why does the speaker mention poor pay?

(a) to emphasize that it is the consequence of administrative failure

(b) to indicate that it is the first thing teachers should consider

(c) to imply that teachers are getting poorly paid

(d) to suggest that it is one of the first things to be mended

6   What can be inferred about the man?

(a) He has seen many Sherlock Holmes movies.

(b) He wants to see the movie based on the book.

(c) He does not like the story of the book.

(d) He has never read the novel before.

Stance

7   Which best describes the attitude of the speaker?

(a) astonished

(b) relieved

(c) supportive

(d) furious

8   Which statement would the speaker likely agree with?

(a) Cost efficiency measures in healthcare have been too extreme.

(b) Old hospitals must be torn down to make way for new ones.

(c) Better training for healthcare professionals is absolutely essential.

(d) Good hospitals will attract more healthcare workers to the province.

9   What is mainly being discussed about the bookstore?

(a) its small size and location

(b) how the man and woman feel about it

(c) its unique collection of books

(d) its shortage of books on Dokdo

10   What is the main topic of the lecture?

(a)

(b)

(c)

(d)

1 Conversation

Which of the following best describes the man's feeling?
(a) satisfied
(b) sad
(c) worried
(d) disappointed

M　Rita, why didn't you _____?

W　I'm sorry, Mr. Taylor. My computer is _____.

M　You didn't save your assignment and the computer crashed, right?

W　Yes, and I didn't have any backup.

M　You've been giving the same excuse _____ _____.

W　Well, Mr. Taylor, this time _____.

M　I hope this is the last time I hear that excuse.

W　_____ again.

M　I've also heard that before.

turn in 건네다, 제출하다　chemistry 화학　assignment 숙제, 과제, 임무　out of order 고장난　save 저장하다, 보관하다　crash 작동하지 않다, 갑자기 기능을 멈추다　backup 백업, 여벌, 지원　excuse 변명, 구실, 핑계　submission 제출(물), 복종, 굴복　genuine 진짜의

2 Monologue

Which is correct about osteoarthritis according to the lecture?
(a) It is primarily caused by obesity.
(b) Its effects cannot be minimized.
(c) It can be prevented only by regular exercise.
(d) It is common among people over 40.

M　In today's talk on geriatrics, we will learn about osteoarthritis. This condition _____, hands, knees and lower back. _____ among most adults above 40, especially in joints that are _____ _____. While obesity is known to aggravate osteoarthritis, particularly in the weight-bearing joints, it is possible for individuals to develop it even if they are not overweight. Currently there is _____ _____ or cure for osteoarthritis, although there are many simple ways _____.

geriatrics 노인병학　osteoarthritis 골관절염　weight-bearing 체중을 지탱하는　lower back 허리 아래쪽　prevalent 널리 퍼져 있는, 보급된
physical activity 신체 활동　obesity 비만　aggravate 악화시키다　cure 치료법　mitigate 누그러뜨리다, 완화하다　severity 가혹, 격렬함

3 Conversation

Why does the man mention Susan's computer?
(a) to tell the woman to take the computer to the service center
(b) to explain that the man has fixed her computer
(c) to suggest the woman buy another computer
(d) to imply that the problem is not very serious

W Can you have a look at my computer?

M Why? Is there a problem?

W _____.

M How long have you had that problem?

W Well, _____ until last night. This morning when I _____, though, I couldn't _____
_____.

M Oh, I see. I think I see what's wrong.

W What is it?

M Do you remember what was wrong with Susan's computer?

W Oh, no.

M Yes. She took it to the service center, but _____.
She had to buy a new one.

W I still want to try to take it to the service center.

have a look at ~을 한번 보다 switch on ~의 스위치를 틀다 access ~에 접근하다, 도달하다 in vain 무익하게, 헛되이

4 Conversation

Which is correct according to the conversation?
(a) The woman will be late for an appointment.
(b) The man has a date with someone at 4:00 p.m.
(c) The woman forgot the location of Middleton Avenue.
(d) The man wants to accompany the woman.

W Ken, what's the time?

M It's 3:30 p.m.

W Oh God. I'll be fired! _____!

M What happened? Why are you _____?

W I have _____ at 4 o'clock.
That client is very important to my boss.

M You still have some time. Don't worry. Where's your meeting?

W It's on Middleton Avenue. _____
_____ at the office first.

M I see why you don't have much time.

W Hey! Could you drive me there?

M I can't. I've got something to do at 4:00 p.m. _____
_____? It will be the fastest way to get there.

W Maybe I should call my boss.

fire 해고하다 rush 돌진하다, 서두르다 in a hurry 급히, 서둘러 location 위치, 소재, 장소 accompany ~와 동행하다, 함께 하다, ~을 동반하다

5 Monologue

Why does the speaker mention poor pay?

(a) to emphasize that it is the consequence of administrative failure

(b) to indicate that it is the first thing teachers should consider

(c) to imply that teachers are getting poorly paid

(d) to suggest that it is one of the first things to be mended

M   In local news, recent figures show that almost 50% of people with teaching degrees from this state do not teach at local schools. _____, they often instead move to larger states _____ _____. Worse, only a very small percentage of new teachers _____ _____, where the need for teachers is greatest. Of the teachers who do begin their careers in local schools, one-quarter reportedly leave within two years. Among the reasons for _____ are poor pay and _____ _____. The Council for Education has responded to these findings by announcing immediate steps to resolve the situation.

figure 수치 teaching degree 교직 학위 elect 고르다, 결정하다 rural 지방의, 시골의 (↔ urban) reportedly 보도에 따르면
attrition 마찰, 마모, (수의) 감소, 축소 inadequate 불충분한, 부적절한 administrative 관리상의, 행정상의

6 Conversation

What can be inferred about the man?

(a) He has seen many Sherlock Holmes movies.

(b) He wants to see the movie based on the book.

(c) He does not like the story of the book.

(d) He has never read the novel before.

M   Hi, what's that book?

W   It's a Sherlock Holmes novel.

M   What's the title?

W   *The Criminal*.

M   Oh! *The Criminal*? Have you seen the movie _____?

W   No, _____.

M   Yes, _____. Can I _____ _____?

W   But you already know the story.

M   Yeah, but _____.

novel 소설 criminal 범인, 범죄자 based on ~에 기초한, ~에 근거한 compare (with) 비교하다, 견주다

7 Monologue

Which best describes the attitude of the speaker?
(a) astonished
(b) relieved
(c) supportive
(d) furious

M My first duty is to remind everyone here that the proceedings of this union meeting are _____.
This binding confidentiality was a part of the legal rules you agreed to when you joined the union. This is also important to our strategy. _____ if the press came to know of it. Now, as you all know the contract negotiations have failed and the company management is _____ _____. They refuse to increase our wages despite the fact that the company _____ _____ this year and gave the board of directors over $30 million in stock options. In this situation I propose that we should _____. Those in favor of this plan please raise your hands.

duty 임무 proceeding 진행, 처리, 의사(록) union 연합, (노동) 조합 strictly 엄격하게 confidential 기밀의, 내밀한 binding 의무적인, 구속력 있는 confidentiality 기밀성, 비밀성 be in jeopardy 위험에 빠지다, 위태롭다 company management 회사 경영진 board of directors 이사진 stock option 스톡옵션, 주식 매입 선택권 strike 파업, 쟁의

8 Monologue

Which statement would the speaker likely agree with?
(a) Cost efficiency measures in healthcare have been too extreme.
(b) Old hospitals must be torn down to make way for new ones.
(c) Better training for healthcare professionals is absolutely essential.
(d) Good hospitals will attract more healthcare workers to the province.

W One more hospital has been demolished _____ _____ of our provincial healthcare system. A look at _____ for treatment and the serious shortage of medical facilities currently in place will show that this was a reckless decision. It has become normal to _____ old hospitals without waiting for new ones to come up. Even where efforts at rebuilding them are underway, work has been delayed _____. If these are the so-called efficiency measures being followed, we can be sure that the bid to improve the healthcare system is _____ _____ and that the prevailing lack of healthcare professionals in this area will continue.

demolish 부수다, 폭파하다 enhance 향상시키다 shortage 부족 underway 진행 중인 bid to do ~하려는 시도, 노력 be doomed to (나쁘게) ~될 운명이다 prevailing 널리 보급되어 있는, 유행하고 있는 tear down 헐다, 부수다 make way for ~에게 길을 비키다, 양보하다

9 Conversation

What is mainly being discussed about the bookstore?

(a) its small size and location
(b) how the man and woman feel about it
(c) its unique collection of books
(d) its shortage of books on Dokdo

M   Have you been to the new bookstore in Jongno?

W   Yes, I went there just last week.

M   _____ ?

W   Well, there's _____, but the collection of books they have is unique.

M   That's true. I found many books on Dokdo _____ _____.

W   Exactly, and _____ since it has so many good books there.

M   Yeah, _____.

---

have been to ~에 가본 적이 있다 ┃ **space** 공간, 장소, 여지 ┃ **collection** 수집(물), 더미 ┃ **unique** 독특한, 특이한, 진기한, 훌륭한 ┃ **rarely** 좀처럼 ~하지 않는
lack of ~의 부족, ~이 없음 ┃ **hardly** 거의 ~않는 ┃ **matter** 문제가 되다, 중요하다 ┃ **feel like -ing** ~하고 싶다 ┃ **shortage** 부족, 결핍

---

10 Monologue

What is the main topic of the lecture?

(a) the cause of changes in Old English
(b) the borrowed words used commonly in English
(c) the evolution of vocabulary in Old English
(d) the history of Modern English vocabulary

M   Old English _____ before it became Middle and then Modern English — the language we use widely today. While some of the changes were in grammar, _____ were in vocabulary. There has not been _____ from Old to Modern English, with some words simply changing in spelling or pronunciation. Rather, during its development English has borrowed very heavily from other languages. It might surprise you to know that only about 20% of the words in the Modern English vocabulary originated in Old English. The remaining 80% comes largely from foreign sources, notably Latin, Greek and Old Norse. _____, a person speaking Old English would be _____ to one speaking Modern English.

---

go through ~을 겪다, 경험하다 ┃ **multiple** 다양한, 복잡한 ┃ **widely** 넓게, 광범위하게 ┃ **linear** 선의, 직선의, 1차원의 ┃ **progression** 진행, 경과, 발달
originate 기원하다, 유래하다 ┃ **Norse** (고대) 노르웨이 사람, 노르웨이 말 ┃ **incomprehensible** 이해할 수 없는 ┃ **borrowed word** 차용어 ┃ **evolution** 발달, 진보, 진화

LISTENING REVIEW 🎧

A Listen to the definitions and write down the words.

1. linear _____
2. o _____
3. c _____
4. d _____
5. e _____
6. p _____
7. b _____
8. j _____

9. s _____
10. i _____
11. r _____
12. a _____
13. a _____
14. o _____
15. e _____
16. g _____

B Choose a sentence that best describes each Korean sentence.

1. Stanley 교수님이 학장 자리에서 사임했다.
   (a) _____
   (b) _____

2. 대부분의 뚱뚱한 미국 사람들이 여분의 살을 없애기 위해 식이요법에 의존한다.
   (a) _____
   (b) _____

3. 미국 사람들은 몸무게가 1960년보다 6파운드 정도 더 나갑니다.
   (a) _____
   (b) _____

4. 이러한 격차가 좁혀질 것 같은 기미는 없습니다.
   (a) _____
   (b) _____

5. 제출이 늦어질 때마다 계속 똑같은 변명을 하는구나.
   (a) _____
   (b) _____

C Listen to three phrases and complete each sentence.

the weight-bearing joints / commonly affects / this condition
1. ➡ This condition commonly affects the weight-bearing joints.

2. _____

3. _____

4. _____

5. _____

D Listen to the following and choose a sentence that has the same meaning.

1. Only a very small percentage of new teachers elect to teach in rural areas.
   (a) _____
   (b) _____

2. Our position would be in jeopardy if the press came to know of it.
   (a) _____
   (b) _____

3. I propose that we should vote on a strike.
   (a) _____
   (b) _____

4. The bid to improve the healthcare system is doomed to failure.
   (a) _____
   (b) _____

5. Only about 20% of the words in the Modern English vocabulary originated in Old English.
   (a) _____
   (b) _____

MEMO

MEMO

Answer Key

Level
3

AIM HIGH 에임하이

Active Curriculum for Successful Listening

LISTENING 리스닝

In-Depth Lab

We're
위아북스

Answer Key

Level
3

AIM HIGH 에임하이

Active Curriculum for Successful Listening

LISTENING 리스닝

In-Depth Lab

We're
위아북스

CHAPTER 01 MAIN IDEA / PURPOSE

VOCABULARY PREVIEW

01. fuel-efficient 연료 효율이 좋은
02. soaring 치솟고 있는
03. commute 출퇴근하다, 통근하다
04. relocate 이전하다, 이동하다
05. facilitate 촉진하다, 손쉽게 하다
06. evaporate 증발하다
07. liberation 해방, 평등
08. notion 개념
09. prevalent 널리 행해지는, 보급된
10. board of directors 이사회
11. appreciably 분명히, 상당히
12. hypnotic 최면의, 최면에 걸린
13. custom-made 주문 제작의, 맞춤의
14. cut down on ~의 소비를 줄이다, 절약하다
15. utility bill 공과금 (고지서)
16. efficiency 효율성
17. coronary 심장의
18. hypertension 고혈압
19. charge 비용을 청구하다
20. appliance 전기기구(제품)
21. vegetation 식물, 초목
22. carbon dioxide 이산화탄소
23. shareholder 주주
24. undergo 경험하다, 견디다

GUIDED LISTENING

1	1. c	2. c	**2**	1. b	2. b
3	1. d	2. a	**4**	1. a	2. d

1 Conversation

M: You got a new car? It really looks good!

W: Yeah, we badly needed a new one. Our old car needed so much gas; we could hardly afford to drive it.

M: I can understand. My car is also old now. I should replace it with a more fuel-efficient model.

W: Well... this car gets over 40 miles to the gallon. I'm glad we bought it. The soaring gas prices are hurting everyone.

M: Actually, I'm thinking of commuting by bus, so that I can at least save on fuel. I'm sure it would save me a lot of money!

W: I agree. My sister has already started biking to work.

M: That's a pretty good idea. I must suggest that to my brother. He doesn't live far from work.

M: 새 차를 샀군요? 정말 멋있어 보이네요!

W: 네, 우리는 정말 새 차가 필요했어요. 예전 차는 기름을 너무 많이 먹었거든요. 우리는 그 차를 운전할 만한 형편이 안 되었다니까요.

M: 이해할 수 있어요. 이제 제 차도 오래됐거든요. 좀 더 연료 효율이 좋은 모델로 바꾸어야겠어요.

W: 음… 이 차는 갤런당 40마일 이상 달려요. 이 차를 구입하게 되어서 기뻐요. 치솟고 있는 휘발유 가격이 모든 사람들을 힘들게 하고 있잖아요.

M: 사실, 저는 버스로 출퇴근을 할까 생각하고 있어요. 그러면 조금이라도 연료를 절약할 수 있지 않을까 해서요. 돈도 많이 절약될 거라고 생각해요!

W: 맞아요. 제 여동생은 벌써 자전거를 타고 회사에 다니기 시작했어요.

M: 그거 정말 좋은 생각이네요. 제 동생에게도 제안해 봐야겠어요. 동생은 회사에서 그리 멀지 않은 곳에 살거든요.

Purpose

1 What are the man and the woman doing in the

conversation?

(a) comparing how energy efficient their cars are

(b) buying a car that uses less amount of gas

(c) talking about ways to overcome high gas price

(d) deciding the most energy efficient way to commute

이 대화에서 남자와 여자가 하고 있는 것은?

(a) 자신들의 차량의 에너지 효율이 어떠한지 비교하기

(b) 기름을 좀 덜 먹는 차량 구입하기

(c) 고유가를 극복하기 위한 방법에 대해 이야기하기

(d) 통근하는 데 있어 가장 에너지 효율이 높은 방법 결정하기

해설 연료 비용이 치솟고 있어서, 그에 대한 의견을 나누고 있는 내용이다. 여자는 기름을 많이 먹는 오래된 차를 새 차로 바꾸었고, 남자는 버스로 통근할 것을 고려하고 있다. 자전거를 타고 출퇴근하고 있는 사람에 대한 언급도 있다. 이를 전체적으로 보면, (c)에 관한 대화임을 알 수 있다.

함정 (a), (b), (d) 모두 잠깐씩 언급된 내용이기는 하지만, 하나의 항목에 지나지 않으므로 정답이 될 수 없다.

Comprehension

2   Which is correct according to the conversation?

(a) A new car is expensive.

(b) The man will start using his bike.

(c) The woman's car is more fuel-efficient.

(d) People will replace their old cars.

이 대화에 따르면 옳은 것은 무엇인가?

(a) 새 차는 비싸다.

(b) 남자는 자전거를 이용하기 시작할 것이다.

(c) 여자의 차가 연료 효율이 좀 더 좋은 차이다.

(d) 사람들은 오래된 차를 교체할 것이다.

해설 여자는 기름을 많이 먹는 오래된 차를 새 차로 바꾸었으므로 (c)의 내용이 옳다는 것을 알 수 있다.

함정 (a) 새 차의 가격에 대해서는 언급된 바가 없다. (b) 자전거를 이용하는 사람은 여자의 자매이며, 이용하게 될 수 있는 사람은 남자의 형제일 것이다. 또한 연료 비용이 올랐다고 해서, 모든 사람들이 여자처럼 연비가 좋은 차로 교체할 것이라고 생각해서는 안 된다. 그러므로 (d)도 정답이 아니다.

어휘 hardly 거의 ~아닌   (can) afford to ~할 여유(형편)가 있다   replace 교체하다, 대체하다   fuel-efficient 연료 효율이 좋은   to the gallon 갤런당, 1갤런으로   soaring 치솟고 있는   commute 출퇴근하다, 통근하다   at least 조금이라도   far from ~에서 아주 먼

2 Conversation

W: Good evening, sir. How may I help you?

M: I have a reservation for a single room. Could you please check?

W: Under what name, sir?

M: Steve Johnson. I reserved it a week ago.

W: Oh yes, here it is. For how long will you be staying here, sir?

M: Maybe a week or so. Actually, my grandma wants to move to another apartment and I came to help her find a new place.

W: Okay. Would you like to meet a real estate agent? I can arrange that for you.

M: Well, I would appreciate that. Thank you.

W: 안녕하세요. 어떻게 도와드릴까요?

M: 싱글룸을 예약했는데요. 체크해 주시겠어요?

W: 어떤 이름으로 하셨나요?

M: Steve Johnson이요. 일주일 전에 예약했어요.

W: 아, 예, 여기 있네요. 여기 얼마나 오랫동안 머무실 것인가요?

M: 아마 일주일 정도요. 실은, 할머니가 다른 아파트로 이사하길 원해서서 새 집을 찾아드리려고 왔어요.

W: 좋습니다. 부동산업자를 만나고 싶으신가요? 약속을 잡아 드릴 수 있어요.

M: 음, 그래 주시면 고맙겠습니다. 감사합니다.

Purpose

1   What is the man doing in the conversation?

(a) looking for a good real estate agent

(b) getting a room at a hotel

(c) confirming a reservation for his grandma

(d) finding a new apartment for his grandma

이 대화에서 남자가 하고 있는 것은?

(a) 좋은 부동산업자 찾기

(b) 호텔에서 객실 얻기

(c) 할머니를 위해 예약 확인하기

(d) 할머니를 위해 새로운 아파트를 찾기

해설 예약했던 호텔에 체크인하면서, 할머니 집을 구해드리러 왔다는 말에 부동산업자를 소개하겠다고 하는 내용의 대화이다. 할머니의 집과 부동산업자에 관한 말들이 있지만, 이 대화에서 남자가 하고 있는 것은 호텔에 체크인하고 하는 것이므로 (b)가 정답이다.

Inference II

2 What can be inferred from the conversation?

(a) The man will leave the hotel soon.

(b) The man will meet a real estate agent.

(c) The woman can not confirm his reservation.

(d) The woman has lived in this area for a long time.

이 대화에서 추론할 수 있는 것은 무엇인가?

(a) 남자는 곧 호텔을 떠날 것이다.

(b) 남자는 부동산업자를 만날 것이다.

(c) 여자는 그의 예약을 확인할 수 없다.

(d) 여자는 이 지역에 오랫동안 살고 있다.

해설 부동산업자를 소개하겠다고 하는 호텔 여직원의 제안에 그래 주면 고맙겠다고 하는 것으로 보아, 남자가 부동산업자를 만날 것이라는 (b)가 정답이다.

함정 남자와 여자는 호텔의 고객과 직원의 관계이며, 여자가 그 지역에서 오랫동안 살았는지에 대한 언급은 없다.

어휘 reservation 예약 real estate 부동산
agent 대리인, 대리점 arrange 조정하다, 마련하다

3 Monologue

M: The sun has a major role in regulating all forms of life found on Earth. Everything on Earth, directly or indirectly, <u>is impacted by the sun</u>. Human activities such as walking, eating and working depend upon sunlight and are adjusted accordingly. Sunlight is <u>essential for crops to grow</u>. The sun directly affects the growth of vegetation by facilitating <u>plants' creation of sugar</u> from water and carbon dioxide. In fact, the very presence of water on Earth is largely due to the sun. <u>Under the sun's rays</u>, water from sources like lakes, rivers and oceans <u>evaporates into the atmosphere</u> to form clouds. These clouds cause rains, thus transporting the water back to Earth — a part of the Earth's "water cycle."

M: 태양은 지구상에서 발견되는 모든 형태의 생명들을 조절하는 데에 주요 역할을 합니다. 지구상의 모든 것들은 직접적으로든 간접적으로든 태양의 영향을 받습니다. 걷고 먹고 일하는 것과 같은 인간의 활동들은 태양빛에 의존하고 그에 순응합니다. 태양빛은 작물이 자라는 데에 꼭 필요합니다. 태양은 식물이 물과 이산화탄소로부터 당을 만들어내도록 촉진시킴으로써 식물의 성장에 직접적으로 영향을 미칩니다. 사실, 지구상의 물의 존재 그 자체가 거의 태양 때문입니다. 태양 광선 아래에서, 호수, 강, 바다와 같은 수원지로부터 물이 대기로 증발되어 구름을 형성합니다. 이러한 구름들이 비를 만들고, 지구상에 그 물을 다시 돌려보내는 것입니다. 이것이 지

구의 "물의 순환"의 한 부분입니다.

Main Idea

1 What is the main idea of the lecture?

(a) The water cycle depends on sunlight.

(b) The sun is needed for farming.

(c) The sun is responsible for the formation of oceans.

(d) The sun has major influence upon Earth.

이 강의의 주제는 무엇인가?

(a) 물의 순환은 태양빛에 의존한다.

(b) 태양은 농업에 꼭 필요하다.

(c) 바다를 형성한 것은 태양 때문이다.

(d) 태양은 지구에 주요한 영향을 미친다.

해설 태양이 지구의 모든 것들에 미치는 영향에 대한 강의이다. 태양은 지구상의 모든 생명과 물의 존재에 영향을 미치고 조절한다는 내용이므로 이 강의의 주제는 (d)이다.

함정 이 강의의 내용 중에 (a), (b), (c) 모두가 언급되어 있기는 하지만, (a), (b), (c)는 전체를 통합하는 주제라기보다는 하나의 예에 해당한다.

Relationship of Ideas

2 What are the two things about the sun that the lecturer focuses on?

(a) the role and the influences of sunlight

(b) the kinds and strength of sunlight

(c) the temperature and the rays of sunlight

(d) the length and brightness of sunlight

강의자가 중점을 두고 있는 태양의 두 가지는 무엇인가?

(a) 태양빛의 역할과 영향

(b) 태양빛의 종류와 세기

(c) 태양빛의 온도와 광선

(d) 태양빛의 길이와 밝기

해설 태양빛이 지구에 미치는 역할과 영향에 관한 내용이다. 지구상의 모든 생명체에 영향을 미치고, 생명에 가장 중요한 물을 만들어내는 것이 태양이라는 것으로 보아 (a)가 정답임을 알 수 있다.

어휘 regulate 조절하다, 조정하다
directly or indirectly 직접적으로든 간접적으로든
adjust 조정하다, 순응하다 accordingly 그에 따라서
crop 작물 vegetation 식물, 초목
facilitate 촉진하다, 손쉽게 하다 sugar 당(糖)
carbon dioxide 이산화탄소 presence 존재
be due to ~ 때문이다 evaporate 증발하다 formation 형성

4 Monologue

W: Today is the era of women's liberation. Although it is a widespread notion, it may be a totally false claim. Women all over the world still <u>face domestic violence</u>, reports UNICEF, which estimates that about 35% of women across the world experience some form of violence at home. It is sad to learn that even educated women fall into this group and, almost always, <u>the offender is her partner</u>. <u>Data from the United Kingdom</u> indicates that one out of every four women undergoes domestic violence during her lifetime. Due to social pressure and <u>lack of awareness among women</u>, the majority of these cases <u>go unnoticed and unreported</u>.

W: 오늘날은 여성 해방의 시대입니다. 그것은 보편화된 개념임에도 불구하고, 완전히 거짓 주장일 수도 있습니다. 전 세계의 여성들은 아직도 가정 폭력을 겪고 있는데, 유니세프의 보고에 의하면, 전 세계의 약 35%의 여성들이 가정에서 이런저런 형태의 폭력을 경험하는 것으로 추정됩니다. 교육을 받은 여성들조차 이런 축에 낀다는 것과 가해자가 거의 대부분이 배우자라니 슬픈 일입니다. 영국에서 나온 자료를 보면, 4명의 여성 중 1명은 살아가는 동안 가정 폭력을 겪는다고 합니다. 사회적 억압과 여성들 사이의 인식 부족 때문에, 이런 사례들 대부분이 간과되고 보고되지 않고 있습니다.

Main Idea

1 What is the main point of the report?

(a) Domestic violence is prevalent worldwide.

(b) There is a lack of awareness among educated women.

(c) UNICEF is planning to fight domestic violence.

(d) The United Kingdom has the highest rate of domestic violence.

이 기사의 요점은 무엇인가?
(a) 가정 폭력은 세계적으로 만연해 있다.
(b) 교육받은 여성들의 의식이 결여되어 있다.
(c) 유니세프는 가정 폭력에 맞서 싸울 계획이다.
(d) 영국은 가정 폭력 비율이 가장 높다.

해설 여성 평등의 시대인데도 불구하고, 세계적으로 가정 폭력에 시달리는 여성들이 많다는 보고이다. 그러므로 요점으로는 (a)가 옳다.

함정 교육받은 여성들도 피해자가 된다는 언급이 있긴 하지만, 이 보고의 요점이 될 수는 없다. 또한 가정 폭력에 시달리는 여성들이 세계적으로는 35%, 영국에서는 4명 중 1명(25%)이라고 했으므로 (d)는 틀린 내용이다.

Comprehension

2 Which is correct according to the report?

(a) Women are the major victims of domestic violence.

(b) Women in developing countries experience more violence.

(c) Many cases of domestic violence are reported nowadays.

(d) 25% of women in the U.K. experience violence at home.

이 기사에 따르면, 다음 중 옳은 것은?
(a) 여성은 가정 폭력의 주된 희생자이다.
(b) 개발도상국의 여성들이 더 많은 폭력을 겪는다.
(c) 가정 폭력의 많은 경우들이 요즘 보고되고 있다.
(d) 영국 여성의 25%가 가정에서의 폭력을 겪는다.

해설 Data from the United Kingdom indicates that one out of every four women undergoes domestic violence during her lifetime.(영국에서 나온 자료를 보면, 4명의 여성 중 1명은 살아가는 동안 가정 폭력을 겪는다고 합니다.)라는 표현에서 (d)가 옳다는 것을 알 수 있다.

함정 (a)와 (b)는 언급된 바가 없으며, (c)는 기사의 내용과 반대된다.

어휘 era 시대 liberation 해방, 평등
widespread 널리 보급되어 있는, 만연한 notion 개념
domestic 가정의 estimate 어림잡다, 추정하다
offender 가해자, 위반자 indicate 가리키다, 시사하다
undergo 경험하다, 견디다
unnoticed 주목되지 않는, 알아채지 않는
prevalent 널리 행해지는, 보급된

PRACTICAL LISTENING

1. c	2. b	3. a	4. a	5. c
6. b	7. b	8. b	9. d	10. d

1

W: I won't be able to attend Sean's show this Sunday morning.

M: Do you have any other plans that day?

W: Well, <u>I'll be out of town</u> from Friday for a business meeting and it <u>doesn't finish until late Saturday night</u>. I'm not sure if I can come back by Sunday.

M: Where's your meeting?

W: In New Hampshire. It's <u>about 4 hours away by plane</u>.

M: Oh, that's too far from here. I don't think you'll <u>get back in time for the show</u>. <u>You'd better call and tell</u> him that.

W: I hope he doesn't get disappointed.

M: I'm sure he'll understand if you bring something for him when you get back.

W: That's something I didn't think of. Thanks and I will definitely get something nice for him.

W: 이번 주 일요일 아침에 Sean의 쇼에 참석하지 못할 거야.

M: 그날 무슨 다른 계획이라도 있니?

W: 업무 회의 때문에 금요일부터 지방 출장을 갈 건데, 토요일 밤늦게까지 끝나지 않을 거야. 일요일까지 돌아올 수 있을지 모르겠어.

M: 회의는 어디서 해?

W: 뉴햄프셔. 비행기로 4시간 정도 떨어진 곳이야.

M: 아, 여기서 너무 멀구나. 쇼 시간에 맞춰서 돌아오지 못할 것 같네. 전화해서 알려주는게 좋을거야.

W: 그가 실망하지 않으면 좋겠는데.

M: 돌아올 때 그에게 선물을 좀 사다 주면 틀림없이 이해해 줄 거야.

W: 그건 내가 생각하지 못했던 거네. 고마워, 좋은 걸 꼭 사다 줘야겠다.

Q Which is correct about the woman according to the conversation?

(a) She is moving to New Hampshire this Friday.

(b) She wants to attend another one of Sean's shows.

(c) She will not be in the city on Saturday.

(d) She is going away to buy something for Sean.

대화에 근거하여 여자에 대한 설명으로 옳은 것은?

(a) 금요일에 뉴햄프셔로 이사할 것이다.

(b) Sean의 다른 쇼에 가고 싶어 한다.

(c) 토요일에 그 도시에 있지 않을 것이다.

(d) Sean에게 무언가를 사주기 위해 멀리 갈 것이다.

해설 여자가 이번 주 일요일 아침에 있을 Sean의 쇼에 참석하지 못하는 이유에 대한 대화이다. 여자는 금요일부터 있을 회의 때문에 뉴햄프셔로 출장을 떠나서 일요일까지 돌아오지 못할 것 같다고 남자에게 말한다. 따라서 여자에 대한 설명으로 옳은 것은 (c)가 된다.

함정 (d) Sean에게 무언가를 사주기 위해 멀리 가는 것이 아니다. 출장 때문에 Sean의 초대를 받아들이지 못하는 것이 미안해서, 돌아오는 길에 Sean에게 무언가를 사달 줄 것이다.

어휘 attend ~에 참석하다, 출석하다 | out of town 도시를 떠나 | business meeting 업무상 회의 | if ~인지 아닌지 | away 떨어져서, 떠나서 | far from ~에서 멀리 |

get back 돌아오다 | definitely 틀림없이

2 Main Idea

M: I'm sorry to inform you, the board of directors, that we have run into problems <u>with the proposed relocation of</u> our company headquarters from Boston to Philadelphia. <u>With a nationwide downturn</u> in the housing and construction market, we anticipated low costs to build in Philadelphia. However, actual construction costs in that city have not only <u>failed to decrease</u>, but actually increased over the last few months. Some board members have recommended moving to a new site in Boulder, Colorado. However, <u>prices there have risen</u> even faster than in Philadelphia and Boulder is far from where we do most of our business. My suggestion is that we give up the current plan for now and relocate when construction costs <u>have fallen appreciably</u> on the East Coast.

M: 이사진 여러분들께 회사 본부를 보스턴에서 필라델피아로 이전하기로 계획된 것과 관련해 문제가 발생했음을 알려드리는 점 죄송하게 생각합니다. 전국적인 주택 및 건설 시장의 침체로 인해, 우리는 필라델피아에서는 건축 비용이 적게 들 것이라고 기대했었습니다. 그러나 필라델피아의 실제 건축 비용이 감소하지 않았을 뿐만 아니라 지난 몇 달 간 사실상 증가하기까지 했습니다. 몇몇 이사진들은 콜로라도의 보울더의 새 부지로 이사하는 게 어떻겠냐고 추천하기도 하셨습니다. 하지만 그곳의 시세는 필라델피아보다 훨씬 빨리 증가했습니다. 게다가 보울더는 대부분의 우리 사업 지역에서 훨씬 멀리 떨어져 있습니다. 때문에 저는 지금으로서는 현재 계획을 포기하고 동부해안 지역 내 건설비용이 분명하게 감소되었을 때 이전할 것을 제안하는 바입니다.

Q What is the speaker's main point in the talk?

(a) A current plan has been thoroughly assessed.

(b) Proposals for a new company site are not viable.

(c) A company's construction project will succeed.

(d) A company's procedures are harming major cities.

이 이야기에서 화자의 요지는?

(a) 현재 계획은 철저한 평가를 거친 것이다.

(b) 회사의 새로운 부지 계획안은 실행이 불가능하다.

(c) 회사의 건설 계획은 성공할 것이다.

(d) 회사의 행정 절차가 주요 도시를 훼손하고 있다.

해설 회사 본사 이전 계획이, 건축 비용의 가격 상승으로 인해 실현 불가능하므로, 일단 이 계획을 보류할 것을 제안하는 내용이다. 따라서 화자의 요지는 (b)가 된다.

(d) 동남아시아에서 들어왔다.

해설 아랍 음악에 대한 일반적인 설명의 강의이다. 아랍 음악이 인도네시아와 동남아시아의 음악에 영향을 미쳤음을 주지시키는 내용의 강의이므로 정답은 (a)이다. "Are you wondering why I've moved from Indonesia ~ impact Indonesia and Southeast Asia significantly." 구문을 통해 강사가 아랍 음악에 대한 설명을 하는 요지를 알 수 있다.

함정 (d) 아랍 음악은 동남아시아에서 들여온 것이 아니라, 인도네시아와 동남아시아의 음악에 영향을 끼쳤다.

어휘 tone 음색, 색조 hypnotic 최면의, 최면에 걸린
lilting (노래 · 목소리가) 경쾌한
sway (전후좌우로) 뒤흔들다, 요동시키다
tradition (전통) 양식, 형태

함정 비용 문제로 인해 본사 이전 계획을 당장 실천할 수 없다고 했다. 그러므로 회사 건설 계획의 성공 여부나 행정 절차의 폐해 여부는 알 수 없다.

어휘 board of directors 이사회 relocation 재배치, 이전
headquarter 본사, 본부 nationwide 전국적인
downturn (경기 등의) 침체, 하강 current 현재의
appreciably 분명히, 상당히
East Coast (미국의) 동해안, 대서양 연안 viable 실행 가능한

3

W: Last week we discussed Indonesian music. In this week's class, I'll be talking about Arabian music. Traditional Arabian music <u>employs rhythms and tones</u> are very unlike those found in the West. Westerners first listening to Arabian music often describe it as "hypnotic" for its lilting tones that almost <u>force the body to begin swaying</u>. Arabian music is what the famous "belly dancers" move to <u>during their performances</u>. Are you wondering why I've moved from Indonesia <u>all the way to the Middle East</u>? The reason is that Arabian musical traditions did impact Indonesia and Southeast Asia significantly. As Arabian traders and religious teachers came to Indonesia <u>after the 7th century</u>, they brought both Islam and Arabian music.

W: 지난주 우리는 인도네시아 음악에 관해 살펴보았습니다. 이번 주 수업에서는 아랍 음악에 대해 얘기하겠습니다. 전통적인 아랍 음악은 리듬을 사용하며 음색은 서구 음악과 상당히 다릅니다. 아랍 음악을 처음 들어본 서양 사람들은 몸이 들썩일 정도로 기분을 고양시키는 경쾌한 음색 때문에 종종 (아랍 음악은) '최면을 거는 것 같다'고 묘사합니다. 아랍 음악은 그 유명한 벨리 댄서들이 공연 중에 사용하는 음악이기도 합니다. 여러분들 제가 인도네시아 음악 강의를 하다가 중동 음악까지 넘어간 이유가 궁금하신가요? 그건 바로 아랍의 음악 양식들이 인도네시아와 동남아시아의 음악에 지대한 영향을 끼쳤기 :때문입니다. 7세기 이후 아랍 무역 상인들과 종교 지도자들이 인도네시아로 오면서 이들이 이슬람과 아랍 음악을 들여왔습니다.

Q Which is correct about Arabian music in the talk?

(a) It inspired music in Indonesia.

(b) It relies heavily on external influences.

(c) It has a rich and varied tradition.

(d) It was brought from Southeast Asia.

이 이야기에서 아랍 음악에 대해 옳은 것은?

(a) 인도네시아의 음악에 영향을 주었다.

(b) 외부 영향에 크게 의존한다.

(c) 풍부하고 다양한 (음악) 전통을 가지고 있다.

4

W: Hello! This is 555-0783. Wendy and Todd <u>are out right now</u>, or can't come to the phone. If you are calling about <u>the apartment advertised for rent</u>, please leave your name and number and we will call you back as soon as we can. <u>Please leave a number</u> that we can use to contact you during the day. If you need <u>directions to the apartment</u>, we are at 457 Andrews Avenue #913 in Groton City, across from the Templeton Movie Theater. If you want to know about the sports car for sale, it's been sold. If you <u>wish to speak to one of us</u>, please leave a message. Thanks, and have a nice day.

W: 안녕하세요. 555-0783번입니다. Wendy와 Todd는 현재 외출 중이거나 전화를 받을 수 없는 상황입니다. 아파트 임대 광고를 보고 전화하셨다면 이름과 전화번호를 남겨주세요. 그러면 가능한 한 빨리 연락 드리겠습니다. 낮에 통화가 가능한 번호를 남겨주십시오. 아파트로 오는 길을 알고 싶으시면, 이곳은 Groton City의 Andrews가 457번지 913호로, Templeton 극장 맞은편입니다. 매매 상품인 스포츠카에 관해 궁금하신 거라면 이미 팔렸습니다. 저희 중 한 사람과 통화하고 싶으시면 메시지를 남겨 주세요. 감사합니다. 좋은 하루 되세요.

Q What should a caller do if interested in the apartment?

(a) to leave a number they can call during the day

(b) to phone either Wendy or Todd directly

(c) to visit at the address given in the message

(d) to leave a message or call back later

전화를 건 사람이 아파트에 관심이 있다면 어떻게 해야 하는가?

(a) 낮에 전화할 수 있는 번호를 남기기

(b) Wendy 또는 Todd에게 직접 전화하기

(c) 메시지에 제시된 주소로 방문하기

(d) 메시지를 남기거나 나중에 다시 전화하기

해설 Wendy와 Todd의 자동 응답기에서 나오는 내용이다. 아파트 임대를 원하는 사람, 스포츠카 구매를 원하는 사람, 직접 전화통화를 하고 싶은 사람에게 각각 메시지를 남겨 놓았다. 본 질문에 해당하는 부분은 아파트 임대에 관한 것이므로 이 부분에 관련해 취해야 할 행동은 (a)가 된다.

함정 여러 가지 사항을 차례로 나열하고 있지만, 질문의 내용을 확인하고 들었다면 아파트 임대에 관한 부분을 쉽게 찾을 수 있다. 스포츠카 구매나 직접 전화통화에 관한 부분은 해당 사항이 아니므로 그냥 지나쳐야 한다.

어휘 **for rent** 임대용의, 세놓는 **contact** 연락(을 취함)
for sale 팔려고 내놓은

5 Purpose

M: Excuse me, waitress.

W: Yes sir. Do you need anything?

M: I asked for <u>a hard-boiled egg</u>, but this one is just soft-boiled.

W: Oh, I'm very sorry. I'll get you another one.

M: Okay, but please <u>tell the chef to make it hard-boiled</u>.

W: Sure, sir. This time <u>there won't be any mistake</u>. Is there anything else I can get you, sir?

M: Just get me a glass of water.

W: <u>I'll be right back with your water</u> and the hard-boiled egg.

M: Thank you, and <u>please make it quick</u>.

M: 여기요.

W: 네, 뭐가 필요하신가요?

M: 완숙으로 삶은 계란을 해 달라고 했는데, 이건 반숙이네요.

W: 어, 정말 죄송합니다. 다른 것으로 가져다드리겠습니다.

M: 알겠어요. 주방장에게 꼭 좀 완숙으로 해달라고 해 주세요.

W: 물론입니다. 이번에는 실수 없도록 할게요. 뭐 다른 필요하신 건 없으십니까?

M: 물 한 잔만 가져다주세요.

W: 물과 완숙 계란을 바로 가져다드리겠습니다.

M: 고맙습니다. 빨리 해 주세요.

Q Why does the man call the woman in the conversation?

(a) to complain about the food and the service

(b) to complain about the bad taste of the food

(c) to correct the order

(d) to demand to see a restaurant's chef

대화에서 남자가 여자를 부른 이유는?

(a) 음식과 서비스에 대해 불평하려고

(b) 맛이 없는 음식에 대해 불평하려고

(c) 주문을 정정해 달라고 하려고

(d) 식당 주방장을 만나게 해 달라고 요구하려고

해설 식당 여종업원과 남자 손님과의 대화이다. 남자는 완숙으로 삶은 계란(hard-boiled egg)을 주문했는데, 반숙(soft-boiled)이 나왔다고 하자, 여자는 미안해 하며 다시 가져다주겠다고 하고 있다. 따라서 정답은 (c)가 된다.

함정 남자는 여자에게 식당 주방장(chef)을 만나게 해달라고 하는 것이 아니라, 주방장에게 완숙으로 삶아 달라는 말을 전해 달라는 것이기 때문에, (d)는 오답이다.

어휘 **ask for** ~을 요구하다
hard-boiled egg 완숙으로 삶은 계란 **soft-boiled** 반숙한
chef 주방장, 요리사 **mistake** 잘못, 착오
make ~을 (…의 상태로) 하다 **quick** 속히, 빨리(=quickly)
complain about ~에 대해 불평(항의)하다 **taste** 맛
correct 고치다, 정정하다 **demand to** ~해달라고 요구하다

6

M: Before we break for lunch, I'd like to speak about the dress code at this employee orientation. Over the last few years, <u>the company dress culture</u> in Canada <u>has changed quite a bit</u>. Now, while we do not <u>impose uniforms</u>, at Altius Inc. all employees <u>are expected to be dressed formally</u>. Men are asked to wear suits and ties, and women can choose between skirts or pantsuits. Every Friday, though, we <u>permit business casual wear</u>. However, jeans, T-shirts and torn or patched clothing are not allowed at any time. We expect you to look like professionals under all circumstances. You must remember that your image and appearance reflects the company to customers, suppliers and shareholders.

M: 점심식사 전에 이번 직원 오리엔테이션에서 복장 규정에 관해 말씀드리고 싶습니다. 지난 몇 년간, 캐나다의 회사 복장 문화가 상당히 바뀌었습니다. 우리 Altius 회사에서는 유니폼 착용 의무는 없습니다만, 모든 직원들은 격식을 갖춘 옷차림을 해야 합니다. 남성 직원들은 양복과 타이, 여성 직원들은 스커트나 바지 정장 차림을 하셔야 합니다. 하지만 금요일에는 비즈니스 캐주얼 차림이 허용됩니다. 그러나 어떤 경우에도 청바지나 티셔츠, 찢어지거나 천을 덧댄 옷차림은 금기시됩니다. 우리는 여러분들께서 언제나 프로다운 모습을 보여 주시기를 기대합니다. 고객과 공급업체, 그리고 주주들에게는 여러분의 이미지나 겉모습이 회사의 이미지로 비쳐진다는 점을 꼭 명심하시기 바랍니다.

Q Which is correct according to the announcement?

(a) Ties are optional for men.

(b) Business casual wear is permitted on Fridays.

(c) Women can choose between skirts and jeans.

(d) Employees must be dressed in company uniforms.

이 공지에 따르면 사실인 것은?

(a) 남성들에게 타이는 선택 사항이다.

(b) 금요일에는 비즈니스 캐주얼 복장 착용이 허용된다.

(c) 여성들은 치마나 청바지 중에서 선택할 수 있다.

(d) 직원들은 회사 유니폼을 입어야 한다.

해설 Altius 회사 직원 오리엔테이션에서의 회사 복장 규정에 대한 공지이다. 일반적으로 남성은 양복과 타이, 여성은 스커트나 바지 정장 차림이 요구되나, 금요일에는 비즈니스 캐주얼 차림이 허용된다고 했으므로 정답은 (b)이다.

어휘 dress code 복장 규정 quiet a bit 상당히, 꽤
impose 강요하다 formally 공식적으로, 격식을 갖춰
pantsuit (여성용) 슬랙스와 재킷이 한 벌이 된 슈트
patched (헝겊 조각 등을) 덧댄 reflect 반영하다, 반사하다
supplier 공급업체 shareholder 주주

7 Purpose

M: You wanted to see me?

W: Yeah. <u>Where have you been</u>?

M: I've been in the garage looking for <u>some tools to fix my bicycle</u>.

W: So, are you done fixing it?

M: I think so. Why?

W: Nothing serious. I saw the chairs in the living room. I thought they are really nice and wanted to ask where you bought them.

M: You know the shop Furniture Mart? The one on Pico Boulevard? <u>I got them there</u>.

W: Did you have them custom-made?

M: No, they <u>sent their representative</u> to look at the interior of our house, so that I'd get chairs <u>that matched the table here</u>.

W: That's a really good service that they provided. Are they expensive?

M: Not at all. They were very reasonable.

W: Sounds good. I may also try getting my dining table from them.

M: 나를 보고자 했나요?

W: 예, 어디에 있었어요?

M: 자전거를 고치기 위해 연장을 좀 찾아보려고 창고에 있었어요.

W: 그래서 다 고쳤나요?

M: 그런 것 같아요. 왜요?

W: 심각한 건 아니고요. 거실에 있는 의자를 봤는데, 그게 정말 좋은 것 같아서 어디에서 샀는지 물어 보고 싶었어요.

M: '가구마트'라는 가게 알죠? 피코 대로에 있는 것이요? 거기서 만든 거 샀어요.

W: 주문 제작한 건가요?

M: 아니요, 우리 집 인테리어를 보러 영업사원을 보냈더라고요. 그래서 여기 탁자에 어울리는 의자를 구할 수 있었어요.

W: 그거 정말 좋은 서비스를 제공하는군요. 가구들은 비싼가요?

M: 아뇨, 전혀 비싸지 않아요.

W: 좋네요. 나도 거기서 식탁을 좀 사야겠어요.

Q Why does the woman want to see the man?

(a) to ask what the man has been doing

(b) to inquire about some furniture she likes

(c) to find out if the bicycle is fixed

(d) to ask about the price of a piece of furniture

여자는 왜 남자를 만나 보고자 하는가?

(a) 남자가 무엇을 하고 있었는지 물어보려고

(b) 그녀가 마음에 드는 의자에 대해 물어 보려고

(c) 자전거가 고쳐졌는지 알아보려고

(d) 가구 가격에 대해 물어 보려고

해설 여자는 남자의 집에서 눈길을 끄는 의자를 보고, 어디서 샀으며, 주문 제작한 것인지, 가격은 어떠한지에 대해 묻고, 남자가 이에 답하는 장면이다. 따라서 정답은 (b)가 된다.

함정 (a) 처음에 뭘하고 있었는지 묻기는 했지만, 그것을 물어 보려고 남자를 보고자 한 것은 아니다. (c) 앞부분에 자전거 수리에 관한 이야기가 나오기는 하지만, 그것은 본론에 들어가기 전의 대화일 뿐이다. (d) 의자에 대한 여러 가지 궁금한 것들을 남자에게 묻고 있는 것이지, 의자의 가격이 주된 화제는 아니다.

어휘 garage 창고 boulevard 대로, 큰 길
custom-made 주문 제작의, 맞춤의
representative 판매 대리인, 세일즈맨 interior 내부, 실내도
provide 주다, 제공하다
reasonable 합리적인, 적당한, (가격이) 비싸지 않은
inquire about ~에 대해 문의하다
a piece of furniture 가구 한 점

8

W: Honey, <u>we've gone over our budget</u> this month.

M: Are you sure? How did that happen?

W: We paid extra this month for Susan's painting classes.

M: Oh, that's right. We need to <u>cut down on our regular spending</u>.

W: Yeah. Why don't we start <u>by reducing our utility bills</u>?

M: Good idea. So, let's not use the heater at night. We can use bigger blankets instead.

W: We could also try to <u>make fewer calls</u> to save money on telephone bills.

M: Right. And we shouldn't eat out this month.

W: Oh, should we <u>cancel the reservation</u> at the restaurant?

M: Mmm, I really wanted to try that restaurant's food. Well, there is always next time.

W: 여보, 우리 이번 달 예산을 초과했어요.

M: 정말이에요? 어떻게 된 거예요?

W: 이번 달 Susan의 그림 수업 때문에 추가로 돈이 더 나갔어요.

M: 아, 그렇군요. 정기지출을 줄여야겠어요.

W: 네. 공과금 줄이는 것부터 시작하는 게 어떨까요?

M: 좋은 생각이에요. 그럼 밤에 히터를 사용하지 말아요. 대신 더 큰 담요를 덮으면 되겠죠.

W: 전화비를 절약할 수 있도록 전화를 더 적게 사용해도 되고요.

M: 맞아요. 그리고 이번 달에는 외식하지 말아야겠어요.

W: 오, 식당 예약을 취소할까요?

M: 음, 그 식당의 음식을 정말로 먹어 보고 싶었는데. 다음에 기회가 있겠죠. 뭐.

Q What do the man and woman decide to do?

(a) to set up a more balanced schedule

(b) to cut back on spending

(c) to improve the efficiency of the heater

(d) to reduce the hours of painting classes

여자와 남자는 무엇을 하기로 결정했는가?

(a) 더욱 균형 잡힌 일정 세우기

(b) 지출 줄이기

(c) 히터의 효율을 높이기

(d) 그림 수업의 시간을 줄이기

해설 이번 달 예산이 초과한 것에 대해 부부가 나누는 대화이다. 예산초과의 원인이 딸의 그림 수업료 때문임을 알자, 부부는 그 초과분을 메우기 위

해서 전기세를 줄이고 전화비를 절약하는 등, 정기지출을 어떡하면 더 줄일 수 있느냐에 대한 대책을 마련하고 있다. 따라서 정답은 (b)이다.

함정 Susan의 그림 수업 시간을 줄이는 것이 아니라, 계속해야 하기 때문에 그 수업료를 채우기 위한 노력들이 이야기되고 있는 것이므로 (d)는 틀린 답이다.

어휘 **go over** (경비 등이 예산을) 초과하다

budget 예산, 경비, 생활비 | **extra** 여분으로, 가외로, 부가적으로

cut down on ~의 소비를 줄이다, 절약하다 | **spending** 소비, 지출

utility bill 공과금 (고지서) | **blanket** 담요, 모포

make a call 전화를 걸다 | **set up** ~을 세우다, 설치하다

efficiency 효율성

---

9 Main Idea

W: Let me now speak about the health issues related to coffee. <u>Though a seemingly simple beverage —</u> ground coffee beans in hot water — coffee in recent years has become a "hot topic" of debate in the medical field. You may have heard that coffee is listed among risk factors for coronary heart disease, which include hypertension and high cholesterol levels. However, there is no direct link between drinking coffee and <u>increased possibility of developing heart disease</u>. Clearly, <u>coffee isn't as bad as it's made out to be</u>. In fact, drinking coffee has some positive health benefits. <u>Research has established</u> that it <u>lowers the risk of developing</u> gall stones and kidney stones.

W: 이제 커피에 관련한 건강 문제에 관해 얘기하겠습니다. 뜨거운 물에 탄 커피 가루는 겉보기에는 단순한 음료처럼 보이지만, 최근 몇 년간 커피는 의학계에서 뜨거운 논쟁거리가 되고 있습니다. 여러분들도 어쩌면 커피가 관상 동맥 질환을 일으키는 위험 요소 목록에 올랐다는 얘기를 들어봤을 것입니다. 여기에는 고혈압이나 높은 콜레스테롤 수치 같은 것이 포함됩니다. 그러나 커피 음용과 심장 질환 발병 가능성 증가 사이에 직접적인 관련은 없습니다. 분명히 말해 커피는 생각하는 것만큼 그렇게 나쁘지 않습니다. 사실, 커피를 마시면 건강상 몇 가지 긍정적인 이점도 있습니다. 연구에 따르면 커피가 담석이나 신장 결석 발병률을 낮추는 것으로 입증되었습니다.

Q What is the speaker's main point in the talk?

(a) Coffee may be even healthier than people thought.

(b) Coffee must be reevaluated as a health drink.

(c) Coffee should not be linked to heart disease.

(d) Coffee has been wrongly considered as a health risk.

이 이야기에서 화자의 요지는?

(a) 커피는 사람들이 생각하는 것보다 더 건강에 좋을 수 있다.

(b) 커피는 건강 음료로 재평가되어야 한다.

(c) 커피는 심장 질환과 연결되어서는 안 된다.

(d) 커피는 건강의 위험 요소로 잘못 인식되어 왔다.

[해설] 커피에 대한 잘못된 인식, 새로운 실험 결과에 대한 내용이다. 커피가 심장 질환을 일으키는 위험 요소로 인식되어 왔지만, 사실 이에 대한 정확한 근거가 없으며, 오히려 건강상의 이점이 있다는 사실이 입증되었다고 밝히고 있으므로 정답은 (d)이다.

[함정] 강의의 요지가 커피의 이로운 점을 열거하는 데 있지 않으므로 (a)나 (b)는 답이 될 수 없다. 또한 커피와 심장 질환과의 관련(c)에 대한 언급은 전체 내용의 일부에 해당하므로 강의의 요지라고 보기 어렵다.

[어휘] ground 빻은, 가루의   coronary 심장의
hypertension 고혈압   establish (사실 등을) 입증하다, 확증하다
gall stone 담석   kidney stone 신장 결석

10

W: My microwave seems to be broken. Do you know somebody who <u>could repair it</u>?

M: You could try Michael's Service Center just down the street.

W: Are they good?

M: Well, I got my DVD player repaired by them. They did a good job and <u>it wasn't expensive</u>.

W: Okay, <u>would they come and pick it up</u>?

M: I'm not sure. You can call them and find out.

W: How do I get the number?

M: You know what? It is not that far and I might be available to take your microwave to the service center this afternoon.

W: Will you do that for me? It is a little heavy for me to carry myself.

M: <u>That's what friends are for</u>.

W: Can I cook something for you when you get back?

M: <u>Sounds fair enough</u>.

W: 전자레인지가 고장 난 것 같아. 고칠 수 있는 사람을 알고 있니?

M: 큰 길 아래쪽에 Michael 서비스 센터에서 알아봐.

W: 잘 하니?

M: 거기서 DVD 플레이어를 수리했는데. 잘 하던데, 비싸지도 않고.

W: 알았어, 거기서 직접 와서 가져갈까?

M: 잘 모르겠어. 전화해서 알아봐.

W: 번호를 어떻게 알 수 있어?

M: 있잖아, 그리 멀지 않으니까, 오늘 오후에 내가 그 서비스 센터에 가져다줄 수 있을 거야.

W: 그렇게 해 줄래? 내가 직접 옮기기에는 좀 무거워서.

M: 친구 좋다는 게 그런 거지.

W: 돌아오면 음식을 만들어 줄게.

M: 상당히 공평한 것 같은걸.

Q   Which is correct according to the conversation?

(a) The woman will exchange her microwave.

(b) The service center charges for pick up service.

(c) The man will take the woman to the service center.

(d) The woman needs an appliance repaired.

대화에 근거하여 옳은 것은?

(a) 여자는 전자레인지를 교환할 것이다.

(b) 서비스 센터는 물품을 가져가는 데 비용을 청구한다.

(c) 남자는 여자를 그 서비스 센터에 데려갈 것이다.

(d) 여자는 전기제품을 수리할 필요가 있다.

[해설] 고장 난 전자레인지에 관한 남녀의 대화이다. 여자는 그것을 어디서 고쳐야 하는지 남자에게 물었으며, 남자는 자신의 DVD 플레이어를 고쳐 본 적이 있는 서비스 센터를 소개해 주고 있다. 따라서 정답은 (d)이다.

[함정] (a) 교환하는 것이 아니라, 수리할 것이다. (b) 서비스 센터가 물품을 가져가는 데 비용을 청구하는지는 알 수 없다. (c) 남자는 여자가 아니라 전자레인지를 여자 대신 그 서비스 센터에 가져갈 것이다.

[어휘] microwave 전자레인지   broken 고장 난, 부러진
repair 수리하다, 고치다   get+목+p.p. ~가 …하게 하다, 시키다
fair 공평한, 정당한   exchange 교환하다, 교체하다
charge 비용을 청구하다   appliance 전기기구(제품)

LISTENING REVIEW

A

1. soaring	2. commute
3. facilitate	4. evaporate
5. notion	6. prevalent
7. downturn	8. appreciable
9. dress code	10. impose
11. shareholder	12. inquire
13. efficiency	14. utility
15. appliance	16. hypertension

1. quickly increasing by a great deal

2. to travel a long distance every day between your home and your place of work

3. to make something easier or more likely to happen

4. to change from a liquid state to a gas because of temperature increases

5. an idea or belief about something

6. It means common.

7. a worsened or less successful state of the economy or an industry

8. It means something is large enough to be important or clearly noticed.

9. the rules about what kind of clothes people are allowed to wear

10. to use your authority to force people to accept something

11. a person who owns shares in a company

12. to ask for information about something

13. the quality of being able to do a task successfully, without wasting time or energy

14. an important service such as water, electricity, or gas that everyone pays for

15. a device or machine in your home that you use to do a job such as cleaning or cooking

16. a medical condition in which a person has very high blood pressure

B

1. a   2. b   3. b   4. a   5. a

1. 돌아오면 뭐 좀 요리해 줄까?

   (a) Can I cook something for you when you get back?

   (b) Can I get something to cook on my way back home?

2. 최근에 커피는 최대 논쟁 거리였습니다.

   (a) Recently, people have been drinking coffee for debates.

   (b) Coffee in recent years has become a "hot topic" of debate.

3. 분명히 말해 커피는 생각하는 것만큼 그렇게 나쁘지 않습니다.

   (a) Clearly, coffee isn't that bad as it used to be.

   (b) Clearly, coffee isn't as bad as it's made out to be.

4. 비용을 아끼기 위해서 전화를 덜 사용할 수 있어요.

   (a) We could try to make fewer calls to save money.

   (b) To save money, we can try to make shorter and briefer calls.

5. 이번 달 예산을 초과했어요.

   (a) We've gone over our budget this month.

   (b) We already got more budget for this month.

C.

1. I've been in the garage looking for some tools.

2. We need to cut down on our regular spending.

3. I may also try getting my dining table from them.

4. We expect you to look like professionals under all circumstances.

5. The reason is that Arabian musical traditions did impact Indonesia.

1. in the garage / looking for some tools/ I've been

2. cut down on / we need to / our regular spending

3. getting my dining table / I may also try / from them

4. under all circumstances / to look like professionals / we expect you

5. that Arabian musical traditions did / the reason is / impact Indonesia

D

1. a   2. b   3. b   4. a   5. a

1. The actual construction costs have failed to decrease.

   (a) The costs for actual construction have not been decreased.

   (b) The construction has failed due to the decreased costs.

2. I'll be out of town from Friday for a business meeting.

   (a) A business meeting will be held in Friday when I'm out of town.

   (b) On Friday, I'll be away for a business meeting.

3. I don't think you'll get back in time for the show.

   (a) You don't have to come back just for the show.

(b) I doubt you're going to make it to the show.

4. If you want to know about the sports car for sale, it's been sold.

   (a) I don't have the sports car any more because it was sold.

   (b) The sports car had been for sale until it was sold.

5. All employees are expected to be dressed formally.

   (a) Formal dress will be expected for all workers.

   (b) All workers should be dressed in any formal occasions.

CHAPTER 02 MAIN TOPIC

VOCABULARY PREVIEW

01. scorching 매우 뜨거운, 찌는 듯한

02. rash *n.* 발진, 뾰루지

03. tolerate 견디다, 참다

04. utilization 이용, 활용

05. candidate 후보자

06. adhere to ~을 지키다, 고수하다

07. congress 의회, 국회

08. courtesy 예의

09. offensive 공격적인, 무례한

10. senator 상원의원

11. eligible 적격의, 자격이 있는

12. descent 혈통, 출신

13. constitute 구성하다

14. blend *n.* 혼합

15. consequence 결과, 결말

16. imperative 필요한, 꼭 해야 할

17. audit *n.* 감사, 검사

18. composite 합성의, 혼합의

19. skeleton 해골, 골격

20. evolve 진화하다

21. deterioration 악화, 노화

22. confine 감금하다

23. thriving 번성하는, 번영하는

24. penalize 유죄를 선고하다

GUIDED LISTENING

1	1. d	2. a	**2**	1. d	2. b
3	1. c	2. c	**4**	1. b	2. d

1 Conversation

M: I've never seen such weather before!

W: I know. I start sweating the moment I go out!

M: Me too! I'd prefer to stay home rather than going out in the scorching heat. What do you do to keep cool?

W: Well, I drink lots of juice to keep myself cool. Sometimes I also go swimming.

M: Pool water doesn't suit me; I get skin rashes from its chemicals. So generally, I sit at home with the air conditioner on.

W: Doesn't your electricity bill get so high that way?

M: It does! But I can't help it. I can't tolerate hot weather.

W: Let's hope the rest of the summer isn't too hot. I'm really looking forward to the cool fall and winter.

M: 전에는 날씨가 이런 적이 없었어요!

W: 알아요, 나가는 순간, 땀에 젖기 시작해요!

M: 저도 그래요! 이렇게 찌는 듯한 더위에서는 외출하는 것보다는 집에 있는 게 좋겠어요. 시원하게 있으려면 무엇을 하세요?

W: 음. 저는 시원하게 있으려면 주스를 많이 마셔요. 수영을 가기도 하고요.

M: 제게는 수영장 물이 잘 안 맞아요. 거기 화학물질 때문에 피부에 발진이 생기죠. 그래서 저는 보통은 에어컨을 켜두고 집에 있죠.

W: 그러면 전기 요금이 꽤 많이 나오지 않나요?

M: 그렇죠! 하지만 할 수 없어요. 저는 뜨거운 날씨를 견디지 못하거든요.

W: 여름이 너무 덥지 않기를 기대해 보죠. 시원한 가을과 겨울이 정말 빨리 오면 좋겠어요.

Main Topic

1 What is this conversation about?

(a) preparing for unusual weather

(b) going swimming

(c) enjoying summer vacation

(d) avoiding summer heat

이 대화는 무엇에 관한 것인가?

(a) 이상 기후 대비

(b) 수영 가기

(c) 여름 휴가 즐기기

(d) 여름의 더위 피하기

해설 너무 더운 날씨에 관한 대화이다. 남자와 여자가 더울 때 무엇을 하는지에 대해 이야기를 나누고 있으므로 정답은 (d)이다.

Detail

2 What is the woman's concern about the man staying home?

(a) the high energy cost

(b) skin rashes

(c) catching a cold

(d) drinking too much water

남자가 집에 머무는 것에 대해 여자가 걱정하는 것은?

(a) 높은 에너지 비용

(b) 피부 발진

(c) 감기에 걸리는 것

(d) 물을 너무 많이 마시는 것

해설 I sit at home with the air conditioner on.(보통은 에어컨을 켜두고 집에 있죠.)라는 남자의 말에 Doesn't your electricity bill get so high that way?(그러면 전기 요금이 꽤 많이 나오지 않나요?)라고 여자가 되묻고 있다. 그러므로 여자는 남자의 전기 요금에 대해 걱정하고 있음을 알 수 있다.

어휘 sweat 땀을 흘리다   the moment ~하자마자, 바로 그때
prefer to ~하는 것을 더 좋아하다
scorching 매우 뜨거운, 찌는 듯한
suit 적합하다   rash 발진, 뾰루지
with the air conditioner on 에어컨을 틀어 놓고
tolerate 견디다, 참다   look forward to ~을 학수고대하다

2 Conversation

W: Do you support Antonio?

M: Yes. He's an intelligent politician — and has done so many things for society.

W: You're correct, but that may not be enough to <u>get him a position at the national level</u>. He may not be able to handle the huge responsibility of leading a nation.

M: I disagree. <u>He's proved his worth as a mayor</u> and I'm sure he'll do well at a higher level as well. Well, who's your favorite?

W: Amanda. She's <u>a well-experienced politician</u> and is <u>well aware of what's going on</u> in Congress.

M: Well, she's been a good senator, but I feel she <u>lacks conviction in her words</u>.

W: That's not true. When she speaks, everyone listens. Whatever she says, she does. I am sure she'll make a good leader.

M: Let's see who gets elected: your candidate or mine!

W: Antonio를 지지하세요?

M: 네. 그는 지적인 정치가이고 사회를 위해 많은 것들을 했잖아요.

W: 맞아요, 하지만 그렇다고 해서 그를 국가 수준의 위치로 받아들이기에는 충분하지 않을 수 있어요. 그는 나라를 이끌어야 하는 막대한 책임을 감당하지 못할지도 모르잖아요.

M: 나는 동의하지 않아요. 그는 시장으로서의 그의 가치를 증명해 보였고, 나는 그가 더 높은 위치에서도 잘 할 거라고 확신해요. 그럼, 당신이 가장 좋아하는 사람은 누구죠?

W: Amanda에요. 그녀는 노련한 정치가이고 국회에서 무슨 일이 어떻게 돌아가고 있는지 잘 알고 있어요.

M: 음, 그녀는 훌륭한 상원의원이지만, 자기 말에 확신이 없는 것 같아요.

W: 그렇지 않아요. 그녀가 말할 때는 모든 사람이 잘 들어요. 그녀는 말하는 것은 무엇이든 실행하죠. 그녀가 훌륭한 지도자가 될 거라고 확신해요.

M: 누가 당선되는지 보자고요. 당신의 후보인지 나의 후보인지!

Main Topic

1 What is this conversation about?

(a) where to visit next time

(b) what to consider when electing

(c) which sporting event to attend

(d) who to support in the election

이 대화는 무엇에 관한 것인가?

(a) 다음 번에는 어디를 방문할지

(b) 선거할 때 고려해야 하는 것

(c) 어느 스포츠에 참여할지

(d) 선거에서 누구를 지지하는지

해설 선거에서 누구를 지지하는지에 관한 대화이다. politician, leading a nation, Congress, senator, leader, elected, candidate 등의 단어만 들어도 정답을 쉽게 찾을 수 있다. 여자와 남자는 각각 다른 후보자를 지지하고 있다는 점도 파악해야 한다.

2   What can be inferred about the two speakers?

(a) They both support the same candidate.

(b) They don't agree with each other.

(c) They don't like either of the candidates.

(d) They think it is not easy to pick one.

대화하고 있는 두 사람에 대해 추론할 수 있는 것은?

(a) 그들은 모두 같은 후보자를 지지한다.

(b) 그들은 서로 의견이 같지 않다.

(c) 그들은 후보자 중 어느 쪽도 좋아하지 않는다.

(d) 그들은 한 사람을 고르기가 쉽지 않다고 생각한다.

해설 남자는 Antonio를, 여자는 Amanda를 지지한다는 내용이다. 서로 자기가 지지하는 후보에 대해 높이 평가를 내리고 있고, 상대편 후보에 대해서는 부정적인 견해를 가지고 있으므로, (b)가 정답이다.

어휘 support 지지하다, 후원하다   intelligent 지성이 있는, 지적인   prove 증명하다   worth 가치   mayor 시장   well-experienced 노련한, 경험이 많은   congress 의회, 국회   senator 상원의원   lack 결핍되다, 부족하다   conviction 확신   whatever ~하는 것은 무엇이든   candidate 후보자

3   Monologue

W: We are delighted to announce the launch of a web board for our consumers. <u>All are invited to post their ads</u>, announce events, share important tips or discuss hot issues online. The services provided to visitors are free of charge. However, we request users to adhere to basic principles for making maximum utilization of the service. The web board <u>is meant for lively debate</u> and free expression of ideas; the participants are requested <u>to show respect and politeness</u> to other visitors. If we <u>find a posting violating the etiquette standards</u> of the board, we may immediately delete it <u>without the poster's permission</u>. Postings should not be offensive, keeping in mind the large and diverse population we cater to.

W: 고객을 위한 웹 게시판이 마련되었다는 것을 알려드리게 되어 기쁘게 생각합니다. 누구든지 광고를 올리거나 이벤트를 공지하거나 중요한 정보를 공유하거나 온라인상에서 핫이슈를 토론할 수 있습니다. 방문자들에게 제공되는 이 서비스는 무료입니다. 그러나 사용자들이 이 서비스를 최대한 활용하기 위한 기본 원칙을 지켜 줄 것을 요청 드립니다. 이 웹 게시판은 활발하게 논쟁하고 자유롭게 아이디어를 표현하기 위한 것입니다. 참여자들은 다른 방문자들에게 존중과 예의를 표해야 합니다. 게시물이 게시판의 예의 기준에 위배된다는 것을 발견하게 되면, 게시자의 동의 없이 즉각 삭

제할 수 있습니다. 게시물은 공격적이어서는 안 되며, 우리가 응대하고 있는 폭넓고 다양한 사람들을 유념해 주시기 바랍니다.

1   What is the announcement mainly about?

(a) how to access the web board for a debate

(b) who is eligible to use the web board

(c) the basic courtesy rules for the web board

(d) fees for using the web board

이 공지는 주로 무엇에 관한 것인가?

(a) 토론을 위해 웹 게시판에 어떻게 들어오는지

(b) 웹 게시판을 이용할 수 있는 사람들이 누구인지

(c) 웹 게시판에 위한 기본 예의 규칙

(d) 웹 게시판을 이용하기 위한 비용

해설 무료 서비스를 하게 된 웹 게시판에 대한 공지이다. 웹 게시판 이용시 지켜야 할 규칙들에 대해 공지하고 있으므로 (c)가 정답이다.

함정 누구나 이용 가능하다고 했으므로 (b)는 오답이다. 또한 이 공지는 웹 게시판을 무료로 이용할 수 있다고 했으므로 (d)를 답으로 착각해서는 안 된다.

2   What would happen to a posting that is offensive?

(a) The person who posted it will be fined.

(b) The person will be kicked out of the board.

(c) The posting will be removed without notice.

(d) The posting will be reported to the police.

공격적인 게시물에는 어떤 일이 일어날 것인가?

(a) 게시한 사람은 벌금을 물게 될 것이다.

(b) 그 사람은 게시판에 들어오지 못하게 될 것이다.

(c) 그 게시물은 공지 없이 삭제될 것이다.

(d) 그 게시물은 경찰에 신고될 것이다.

해설 뒷부분의 we may immediately delete it without the poster's permission(게시자의 동의 없이 즉각 삭제할 수 있습니다)이라는 내용으로 보아 (c)가 정답임을 알 수 있다.

어휘 launch 시작, 착수   board 게시판   consumer 소비자   post 게시하다, 알리다   share 공유하다   free of charge 무료인   adhere to ~을 지키다, 고수하다   principle 원칙, 원리   utilization 이용, 활용   debate 토론   participant 참여자, 참가자   violate 어기다, 침해하다   permission 허가, 허락   offensive 공격적인, 무례한   cater to ~의 요구에 응하다   access 접근하다, 들어오다   eligible 적격의, 자격이 있는   courtesy 예의

4 Monologue

M: The population of the United States is racially mixed in composition. There are people of different ethnic descents and cultures. In today's class, we will look into the details of diversity in the American population and the groups that constitute it. Except for Native Americans, most of the American population emigrated from different parts of the world. A majority of the non-Native Americans are Anglo-Scottish, Irish, French or Dutch. Some large groups also have their origins in Italy, Germany and Canada. There are also people from Africa, Eastern Europe, Asia, and Latin America that constitute a small group of Americans. On the whole, the American population is diverse and has a blend of many ethnic groups.

M: 미국의 인구는 구성에 있어서 인종적으로 혼합되어 있습니다. 다양한 인종의 출신과 문화권의 사람들이 있습니다. 오늘 수업에서 우리는 미국 인구의 다양성에 대한 세부사항과 그것을 구성하는 집단들에 대해 고찰해 볼 것입니다. 미국 원주민을 제외하면, 미국 인구의 대부분은 세계 각 지역에서 이주해 왔습니다. 원주민이 아닌 미국인들 중 대다수는 앵글로 스코틀랜드계, 아일랜드계, 프랑스계와 네덜란드계입니다. 몇몇 다수 인종은 이탈리아, 독일, 캐나다에 혈통을 둔 집단입니다. 미국인 중 소수 그룹을 이루고 있는 아프리카, 동부 유럽, 아시아, 라틴 아메리카에서 온 사람들도 있습니다. 전체적으로 볼 때, 미국 인구는 다양하며 다민족 혼합체입니다.

Main Topic

1 What is the subject of the lecture?

(a) the history of blended American culture

(b) the diverse ethnic composition of the U.S. population

(c) immigration policies in the United States

(d) the proportion of the Anglo-Scottish population in the American population

이 강의의 주제는 무엇인가?
(a) 미국 혼합 문화의 역사
(b) 미국 인구의 다양한 인종 구성
(c) 미국의 이민 정책
(d) 미국 인구 중 앵글로 스코틀랜드계의 비율

해설 앞부분에 미국 인구의 다양성(diversity in the American population)에 대해 고찰해 볼 것이라고 했으므로 정답은 (b)이다. 처음부터 끝까지 이에 대한 설명이 계속되고 있다.

Comprehension

2 Which is correct according to the lecture?

(a) The largest racial groups are German and French.

(b) White American is the largest racial group.

(c) Latin American population is the largest minority group.

(d) A majority of non-Native Americans are Europeans.

이 강의에 따르면 다음 중 옳은 것은?
(a) 가장 많은 인종 집단은 독일계와 프랑스계이다.
(b) 백인계 미국인이 가장 큰 인종 집단이다.
(c) 라틴 아메리카 인구가 소수 집단 중 가장 크다.
(d) 원주민이 아닌 미국인들 중 다수가 유럽 사람이다.

해설 원주민이 아닌 미국인들 중 다수는 앵글로 스코틀랜드, 아일랜드, 프랑스와 네덜란드계라고 했으므로, (d)가 옳다는 것을 알 수 있다.

함정 소수 그룹에 아프리카, 동유럽, 아시아, 라틴 아메리카에서 온 사람들이 있다는 말은 있지만, 그 중 라틴 아메리카 인구가 가장 크다는 언급은 없으므로 (c)는 오답이다.

어휘 racially 인종적으로   composition 구성
ethnic 인종의, 민족의   descent 혈통, 출신   detail 세부사항
diversity 다양성   constitute 구성하다
except for ~을 제외하면   emigrate 이주하다
majority 대부분, 대다수
Anglo-Scottish 앵글로 스코틀랜드 사람(의)
Irish 아일랜드 사람(의)   Dutch 네덜란드 사람(의)
on the whole 전체로 보아서, 대체로   proportion 비율
blend 혼합

PRACTICAL LISTENING

1. c	2. c	3. b	4. a	5. c
6. b	7. a	8. c	9. d	10. d

1 Main Topic

W: The government has decided to conduct an extensive investigation into the cargo truck industry. This follows the high numbers of cargo trucks reported to have failed random safety inspections by state troopers, along with 200 major truck accidents this year alone. Since cargo trucks carry 75% of the goods in the United States, and truck accidents often have horrific consequences, it is imperative that they operate safely at all times. Officers from the Transportation

Department will begin inspecting several major cargo truck companies starting next week. This will include mechanical and safety checks on the vehicles as well as audits of service records. Companies which are found to be <u>in violation of major safety rules</u> will be given 30 days to correct their problems or <u>be forced to suspend operations</u>.

W: 정부는 화물 트럭 산업에 대한 전면적인 조사를 실시하기로 결정했습니다. 이는 올해만 200건의 큰 트럭 사고가 발생한 것과 더불어, 대다수의 화물 트럭이 주 경찰의 무작위 안전 검사를 통과하지 못한것으로 보고됨에 따라 결정된 사항입니다. 이들 화물 트럭이 미국 물자의 75%를 운반하며, 트럭 사고들이 종종 무서운 결과를 초래하기 때문에 이들 화물 트럭은 항상 안전운행을 해야 할 필요가 있습니다. 교통부 공무원들은 다음 주부터 몇몇 주요 화물 트럭 회사에 대한 조사를 실시할 것입니다. 여기에는 운행 기록에 대한 감사뿐 아니라 화물차에 대한 기계 조사와 안전 조사까지 포함될 것입니다. 주요 안전 규칙을 위반한 것으로 발각되는 회사들은 30일간의 문제 시정 기간이 주어지거나 강제 운행 중단 조치를 받을 수 있습니다.

Q What is the news report mainly about?

(a) complaints regarding safety in cargo trucks

(b) the growing number of trucks that are not roadworthy

(c) government action to make cargo trucks safe

(d) measures taken by cargo companies to improve services

이 뉴스는 주로 무엇에 관한 것인가?

(a) 화물 트럭 안전에 관한 불만

(b) 도로에 적합하지 못한 트럭 수의 증가

(c) 화물 트럭 안전을 위한 정부 조치

(d) 서비스 개선을 위한 트럭 회사의 조치

해설 화물 트럭 안전사고가 증대됨에 따라 정부에서 이를 시정하기 위해 전면적인 조사를 시행키로 했다는 소식을 전하고 있으므로 전체 요지는 (c)이다.

함정 (a) 트럭 회사에 대한 정부의 감사 조치는 빈번한 트럭 사고에 대한 염려 때문이지 트럭 안전에 대한 불만이 제기되었기 때문이 아니다. (b) 트럭이 도로 운행에 적당하지 않다거나 (d) 트럭 회사가 자체적으로 서비스 개선을 위해 노력하고 있다는 내용은 언급되지 않았다.

어휘 conduct 수행하다, 처리하다 | extensive 넓은, 광대한 범위의 | cargo truck 화물 트럭 | random 무작위의 | state trooper 주(州) 경찰관 | goods 물지, 상품 | consequence 결과, 결말 | imperative 필요한, 꼭 해야 할 | transportation department 교통부 | audit 감사 | service (교통 기관 등의) 운행, 편도

2

M: Sharon, I need your advice on something.

W: Sure. What is it?

M: The day after tomorrow is <u>my nephew's birthday. What gift would be good</u> for him?

W: Well, how old is he?

M: He's seven years old.

W: Do you know what he is interested in?

M: Well, his mom told me he likes reading, but I was thinking of getting him an MP3 player or some games. I'm not sure what <u>kids in that age group</u> would like.

W: Why don't you get him <u>a good educational book</u>? That will make his mom happy, too. You could find those in any bookshop.

M: That's a good idea. I'll have to ask my girlfriend to look for one since <u>I will be stuck at the office</u> until late.

M: Sharon, 너의 조언이 필요해.

W: 응, 원데?

M: 모레가 조카 생일인데, 무슨 선물이 좋을까?

W: 음, 몇 살인데?

M: 7살이야.

W: 그 애가 뭐에 관심이 있는지 알고 있니?

M: 음, 걔네 어머니가 그러는데, 책 읽는 것을 좋아한다지만, 나는 MP3 플레이어나 게임을 사 줄까 생각하고 있었어. 그 나이의 아이들이 무엇을 좋아하는지 잘 모르겠어.

W: 좋은 교육용 책을 사주는 게 어떨까? 그러면 그 애의 엄마도 좋아할 거야. 어느 서점엘 가도 그런책들을 찾을 수 있을 거야.

M: 좋은 생각이야. 나는 오늘 늦게까지 회사 일로 바쁘니까, 여자친구에게 하나 찾아봐 달라고 부탁해야겠다.

Q What will the man probably do in the afternoon?

(a) go to a children's bookstore

(b) take the woman shopping

(c) work at the office

(d) give his nephew a birthday party

남자는 오후에 아마도 무엇을 할 것인가?

(a) 어린이 서점에 가기

(b) 여자를 쇼핑에 데려가기

(c) 사무실에서 일하기

(d) 조카에게 생일 파티 해 주기

조카의 생일 선물에 대한 남녀의 대화이다. 남자가 여자에게 조카 생일 선물로 무엇이 좋을지 조언을 구하자, 여자는 교육용 도서를 추천한다. 이에 남자는 자기는 바쁘니까, 여자친구에게 부탁해야겠다고 한다. 마지막 말 since I will be stuck at the office until late에서 남자는 오후에 늦게까지 사무실에서 일할 것임을 알 수 있다.

advice 충고, 조언 | the day after tomorrow 모레 |
nephew 조카 | educational 교육의, 교육적인 |
look for ~을 찾다

3

W: In this lecture we will discuss methods followed to protect aircraft from lightning. Aircraft bodies are generally made of aluminum, which is a good conductor of electricity. Modern aircraft, however, tend to use composite materials for their exteriors. These kinds of materials are made up of layers of conductive fibers devised to carry lightning currents. Since aircraft design ensures that there is no gap in conduction paths, a lightning current travels along the skin of the aircraft before exiting at an extremity like the tail or wing tip.

W: 이번 강의에서는 항공기를 번개로부터 보호하기 위해 취하는 방법을 논의해 보겠습니다. 항공기 본체는 일반적으로 알루미늄으로 만들어져 있는데, 전기 전도가 아주 잘되는 물질입니다. 그러나 현대의 항공기는 바깥 표면에 혼합 물질을 사용하는 경향이 있습니다. 이런 종류의 물질은 번개 전류가 통하도록 고안된 전도 섬유층으로 이루어져 있습니다. 항공기 디자이너는 전도 경로에 틈이 없도록 되어 있으므로 번개 전류는 항공기의 외판을 통과하다가 꼬리나 날개 끝과 같은 양끝에서 빠져나갑니다.

Q   Which is correct according to the lecture?

(a) Conduction paths are engineered without composite fibers.

(b) Aircraft skins are designed to conduct electricity.

(c) Aircraft are frequently harmed by lightning strikes.

(d) Lightning cannot damage fast-flying aircraft.

강의에 따르면 맞는 것은?

(a) 전도 경로는 혼합 섬유 없이 만들어진다.

(b) 항공기 바깥 표면은 전기가 통하도록 설계된다.

(c) 항공기는 번개 때문에 자주 피해를 입는다.

(d) 번개는 빠른 속도의 항공기에는 피해를 줄 수 없다.

항공기를 번개로부터 보호하는 방법에 관한 내용이다. 항공기 바깥 표면을 전기 전도가 높은 알루미늄에서, 전류가 바깥쪽으로 흐르다가 양끝으로 나가게 하는 혼합 물질로 바꾸고 있다는 내용이다.

(c) 항공기가 번개 때문에 자주 피해를 입는다는 언급은 나와 있지 않다.

aircraft 항공기 | lightning 번개 | conductor 전도체 |
composite 합성의, 혼합의 | exterior 외부, 표면 |
conductive 전도성의 | fiber 섬유, 섬유질 |
devise 고안하다, 발명하다 | carry (전기 등을) 통하게 하다, 흘리다 |
exit 나가다 | extremity 끝, 말단 | wing tip (비행기의) 날개 끝

4   Main Topic

W: You seem to be in good spirits. What are you listening to?

M: Trance, a new pop music band.

W: I haven't heard of them but this song sounds quite familiar.

M: It's becoming very popular among music-lovers, so you've probably heard it on the radio.

W: Would you mind turning it up? It sounds good.

M: Well, all their songs are.

W: Then, I may buy that CD as well. Or, can I download them from any music site?

M: I heard this site called "Melon" downloads MP3s at reasonable prices. You can probably get some discounts if you become a member or something.

W: That sounds good enough. Thanks a lot.

W: 기분이 좋아 보이네, 뭘 듣고 있는 거야?

M: '트랜스,' 새로운 팝뮤직 밴드야.

W: 들어본 적은 없지만, 이 노래는 정말 귀에 익은데.

M: 음악애호가들 사이에서는 아주 많은 인기를 얻고 있는 곡이라서 아마 너도 라디오에서 들어 봤을 거야.

W: 소리 좀 키워 볼래? 좋은데.

M: 노래들이 다 좋아.

W: 그럼 나도 그 CD를 사야겠다. 아니면, 음악 사이트에서 다운로드받을 수 있을까?

M: 내가 듣기로는 '멜론'이라는 이 사이트가 적절한 가격에 MP3를 다운로드한다고 하던데. 회원인가 뭐 그런 걸로 가입하면 아마 할인도 될 거야.

W: 괜찮네. 정말 고마워.

Q   What is the topic of the conversation?

(a) a band the man is listening to

(b) an Internet site where music can be bought

(c) how to find good music to listen to

(d) recent trends in popular music

5

W: The largest and most <u>complete skeleton</u> of a Tyrannosaurus Rex ever found belongs to "Sue," a dinosaur. Researchers are finding evidence from it to show that dinosaurs may be more closely <u>related to birds than to reptiles.</u> <u>Among its bones</u> is a furcula or wishbone, typical of a bird's genital structure. No other T-Rex skeleton found previously has featured this wishbone. Sue's furcula, however, is <u>evidence for the hotly debated theory</u> that birds <u>may have evolved from meat-eating dinosaurs.</u>

Q What can be implied from the lecture?
(a) The T-Rex used to feed primarily on birds.

(b) Wishbones were commonly seen in dinosaurs.

(c) Reptiles do not have furcula bones.

(d) Sue's skeleton proves an evolutionary link to reptiles.

6 Main Topic

M: <u>I need to take a day off</u> some day this week.

W: Not a problem. Are you <u>planning to go somewhere</u>? A vacation?

M: Not exactly. I have to take my son to the dentist, Dr. Ibrahim, most likely.

W: Does he have any problems?

M: Yes, <u>he's been complaining of toothache</u> for the last three days.

W: Again?

M: No. That was my first son, and this time it is my second.

W: I see. Have you made an appointment already?

M: Not yet. <u>I'll make it on my day off</u>.

W: You'd better make it now. The doctor <u>might not be available</u> that day.

M: Yeah. I will find out when I can get a day off and then I will call the dentist.

M: 이번 주에 하루 일을 쉬어야 해요.

W: 괜찮아요. 어딘가 갈 계획이에요? 휴가?

M: 그런 건 아니고요. 이브라힘인가 하는 치과에 아들을 데려가야 할 것 같아요.

W: 무슨 문제라도 있나요?

M: 네, 3일 전부터 치통을 호소해서요.

W: 또요?

M: 아니에요. 지난번엔 큰 아들이었고, 이번엔 둘째 아들이에요.

W: 알겠어요. 예약은 해 둔 거예요?

M: 아직 안 했어요. 쉬는 날 하려고요.

W: 지금 하는 게 좋을것 같은데요. 그 날 의사가 안 될 수도 있잖아요.

M: 네, 언제 쉴 수 있는지 알아보고 의사에게 전화해야겠네요.

Q   What is the conversation mainly about?

(a) how long the man will be away from work

(b) why the man needs a day off

(c) where the man is going on his vacation

(d) which dentist is the best to see

대화는 주로 무엇에 관한 것인가?

(a) 얼마 동안 남자가 일을 쉬는지

(b) 왜 남자가 하루 일을 쉬어야 하는지

(c) 남자가 어디로 휴가를 가는지

(d) 어느 치과가 가장 진찰을 잘하는지

해설 이번 주에 하루 일을 쉬겠다고 하는 남자에게 여자가 이유를 묻고 있는 장면이다. 이에 남자는 아들이 치통을 호소해서 쉬는 날 치과에 데려가야 하기 때문이라고 이유를 밝힌다. 따라서 정답은 (b)가 된다.

함정 남자는 이브라힘인가 하는 치과의사에게 아들을 데려갈 계획이라고만 말한 것이지, 어느 치과의사가 진료를 가장 잘하는지에 대해서는 전혀 언급이 없다. 따라서 (d)는 정답이 아니다.

어휘 take a day off 하루 휴가를 얻다   vacation 휴가
not exactly 반드시 그렇지는 않다, 조금 틀리다
take 사람 to 사람을 ~로 데리고 가다   dentist 치과의사
complain of (고통·병의 상태를) 호소하다   toothache 치통
make an appointment 약속하다   day off 비번일, 휴일
away 부재중, 결석(결근)하여

7

M: Bone deterioration is an increasing cause for concern among the elderly, especially women, with many patients having this complaint being confined to bed. Lindford University scientists recommend high-stress exercises like lifting weights as being perhaps the ideal way to develop and improve bone density. In the course of their study, they rated different exercises for the stress they placed on a bone. This helped them conclude that bone maintenance requires high-load and high-stress activities like lifting weights rather than exercises like jogging.

M: 뼈의 노화는 중년 중에서도 여성에게 점점 늘어나는 관심사입니다. 많은 환자들이 침대에 묶여 있는 것을 불만스러워하죠. Lindford 대학교 과학자들은 골밀도를 높이는 가장 좋은 방법으로 역도 같은 고압박 운동을 추천합니다. 연구 과정 중 연구자들은 여러가저 운동들이 뼈에 가하는 강도를 평가해 보았습니다. 이 연구에서 뼈를 유지하려면 조깅보다는 역도 같은 고압박 활동이 좋다는 것이 밝혀졌습니다.

Q   What can be inferred from the lecture?

(a) Some exercises can be more beneficial for people at certain ages.

(b) Lifting weights helps in many types of health problems.

(c) Bone deterioration has largely become a concern for young women.

(d) Health experts are recommending various exercises to their members.

강의에서 추론할 수 있는 것은?

(a) 어떤 운동은 특정 연령층의 사람들에게 더 유익할 수 있다.

(b) 역도는 여러 가지 건강 문제에 도움이 된다.

(c) 뼈의 노화는 젊은 여성에게 폭넓은 고민거리이다.

(d) 운동 전문가들은 회원들에게 다양한 운동을 추천하고 있다.

해설 중년 여성의 뼈 노화를 막는 운동에 대한 설명이다. 화자는 골밀도를 높이는 가장 좋은 운동으로 역도와 같은 고압박 운동이 좋다는 연구 결과를 소개하고 있다. 그러므로 어떤 운동이 특정 연령층의 사람들에게 더 유익할 수 있다는 것을 알 수 있다.

함정 오답인 (b)는 본문에서 골밀도에 역도가 좋다고 했지, 모든 건강의 해결책이라고 하지는 않았다. 또한 뼈의 노화는 중년 여성에게서 나타나는 문제이므로 (c)의 young은 elderly가 되어야 맞다.

어휘 deterioration 약화, 노화   concern 관심, 염려
the elderly 중년 사람들   confine 감금하다
high-stress 고압박의   bone density 골밀도

8

M: Jeannie, I'm glad to see you!

W: Hi, Steve. What brings you here?

M: I'm a real estate agent, and came here to close a deal with a client. And you? Why are you here?

W: I'm planning to buy an apartment. So I came here to have a look at a few of them.

M: Okay. Are you going through a real estate agent?

W: Yes, he should be here any moment.

M: Okay, let me know if you need any help.

W: Sure, I'll let you know. Thank you.

....

M: Jeannie, 만나서 반가워!

W: 안녕, Steve. 여기 어떻게 왔어?

M: 나는 부동산 중개인이라서, 고객과의 거래를 체결하러 왔어. 너는? 여기 왜 온 거니?

W: 아파트를 구매할 계획이야. 그래서 좀 둘러보려고 왔어.

M: 그렇구나. 부동산 중개인의 소개를 받을 거니?

W: 응, 곧 올 거야.

M: 알았어. 도움이 필요하면 알려 줘.

W: 물론이야. 알려 줄게. 고마워.

....

Q Which is correct about the man according to the conversation?

(a) He is selling an apartment to the woman.

(b) He is planning to show various apartments to the woman.

(c) He is working as a real estate agent.

(d) He is going to help the woman find a good house.

....

이 대화에 의하면 남자에 대해 옳은 것은?

(a) 여자에게 아파트를 팔고 있다.

(b) 여자에게 여러 아파트를 보여 줄 계획이다.

(c) 부동산 중개인으로 일하고 있다.

(d) 여자가 좋은 집을 찾도록 도울 것이다.

해설 남녀가 서로 이곳에 온 이유에 대해 묻고 답하는 대화이다. 남자는 현재 부동산 중개인(a real estate agent)으로 일하고 있고, 고객과 계약을 하러 왔으며, 여자는 아파트를 사기 위해 다른 중개인을 통해 알아보러 왔다고 이야기한다. 따라서 정답은 (c)이다.

함정 남자는 다른 손님과의 계약 체결을 위해 이곳에 왔다가 우연히 여자를 만난 것이다. 따라서 여자에게 아파트를 보여 줄 목적으로 온 것이 아니기 때문에 (b)는 정답이 아니다. 또한 여자는 다른 부동산 중개인과 함께 집을 알아보러 온 것이므로, 남자가 여자에게 좋은 집을 구해 주려고 돕고 있는 상황은 아니다. 따라서 (d)도 역시 정답이 될 수 없다.

어휘 bring ~을 오게 하다, 가져오다 |
real estate agent 부동산 중개인 |
close 종결하다, 마치다, 체결하다 | deal 거래, 흥정, 계약 |
have a look at ~을 한번 보다 |
any moment 어느 때라도, 언제든지, 당장이라도

9 Main Topic

W: Moving on to other news, India's growing divorce rate is benefiting not just law firms but also the thriving business of marital investigation. Divorce was traditionally rare in India, due to cultural and religious restrictions. Now, however, the country is experiencing one of the fastest-growing divorce rates in Asia. Detective agencies have thrived in this new situation, particularly since the common law system that India inherited from Britain penalizes adulterous spouses during divorce cases. Some detective agencies with the services of former policemen, journalists and security personnel like bodyguards are reportedly making large profits. It seems that suspicious spouses are undeterred by the fee charged for investigation, which can be the equivalent of USD 1,800.

....

W: 다음 뉴스입니다. 인도의 이혼율 증가는 법률회사뿐 아니라 번창하는 결혼 생활 수사 사업에도 이익이 되고 있습니다. 문화적, 종교적 속박 때문에 전통적으로 인도에서 이혼은 매우 드문 일이었습니다. 그러나 현재 인도는 아시아에서 가장 빠른 이혼 증가율을 보이고 있습니다. 이런 새로운 상황 속에서 사설 탐정소(흥신소)가 번창하고 있습니다. 이는 특히, 영국 법을 물려받은 인도의 관습법에 따라 이혼 소송의 경우에 불륜을 저지른 배우자에게 불리한 판결이 나기 때문입니다. 전직 경찰, 저널리스트, 그리고 보디가드 같은 보안 인력 출신을 고용한 일부 탐정 사무소는 상당한 이익을 내고 있다는 보고가 있습니다. (배우자를) 의심하는 남편이나 아내들은 미화로 약 1,800달러에 달하는 수사비용이 청구되어도 이(수사 유혹)를 뿌리칠 수 없는 모양입니다.

....

Q What is the news report mainly about?

(a) huge expenses incurred during divorce in India

(b) marriages in India that largely end in divorce

(c) corruption that has grown in Indian detective organizations.

(d) private investigation agencies that are profiting from divorce in India.

....

이 뉴스 보도는 주로 무엇에 관한 것인가?

(a) 인도에서 이혼하는 동안 초래되는 막대한 비용

(b) 대개는 이혼으로 끝나는 인도의 결혼

(c) 인도 탐정 조직들에서 늘어나는 부패

(d) 인도에서 이혼으로 인해 이익을 보는 사립 수사 기관들

해설 전통적으로 이혼이 터부시되어 왔던 인도에서 최근 이혼율이 승가하면서 법률 회사와 탐정 수사 사업이 번창하고 있다는 뉴스이다. 따라서 뉴스의 주된 내용은 (d)가 된다.

함정 (a) 배우자 수사에 적지 않은 돈이 들어가고는 있지만, 이로 인해 인

도 사람들이 막대한 비용 손실을 초래하고 있다고까지 보는 것은 지나친 억측이다. (b) 이혼율이 증가하고는 있지만 대부분의 결혼이 이혼으로 끝난다고 단정할 수는 없다. (c)에 대한 언급은 없다.

어휘 **divorce rate** 이혼율 | **thriving** 번성하는, 번영하는 |
marital 결혼의, 결혼 생활의, 부부의 | **restriction** 규제, 속박 |
detective agency 탐정 사무소, 흥신소 |
common law 관습법, 불문율 |
penalize 유죄를 선고하다, 불리한 입장에 두다 |
adulterous 불륜의, 간통의 | **spouse** 배우자 |
case 판례, 소송 사건 | **undeterred** 저지되지 않은, 말리지 못한 |
equivalent 상응하는, 같은 가치의

10

W: Hi, Dad. Sorry, I'm late. <u>I was held up</u> at the office.

M: It's alright. I'm glad to see you.

W: Me too. It's been so long since we met.

M: Yeah. Where's George? <u>Is he still touring</u>?

W: No, he's at home with the kids.

M: I was expecting him to come. It's been a long time <u>since we saw each other</u>.

W: Actually <u>he was all set to come</u>, but this babysitter who was supposed to come <u>couldn't make it</u>. And then we called my mom to see if she can take care of the kids, but she wasn't home.

M: I understand. I'll try to meet him sometime this week.

W: 안녕, 아빠. 늦어서 죄송해요. 사무실에서 꼼짝 못했어요.

M: 괜찮다. 보게 되어 반갑구나.

W: 저도요. 정말 오랜만이죠.

M: 그래. George는 어디 있니? 아직 여행 중이니?

W: 아뇨, 애들하고 집에 있어요.

M: George가 나올 것이라고 생각하고 있었는데. 서로 안 본 지가 꽤 됐구나.

W: 실은 오려고 만반의 준비를 했었는데, 아기를 돌봐 주기로 했던 사람이 오지 못했어요. 그래서 어머니에게 아이들을 봐 줄 수 있는지 여쭤 보았지만, 집에 안 계시더라고요.

M: 이해한다. 이번 주 언제 만나 봐야겠구나.

Q Why couldn't George come?

(a) He was touring.

(b) He was held up at the office.

(c) He had to go to see the woman's mom.

(d) He couldn't find someone to babysit.

George는 왜 오지 못했나?

(a) 여행 중이었다.

(b) 사무실에서 꼼짝 못했다.

(c) 여자의 엄마를 보러 가야 했다.

(d) 아이들을 돌볼 사람을 찾지 못했다.

해설 오랜만에 만난 아빠와 딸의 대화이다. 아빠는 사위인 George도 함께 오리라 기대했지만, 아기 봐 줄 사람(babysitter)을 구하지 못한 탓에 George는 아이들과 함께 집에 있어야 해서 오지 못했다고 이유를 설명하고 있다. 따라서 정답은 (d)가 된다.

함정 여자가 사무실 일로 꼼짝하지 못해서 늦게 왔다고 말하고 있는 것이지, George가 그런 것은 아니기 때문에 (b)는 정답이 아니다.

어휘 **hold up** 정지하다, 서다, ~을 방해하다, 막다, 지연시키다 |
tour 관광 여행하다, 느린 속도로 달리다 |
expect ~을 기대하다, 기다리다 | **all set** 만반의 준비가 되어 |
babysitter 아이 봐주는 사람 | **take care of** ~을 보살피다, 돌보다

LISTENING REVIEW

A

1. rash	2. tolerate
3. mayor	4. conviction
5. adhere to	6. courtesy
7. constitute	8. cater
9. eligible	10. descent
11. imperative	12. audit
13. marital	14. trend
15. skeleton	16. evolve

1. an area of red spots that appears on your skin

2. to accept a situation or person although you do not particularly like them

3. the person who has been elected to represent the city or town for a fixed period of time

4. a great confidence in your beliefs or opinions

5. to act in the way that a rule or agreement says you should

6. politeness, respect, and consideration for others

7. to set up or establish according to law or provision

8. to provide all the things that they need or want

9. being qualified or able to do something

10. origin or ancestry of a person's family background

11. extremely necessary or required

12. official examination of the accounts in order to make sure that they have been done correctly

13. of or relating to the state of marriage

14. a change or development towards something new or different

15. the framework of bones in your body

16. to change and develop gradually into different forms

B

1. b 2. a 3. b 4. b 5. a

1. 서로 안 본 지가 꽤 됐구나.

   (a) We have not known each other for a long time.

   (b) It's been a long time since we saw each other.

2. 어머니한테 아이들을 봐 줄 수 있는지 여쭤 보았어요.

   (a) We called my mom to see if she can take care of the kids.

   (b) My mom asked if she could take care of our children for me.

3. 이 나라는 가장 빠른 이혼 증가율을 보이고 있습니다.

   (a) The fastest-growing divorce rates can indicate the growth of the country.

   (b) The country is experiencing one of the fastest-growing divorce rates.

4. 그는 3일 전부터 치통을 호소했어요.

   (a) He's been asking about the toothache for the last three days.

   (b) He's been complaining of toothache for the last three days.

5. 뼈를 유지하려면 고압박 활동이 요구된다.

   (a) Bone maintenance requires high-load and high-stress activities.

   (b) High-load and high-stress activities require bone maintenance.

C

1. I will find out when I can get a day off.

2. Sue's furcula is evidence for the hotly debated theory.

3. Can I download them from any music site?

4. This site called "Melon" downloads MP3s at reasonable prices.

5. Modern aircraft tend to use composite materials for their exteriors.

1. I will find out / a day off / when I can get

2. is evidence / for the hotly debated theory / Sue's furcula

3. downloaded them / Can I / from any music site

4. at reasonable prices / this site called "Melon" / downloads MP3s

5. tend to use composite materials / for their exteriors / modern aircraft

D

1. a 2. a 3. a 4. b 5. b

1. Why don't you get him a good educational book?

   (a) You should buy him a book that is educational.

   (b) You can have him read a good book for his education.

2. I'll have to ask my girlfriend to look for one.

   (a) My girlfriend might be able to find one.

   (b) I will have to find one for my girlfriend.

3. Companies found to be in violation of safety rules will be given 30 days.

   (a) 30 days will be given to a company that violated safety rules.

   (b) The company's violated safety rules for the given 30 days.

4. We will look into the details of diversity in the American population.

   (a) We will discuss various details about the American population.

   (b) The diversity of the American will be discussed in detail.

5. We may immediately delete it without the poster's permission.

   (a) Immediate permission from the poster will be deleted.

   (b) We will not ask the poster's permission for immediate deletion.

VOCABULARY PREVIEW

01. electrical circuit 전기회로

02. undisputed 의심할 여지없는, 당연한

03. disperse 흩뜨리다, 산재하다

04. eliminate 제거하다, 없애다

05. intensive 강한, 강렬한

06. witchcraft 마법, 주술

07. spell *n.* 주문

08. rationale 이론적 근거(설명), 원리

09. reunion 동창회, 재회

10. sweep 쓸어 내다, 쓸어버리다

11. virtually 사실상, 실제로

12. postulate 요구하다, 주장하다

13. flurry 눈보라

14. treacherous 위험한, 불안정한

15. bachelor 미혼(독신) 남성

16. intersperse 흩뜨리다, 산재시키다

17. amnesia 기억 상실

18. discretion 선택의 자유, (자유) 재량, 결정권

19. stroke 뇌졸중

20. faint 기절하다, 졸도하다

21. sprain ~을 삐다

22. reputation 명성, 평판

23. conceive 생각하다, 계획하다

24. tremendous 굉장한, 거대한

GUIDED LISTENING

1 1. b 2. c **2** 1. d 2. d

3 1. c 2. b **4** 1. d 2. b

1 Conversation

W: Hi, where can I get a refund?

M: Right here, ma'am. Do you have a receipt?

W: Yes. Here it is.

M: Thank you. Is there any problem with the toaster?

W: Yes, it doesn't toast anything — even if you keep something inside it for half an hour.

M: Oh, there might be some problem with its electrical circuits. Do you want us to repair it and give it back to you?

W: Yes, that would be nice. How long will it take?

M: Just ten to fifteen minutes. You can have a seat in the waiting room.

W: 안녕하세요. 어디서 환불을 받을 수 있나요?

M: 바로 여기예요. 영수증을 가지고 계신가요?

W: 예. 여기 있어요.

M: 감사합니다. 토스터에 무슨 문제가 있습니까?

W: 네. 아무것도 구워지지가 않아요. 30분을 넘어 두어도 안 되더라고요.

M: 아, 전기회로에 문제가 있는 것 같군요. 저희가 수리해서 돌려 드릴까요?

W: 예. 그게 좋겠군요. 얼마나 걸릴까요?

M: 10분에서 15분이면 돼요. 대기실에서 앉아 계세요.

Detail

1 What does the woman want to do?

(a) to get a refund

(b) to have an item repaired

(c) to replace a toaster

(d) to buy a new toaster

여자가 바라는 것은 무엇인가?

(a) 환불받기

(b) 제품 수리받기

(c) 토스터 교체하기

(d) 새로운 토스터 구입하기

<u>해설</u> 토스트를 굽는 기계가 작동하지 않아, 환불 해주는 곳을 찾는 여자와 직원간의 대화이다. 여자는 토스터를 수리해서 다시 가져가기를 바라고 있으므로 정답은 (b)이다.

<u>함정</u> 여자의 첫 번째 말, 어디서 환불을 받을 수 있나요?(Hi, where can I get a refund?)라는 것에서 무조건 환불을 원한다고 생각하여 (a)를 답으로 고르면 안 된다.

Detail

2 What is the problem?

(a) It takes too long to toast bread.

(b) It burns bread.

(c) It doesn't toast bread well.

(d) It has no electrical circuits.

무엇이 문제인가?

(a) 빵을 굽는 데 시간이 너무 오래 걸린다.

(b) 빵이 탄다.

(c) 빵을 잘 굽지 못한다.

(d) 전기회로가 없다.

<u>해설</u> 여자의 it doesn't toast anything(아무것도 구워지지가 않아요.)라는 말에서 정답을 알 수 있다. 30분을 넣어두어도 빵이 구워지지 않아서, 다시 가져온 것이므로 정답은 (c)이다.

<u>어휘</u> refund 환불, 반품 | receipt 영수증 | toast 굽다 | electrical circuit 전기회로 | have a seat 앉다 | waiting room 대기실

2 Conversation

(Telephone rings.)

M: This is Orange Taxi. How may I help you?

W: Can somebody <u>pick me up and drop me</u> by the Trade Globe Center? I have a meeting there at four o'clock.

M: What time do you <u>want us</u> to pick you up, ma'am?

W: In 15 minutes. It's <u>a twenty-minute drive</u> from here and it's already three o'clock. I want to get there a little earlier <u>so I can have some time to grab a sandwich</u> before I go in.

M: <u>Where are you calling from</u>, ma'am?

W: I'm here at 151 Fifth River Avenue.

M: We can have a taxi there in half an hour, if you can wait until then.

W: Okey, but don't take longer than half an hour.

(전화벨이 울린다.)

M: 오렌지 택시입니다. 어떻게 도와드릴까요?

W: 저를 태워서 무역세계센터까지 데려다 줄 수 있나요? 거기서 4시에 회의가 있거든요.

M: 몇 시에 모시러 갈까요?

W: 15분 내로요. 여기서 운전해서 20분 거리이고, 벌써 3시네요. 좀 일찍 도착하고 싶어요. 그래서 들어가기 전에 샌드위치라도 좀 먹으려고요.

M: 어디에서 전화하시는 거죠?

W: 여기는 Fifth River가 151번지입니다.

M: 기다려 주신다면, 30분 안에 택시를 거기로 보내겠습니다.

W: 좋아요. 하지만 30분 이상 걸리면 안 돼요.

Detail

1 What time will the woman arrive at the Trade Globe Center?

(a) 4:00

(b) 3:45

(c) 3:30

(d) 3:50

여자는 무역 세계 센터에 몇 시에 도착할 것인가?

(a) 4:00

(b) 3:45

(c) 3:30

(d) 3:50

<u>해설</u> 콜택시를 부르는 통화 내용이다. 여자가 있는 곳에서 목적지까지는 20분 거리라는 말이 있고, 마지막 부분에 택시가 여자가 있는 곳까지 가는 데에는 30분 걸린다는 내용이 있다. 지금이 3시이므로 여자가 목적지에 도착하게 될 시간은 3시 50분이 될 것이다.

<u>함정</u> 4시, 15분, 20분, 3시, 5번가 등 숫자가 많이 나오고 있다. 무엇이 문제화되었는지 파악하고, 정확히 들어야 한다. 간단한 계산이 되어야 하는 문제이므로 메모도 잘 해둔다.

Detail

2 Why does the woman want to arrive there earlier?

(a) She doesn't want to be late for the meeting.

(b) She has to prepare something before the meeting.

(c) She has to buy something for the meeting.

(d) She wants to eat something before the meeting.

여자는 왜 그곳에 좀 더 일찍 가고 싶어 하는가?

(a) 여자는 회의에 늦고 싶지 않다.

(b) 여자는 회의 전에 뭔가 준비해야 한다.

(c) 여자는 회의를 위해 뭔가를 사야 한다.

(d) 여자는 회의 전에 뭔가를 먹고 싶어 한다.

해설 중간 부분의 여자의 말, I want to get there a little earlier so I can have some time to grab a sandwich before I go in.(좀 일찍 도착하고 싶어요. 그래서 들어가기 전에 샌드위치라도 좀 먹으려고요.)에서 답을 알 수 있다.

어휘 pick ~ up ~를 데리러 오다
a twenty-minute drive 20분 운전 거리
grab 급히 잡다 cf. grab a sandwich 간단하게(빨리) 샌드위치를 먹다(사다) half an hour 30분

3 Monologue

M: Exercise is important for our well-being. Although it is <u>an undisputed fact</u>, not many people are able to take time out for a little workout, due to their busy schedules. Many people <u>feel guilty about it</u> and try to exercise as much as possible on the weekends. However, this way of exercising is not a healthy option. Experts suggest that people who have busy weekdays should try to be physically active as much as possible <u>throughout the day</u>. For example, <u>it is better to take the stairs than riding elevators</u>. People can choose to walk short distances rather than to take cars. These small activities <u>dispersed throughout the day</u> may <u>eliminate the need for heavy exercise</u> on the weekends.

M: 운동은 건강에 중요합니다. 이것은 의심할 여지없는 사실이지만, 많은 사람들이 바쁜 일정 때문에 약간의 운동을 위한 시간도 내지 못하고 있습니다. 많은 사람들이 그러한 것에 대해 죄의식을 느껴서 주말에 가능한 한 많이 운동하려고 합니다. 하지만 이런 식으로 운동하는 것은 건강에 좋은 선택이 아닙니다. 전문가들은 평일에 바쁜 사람들은 하루 종일 가능한 한 많이 신체활동을 해야 한다고 제안합니다. 예를 들어, 승강기를 타기보다는 계단을 걸어 올라가는 것이 더 좋습니다. 짧은 거리라면 차를 타고 가기보다는 걸어가는 것을 택할 수 있습니다. 하루 종일 틈틈이 이러한 작은 활동들을 하면 주말에 힘겨운 운동을 해야 하는 필요가 없을 것입니다.

Detail

1 What do many people feel guilty about?

(a) not exercising at all throughout the week

(b) having busy schedules during the weekdays

(c) not taking time out for a little workout

(d) not exercising during the weekends

많은 사람들이 무엇에 죄의식을 느끼는가?

(a) 일주일 내내 전혀 운동을 하지 않는 것

(b) 주중에 일정이 바쁜 것

(c) 운동하기 위해 조금이라도 시간을 내지 못하는 것

(d) 주말에 운동하지 않는 것

해설 앞부분의 not many people are able to take time out for a little workout(많은 사람들이 약간의 운동을 위한 시간도 내지 못하고 있습니다.)와 Many people feel guilty about it(많은 사람들이 그러한 것에 대해 죄의식을 느껴서)의 내용에서 정답을 알 수 있다.

함정 주중에 전혀 운동을 못하는 것에 죄의식을 느껴서 주말에 격하게 운동하려 한다는 것이므로 (a)의 일주일 내내는 아니다.

Comprehension

2 Which type of exercise is good for busy people?

(a) limited exercise on the weekend

(b) moderate exercise through the day

(c) intensive exercise every day

(d) light exercise in the office

바쁜 사람들에게 좋은 운동 형태는 무엇인가?

(a) 주말에만 제한적으로 하는 운동

(b) 하루 일과에서의 적당한 운동

(c) 매일 매일의 강도 높은 운동

(d) 사무실에서의 가벼운 운동

해설 운동의 중요성에 관한 담화이다. 바쁜 일정 때문에 매일 규칙적으로 운동하지 못하는 사람들을 위한 조언이 나와 있다. 일과 중에 계단 오르기, 짧은 거리 걷기 등의 조언이 나와 있다. 그러므로 정답은 (b)이다.

함정 (a)의 주말에만 하는 제한된 운동은 건강에 좋은 선택이 아니라고 했다. 그리고 (d)는 언급되지 않았다.

어휘 undisputed 의심할 여지없는, 당연한 | workout 운동, 연습 | due to ~ 때문에 | as much as possible 가능한 한 많이 | option 선택 사항 | expert 전문가 | disperse 흩뜨리다, 산재하다 | eliminate 제거하다, 없애다 | throughout the day 종일 | limited 한정된, 제한된 | intensive 강한, 강렬한

4 Monologue

W: The Yoruba are a West African ethnic group and like many others, this group also <u>has strong faith in witchcraft</u>. According to people from the Yoruba tribe, magic spells and other types of witchcraft can be used to harm others. Although there might be <u>no logical rationale behind the practice</u>, the Yoruba people tend to believe it. According to their belief system, wild rabbit fur <u>contains very powerful magic</u>: the Yoruba believe it <u>protects a house from fire</u>, if hung outside it. It is very common to find wild rabbit fur outside Yoruba houses. Some may <u>seriously doubt whether</u> such witchcraft practices work or not, but the Yoruba people retain their belief that they do.

W: 요루바족은 서부 아프리카의 인종이며, 많은 다른 부족처럼 이 부족 또한 주술에 대한 강한 믿음을 가지고 있습니다. 요루바족의 사람들에 의하면, 마법의 주문과 기타 형태의 주술은 다른 사람들을 해를 입히는 데 사용될 수 있습니다. 그러한 관행 뒤에는 논리적인 이론적 근거가 없더라도, 요루바 사람들은 그것을 믿는 경향이 있습니다. 그들의 믿음 체계에 따르면, 야생 토끼털에는 매우 강력한 마술이 있는데, 요루바 사람들은 그것을 밖에 걸어 두면 집에 화재가 생기는 것을 막아 준다고 믿습니다. 요루바족의 집 밖에 야생 토끼털이 걸려 있는 것을 보는 것은 아주 흔한 일입니다. 어떤 사람들은 그러한 주술 관행이 효과가 있는지 없는지 심각하게 의심할지 모르지만, 요루바 사람들은 그것이 효과가 있다는 믿음을 잃지 않고 있습니다.

Detail

1 How do the Yoruba use wild rabbit fur?

(a) They use it to put magic spells on others.

(b) They use it to acquire bigger houses.

(c) They use it to attack other tribes.

(d) They use it to protect their homes from fire.

요루바 사람들은 야생 토끼털을 어떤 용도로 사용하고 있는가?

(a) 다른 사람들에게 주문을 걸기 위해 사용한다.

(b) 더 큰 집을 얻기 위해 사용한다.

(c) 다른 부족을 공격하기 위해 사용한다.

(d) 집에 불이 나지 않게 하기 위해 사용한다.

해설 the Yoruba believe it protects a house from fire라는 표현에서 정답을 알 수 있다. 즉 요루바 사람들은 야생 토끼털이 집에 불이 나지 않게 해 준다고 믿는다는 것을 알 수 있다.

함정 (a), (b), (c)는 언급되지 않은 내용이다. 하지만 정답을 찾기 위해서는 중간에 언급되는 내용을 놓치면 안 된다.

Function

2 Why does the speaker mention wild rabbit fur?

(a) to show what the Yoruba people believed the most

(b) to illustrate the strong faith of the Yoruba in witchcraft

(c) to explain that it was the most common type of witchcraft

(d) to imply that wild rabbits were hunted the most

화자가 야생 토끼털을 언급하고 있는 이유는 무엇인가?

(a) 요루바 사람들이 가장 믿고 있는 것이 무엇인지 보여 주려고

(b) 요루바족의 주술에 대한 강한 믿음을 예증하려고

(c) 그것이 가장 흔한 주술이라는 것을 설명하려고

(d) 야생 토끼가 가장 많이 사냥되고 있다는 것을 암시하려고

해설 요루바족의 주술에 대한 믿음에 관한 내용이다. 그 예로, 야생 토끼털을 집 밖에 걸어 두면 집에 화재가 발생하는 것을 막아 준다고 믿어서, 그런 광경을 흔히 볼 수 있다고 했다. 그것을 예로 들어 주술에 대한 요루바 사람들의 강한 믿음을 설명하고 있으므로 (b)가 답이다.

어휘 Yoruba 요루바족 (Guinea 지방에 사는 흑인)
ethnic 인종의, 민족의 ｜ witchcraft 마법, 주술 ｜ spell 주문 ｜
be used to ~하는 데에 사용되다 ｜ logical 논리적인 ｜
rationale 이론적 근거(설명), 원리 ｜ practice 관행 ｜
tend to ~하는 경향이 있다 ｜ fur 털 ｜
protect A from B A를 B로부터 보호하다 ｜
work 효과가 있다, 작용하다 ｜
retain 보류하다, 계속 실행하다, 잊지 않고 있다 ｜
acquire 얻다, 획득하다

PRACTICAL LISTENING

1. c	2. d	3. d	4. d	5. b
6. a	7. c	8. c	9. c	10. c

1

M: Good morning, ma'am. How may I help you?

W: I'd like <u>to get this jacket exchanged for a sweatshirt</u>.

M: Okay. Have a look at the sweatshirts available here.

W: Do I have to <u>pay anything extra</u> for the sweatshirt?

M: Yes, <u>if it's priced higher than</u> the jacket.

W: Oh, okay. Do you also give refunds if I want?

M: Yes, of course. But, <u>in either way</u>, you will have to <u>have the receipt with you</u>.

W: I think I put that in the pocket of the jacket. Would you look for it for me please?

M: Sure. Wait a moment. Here it is. Now, have you found anything you would like to get?

W: Yes, I have. Here it is.

M: 안녕하세요. 무엇을 도와드릴까요?

W: 이 재킷을 스웨트 셔츠로 바꾸고 싶은데요.

M: 알겠습니다. 여기에 있는 스웨트 셔츠들을 한번 보시죠.

W: 스웨트 셔츠로 바꾸려면 추가로 돈을 더 내야 하나요?

M: 네, 이 재킷보다 더 비싸다면요.

W: 아, 그렇군요. 원하면 환불도 받을 수 있나요?

M: 네. 물론입니다. 하지만 어떻든지 영수증을 가지고 계셔야 할 것입니다.

W: 그 재킷의 주머니에 넣어둔 것 같아요. 한번 살펴봐 주시겠어요?

M: 음, 잠깐만요. 여기 있어요. 마음에 드시는 것을 찾으셨나요?

W: 음, 찾았어요. 여기 있어요.

Q What is the woman doing in the conversation?

(a) trying to find a jacket that she likes

(b) finding a sweatshirt whose price is either equal or lower

(c) getting a sweatshirt in exchange for a jacket

(d) getting a refund for the jacket she bought

대화에서 여자는 무엇을 하고 있는가?

(a) 마음에 드는 재킷을 찾아보기

(b) 가격이 같거나 더 싼 스웨트 셔츠 찾아보기

(c) 재킷을 스웨트 셔츠로 교환하기

(d) 구입했던 재킷에 대해 환불받기

해설 여자는 구입한 재킷을 다른 스웨트 셔츠로 교환하거나 환불받을 수 있는지 물어 보고 있다. 스웨트 셔츠가 재킷보다 비싼 경우를 대비해 환불 가능한지 묻고 있으므로 (c)가 정답이다.

함정 마음에 드는 교환할 물건을 골랐으므로 (d)는 답이 될 수 없다.

어휘 ma'am 점원이 여자 손님을 부르는 말

exchange (for) ~로 교환(교체)하다, 환전하다

sweatshirt 두껍고 헐거운 캐주얼 셔츠, 스웨트 셔츠

have a look at ~을 훑어보다, 한번 슬쩍 보다

available 이용할 수 있는, 유효한   extra 여분의, 추가의, 특별한

price 값을 매기다   refund 환불, 반환, ~을 갚다, 환불하다

receipt 영수증   in exchange for ~대신에, ~과 교환하여

2 Detail

M: Your friend told me that you're going to a party.

W: Yes, it's a school reunion.

M: Great! I'm sure you're excited.

W: Yes, because I'll be meeting my high school sweetheart.

M: But will he recognize you? It's been more than ten years now.

W: That's exactly what I'm worried about. I've

changed a lot since high school and I'm so worried that he won't recognize me.

M: That is not bad.

W: What do you mean?

M: I mean you will be a surprise to him then. Go up to him and let him know who you are if he does not recognize you.

W: Yeah. That's not a bad idea.

M: Well, good luck and I hope you have a good time there.

M: 네가 파티에 갈 거라고 네 친구가 그러던데.

W: 응, 학교 동창회야.

M: 멋지네! 흥분되겠는걸.

W: 응, 고등학교 때 남자친구를 만날 거거든.

M: 근데 그 사람이 널 알아볼까? 10년도 더 지났잖아.

W: 나도 바로 그게 걱정이야. 나는 고등학교 이후에 정말 많이 변해서 그가 나를 알아보지 못할까봐 너무 걱정돼.

M: 나쁘지는 않네.

W: 무슨 말이야?

M: 그러니까 내 말은 그를 놀라게 할 수 있다는 거야. 그에게 다가가서, 그가 너를 알아보지 못하면 네가 누군지 알려줘.

W: 응, 나쁜 생각은 아니네.

M: 음, 행운을 빌어. 그리고 좋은 시간 보내기를 바랄게!

Q What is the woman's concern?

(a) that she is not able to go to the school reunion party

(b) that she has to meet her high school friends

(c) that she has not changed a bit after high school

(d) that her old boyfriend will not remember her

여자의 걱정은 무엇인가?

(a) 그녀가 동창회에 갈 수 없을까봐

(b) 그녀가 고등학교 친구들을 만나야 할까봐

(c) 그녀가 고등학교 이후에 별로 변하지 않았을까봐

(d) 그녀의 옛날 남자친구가 그녀를 기억하지 못할까봐

해설 곧 있을 여자의 동창회에 관한 남녀의 대화이다. 여자는 학교 동창회에서 예전 남자친구를 만날 수 있게 되어 매우 들떠 있다. 하지만 고등학교를 졸업한 지 10년도 더 됐고, 그 사이에 여자는 많이 변했기 때문에, 남자친구가 자신을 알아보지 못할 거라고 말하고 있다. 따라서 정답은 (d)이며, 나머지는 대화의 내용상 전혀 맞지 않는 말들이다.

어휘 reunion 동창회, 재회   sweetheart 애인, 연인

recognize ~을 보고 알아보다, 분간하다, 인정하다   concern 걱정

3

M: It's a pleasure to announce that the Bottle-nose Dolphin has been <u>brought back from the verge of extinction</u>. Our maritime research reveals that the dolphin population here has increased by 12% over the past 18 years in the animal's natural habitats. This has been despite the fact that large numbers of dolphins continue to be caught accidentally in tuna nets, especially "drag" nets <u>that sweep virtually everything</u> out of the ocean in front of them. In spite of these challenges, <u>it's heartening to know</u> that the Bottle-nose <u>has good prospects for survival</u>. Some scientists postulate that the Bottle-nose, a highly intelligent creature, may even have learned <u>how to avoid the nets</u>.

M: 청백돌고래가 멸종의 위기로부터 되살아났다는 사실을 알리게 되어 기쁩니다. 저희 해상 연구에 따르면 이곳 동물 자연 서식지 내 돌고래 개체 수가 지난 18년간 12퍼센트 증가했습니다. 다량의 돌고래가 뜻하지 않게 참치용 그물망, 특히 자기 앞바다의 거의 모든 것들을 끌어내다시피 잡아내는 예인망에 끊임없이 잡히고 있는 실정에도 불구하고 말입니다. 이런 난관에도 불구하고 청백돌고래가 생존 가망이 있다는 것을 알게 되어 상당히 고무적입니다. 일부 과학자들은 대단히 지능적인 생물인 청백돌고래가 그물망을 피하는 방법을 터득한 것일지도 모른다고 주장하고 있습니다.

Q Which of the following is correct according to the talk?

(a) Bottle-nose Dolphins have dwindled over the years.

(b) Some types of dolphins have learned to avoid tuna nets.

(c) Human beings are causing the destruction of dolphin habitats.

(d) Bottle-noses are no longer under the threat of extinction.

이 담화의 내용으로 보아 올바른 것은?

(a) 청백돌고래 수가 수년간 점차 감소했다.

(b) 몇몇 고래들은 참치 그물망을 피하는 방법을 터득했다.

(c) 인간이 돌고래 서식지를 파괴하고 있다.

(d) 청백돌고래는 더 이상 멸종 위기에 놓여 있지 않다.

해설 청백돌고래의 개체수가 증가했음을 알려 주는 내용의 이야기이다. 화자는 청백돌고래가 갖은 난관에도 불구하고 개체수가 줄지 않고 증가했다고 주장하고 있으므로 정답은 (d)이다.

함정 (a)는 사실과 반대이며, (c)는 언급되지 않았다. (b)는 일부 과학자들의 예측이지 증명된 사실이 아니므로 정답이 될 수 없다.

어휘 Bottle-nose Dolphin 청백돌고래 | the verge of ~의 직전, ~의 가장자리 | extinction 멸종, 절멸 | maritime 바다의, 해운상의 | reveal 드러내다, 폭로하다 |

natural habitat 자연 서식지 | drag net 저인망, 예인망, 후릿그물 | sweep 쓸어내다, 쓸어버리다 | virtually 사실상, 실제로 | heartening 기운 나게 하는, 고무적인 (hearten v. 고무하다, 기운 나게 하다) | prospect 가망, 기대, 예상 | postulate 요구하다, 주장하다

4 Detail

W: Hi, I need information <u>about your tour packages</u>.

M: Okay, what would you like to know?

W: I saw your ad in the newspaper <u>about two-week group tours</u> to Egypt.

M: Oh, the tours are so popular among many families.

W: What is the number of people required for the trip?

M: <u>Ten or more is required</u> for that two-week tour.

W: Oh I see. When does the tour start?

M: We leave the last Friday of the month.

W: Okay. I would like <u>to reserve that package</u> for twelve members from my class for next month. Is twelve big enough?

M: Sure. Would you please <u>fill in the details in this form</u>?

W: Can I borrow a pen?

W: 안녕하세요, 여행 상품에 대한 정보가 필요한데요.

M: 네, 무엇을 알고 싶으세요?

W: 신문에서 이집트행 2주 단체 여행에 관한 광고를 봤어요.

M: 아, 그 여행은 가족들에게 매우 인기가 있죠.

W: 그 여행에 필요한 인원은 어떻게 되죠?

M: 그 2주간의 여행에는 10명 이상의 인원이 필요해요.

W: 아, 알겠습니다. 언제 출발하나요?

M: 매달 마지막 금요일에 떠납니다.

W: 좋아요. 다음 달 우리 반 학생들 중 12명을 위해 그 패키지를 예약하고 싶어요. 12명이면 충분한가요?

M: 물론이죠. 이 양식에 자세한 사항을 기입해 주시겠어요?

W: 펜 좀 빌릴 수 있을까요?

Q What does the woman want to know about?

(a) information on special packages available for families

(b) brochures for tours so that she can leave as early as she can

(c) inexpensive ways to tour around Egypt with her family members

(d) the minimum number of people for the tour and

the schedule

여자가 알고 싶어 하는 것은 무엇인가?

(a) 가족을 위한 특별 패키지 상품에 대한 정보

(b) 가능한 한 빨리 떠날 수 있는 여행의 안내책자

(c) 가족들과 함께 이집트를 여행할 수 있는 저렴한 방법

(d) 여행에 필요한 최소한의 인원수와 스케줄

해설 여행 상품에 관해 물어 보는 여자와 이에 답하는 여행사 남자 직원과의 대화 내용이다. 여자는 신문에서 본 이집트행 단체 여행의 필수인원에 대해 묻고 있다. 10명 이상이라고 하자, 출발 일자를 확인한 뒤 12명을 예약하고 있다. 따라서 정답은 (d)가 된다.

함정 (a)와 (b)는 전혀 언급되지 않았다. 여자가 묻고 있는 여행이 요즘 가족들에게 인기가 있는 상품이라는 남자의 대답이 있기는 하지만, 저렴한 상품인지에 대한 언급이 없고 여자가 알고 싶어한 내용도 아니므로 (c)도 역시 정답과 거리가 멀다.

어휘 package 일괄상품, 소포, 포장한 상품 |
require ~을 필요로 하다 | leave 떠나다 | reserve 예약하다 |
fill in ~을 메우다, (서류에) 적어 넣다 |
detail 세부, 상세, 자세한 사항 | form (문서의) 양식, 서식 |
brochure 팸플릿, 소책자 | minimum 최소한의

5 Detail

W: Good morning, this is Nina with today's weather forecast. The recent warm spell has passed, so get ready for lower temperatures throughout the region. You will do well to put on a warm coat and boots for the coming days. The colder weather will start today. Central areas of the state will experience cloudy skies and snow flurries with a high of about 2 degrees Celsius in the afternoon. In the southern areas, watch out for showers and thunderstorms with a high of 3 degrees. The south may also experience rain mixed with ice, which will create treacherous road conditions. The state will have lows ranging between minus 6 and minus 8 degrees.

W: 안녕하십니까. 오늘의 일기 예보의 Nina입니다. 최근 한동안의 온화한 기후는 끝나고 전 지역에 걸쳐 낮은 기온에 대비하셔야겠습니다. 앞으로 며칠 동안은 따뜻한 외투와 부츠를 착용하시는 게 좋을 것입니다. 추운 날씨가 오늘부터 시작될 것입니다. 우리 주의 중부 지역은 날씨가 흐린 가운데 오후에는 최고 영상 2도까지 오르며 눈보라가 있을 것으로 예상됩니다. 남부 지역은 소나기와 천둥 번개를 동반한 강한 바람이 불 것으로 보이니 조심하십시오. 최고 기온은 영상 3도입니다. 남부 지역은 또한 우박이 섞인 비가 올지도 모릅니다. 때문에 도로 상황이 위험할 수도 있습니다. 우리 주의 최저 기온은 영하 6도에서 영하 8도 사이일 것으로 보입니다.

Q What weather conditions can southern areas expect?

(a) clear and dry conditions

(b) showers and thunderstorms

(c) flurries and cloudy skies

(d) rainfall over 4 centimeters

남부 지역의 예상 날씨는?

(a) 맑고 건조한 날씨

(b) 소나기와 강풍을 동반한 뇌우

(c) 눈보라와 흐린 하늘

(d) 4센티미터가 넘는 강우

해설 지역별 오늘의 일기 예보이다. 남부 지역은 소나기와 천둥 번개를 동반한 강한 바람, 또한 우박이 섞인 비가 예상된다고 했으나 강우량에 대한 언급은 없었다. 정답은 (b)이다. 또한 (c)는 중부 지역의 예상 날씨이다.

어휘 spell (날씨 등의) 계속되는 기간 | region 지역 |
put on ~을 입다 | flurry 눈보라 | shower 소나기 |
thunderstorm (강풍이 따르는) 뇌우 |
treacherous 위험한, 불안정한 | low 최저 기온

6

M: Now that you've been married for two years, what's your opinion of it?

W: Well, it's like a team of two people working towards the same goal.

M: That's good. But how about giving space to each other?

W: Certainly, that's important for personal growth.

M: Yet not many people understand that, and I've seen so many marriages not work well because of that.

W: That's not always correct. Is that the reason stopping you from getting married?

M: Yeah, and I'm quite happy with my bachelor status. At least I'm free to do whatever I want.

M: 결혼한 지 2년 정도 되었는데, 결혼이 뭔 것 같아요?

W: 음, 같은 목표를 향해 움직이는 두 사람으로 이루어진 하나의 팀 같아요.

M: 좋군요. 그런데 서로의 영역을 인정해 주는 건 어때요?

W: 그래야죠. 그건 개인의 발전을 위해 중요한 거예요.

M: 하지만 그걸 이해하는 사람들은 많지 않잖아요. 그리고 그것 때문에 너무 많은 결혼생활이 원만하지 못한 걸 봐 왔어요.

W: 항상 그런 건 아니에요. 당신이 결혼을 하지 않는 이유가 그건가요?

M: 네, 그리고 나는 독신 생활에 꽤 만족해요. 적어도 내가 원하는 것은 뭐든지 자유롭게 할 수 있거든요.

Q Which is correct according to the conversation?

(a) The man is pretty satisfied with his single life.

(b) The woman has a problematic marriage.

(c) The woman has been married for the last five years.

(d) The man wants to get married at the earliest possible time.

대화에 근거하여 옳은 것은?

(a) 남자는 자신의 독신 생활에 상당히 만족한다.

(b) 여자의 결혼 생활은 문제가 있다.

(c) 여자는 결혼한 지 5년 됐다.

(d) 남자는 가능하면 빨리 결혼하길 원한다.

해설 결혼 2년차 여자와 독신 남자가 결혼에 대한 서로의 견해를 이야기하고 있는 장면이다. 여자는 부부란 같은 목표를 향해 나아가는 팀과 같으며, 개인의 성장을 위해 서로의 영역을 인정해야 한다고 여기면서 긍정적인 결혼생활을 유지하고 있는 것으로 보인다. 하지만 남자는 주위에서 그렇지 못한 부부들을 많이 봤기 때문에, 지금의 독신 상태에 만족하고 있으며, 자유롭게 자신이 원하는 것을 할 수 있다는 것에 매우 만족해하고 있다. 따라서 정답은 (a)이다.

어휘 now that ~이므로, ~이기 때문에 towards ~을 향하여 space 공간, 우주, 장소, 거리, 간격 personal 개인의, 사적인 work well 잘 되어가다 stop 사람 from ~에게 …을 못하게 하다 bachelor 미혼(독신) 남성 status 지위, 신분, 상태 free to 자유롭게 ~할 수 있는 whatever ~하는 것은 뭐든지 single 혼자의, 독신의 problematic 문제가 있는 get married 결혼하다

7 Detail

W: Now, I'm going to speak about a common device used in cinema — the flashback. It is used to present information in past events by stopping briefly the linear flow of a film narrative. Flashbacks give filmmakers greater scope for narrating their stories. Apart from providing background, they produce multiple perspectives to events in the film and add intensity to both story and character. Flashbacks can be interspersed throughout a film, or sometimes emerge at a critical point, such as when a main character with amnesia suddenly remembers who he is and how he became amnesiac. Sometimes a film is composed almost entirely of one long flashback: Mel Gibson's *The Patriot* is a good example.

W: 이제 영화에서 사용되는 일반적인 장치인 플래시백에 관해 말씀드리겠습니다. 이 플래시백 기법은 영화의 이야기 부분에서 직선적인 설명의 흐름을 잠시 중단하고 과거 사건들에 대한 정보를 내놓는 데 사용됩니다. 플래시백 기법은 영화제작자들에게 자신들의 이야기를 풀어내는 데 대단히 큰 돌파구가 됩니다. 배경 설명을 주는 것과는 별도로, 이들은 영화 속 사건들에 대한 다양한 관점을 만들어내며, 스토리와 캐릭터 모두에 강렬함을 부여합니다. 플래시백은 영화 전체를 통해 산발적으로 존재할 수 있으며 때로 기억력을 상실한 주인공이 갑자기 자신이 누구이며 어쩌다 기억력을 잃었는지 기억해내는 것과 같은 중요 시점에서 사용되기도 합니다. 때때로 어떤 영화는 거의 전체가 하나의 긴 플래시백으로 구성되어 있기도 합니다. 멜 깁슨의 영화 'The Patriot'가 좋은 예입니다.

Q Why are flashbacks mainly used according to the lecture?

(a) to interrupt a narrative that provides background

(b) to serve to raise an audience's expectations

(c) to help to present different perceptions in a narrative

(d) to show how characters evolve from the past

이 강의에 따르면 플래시백이 사용되는 주된 이유는?

(a) 배경을 제시하는 이야기를 방해하기 위해

(b) 관객의 기대치를 높이는 데 기여하기 위해

(c) 이야기 속에 서로 다른 관점을 제시하는 데 도움을 주기 위해

(d) 영화 속 인물이 과거로부터 어떻게 변화되어왔는지를 보여 주기 위해

해설 영화 속에 자주 등장하는 플래시백 기법을 설명하는 강의이다. 과거 장면으로의 전환을 나타내는 이 기법은 영화 속 사건들에 대한 다양한 관점을 만들어내며, 스토리와 캐릭터 모두에 강렬함을 부여한다는 설명 (they produce multiple perspectives to events)에서 정답이 (c)임을 알 수 있다.

함정 플래시백 기법을 통해 스토리나 캐릭터에 강렬한 인상을 심어 준다고 했으므로 이야기를 방해한다는 (a)는 사실과 다르다. (b)는 언급된 바가 없으며, (d)는 플래시백 기법을 사용하는 한 예로, 주된 특징은 아니라는 데에 주의한다.

어휘 flashback (영화 등에서의) 과거 장면으로의 순간적 전환 기법 narrative 이야기, 설명 scope 기회, 배출구 perspective 견해, 관점 intersperse 흩뜨리다, 산재시키다 emerge 나타나다 amnesia 기억 상실 be composed of ~으로 구성되다 interrupt 방해하다 evolve 발전하다, 진화하다

8

M: A pilot program is in progress for a new elementary school testing system for kids in New Zealand. This could lead to a less stressful testing of children in this school level beginning next year. The government seeks to make testing more flexible and reduce pressure on children by placing greater importance on the discretion of teachers. Teachers under this new system will be able to judge which types of tests might be best for which types of classes or students. Teachers will also be able to decide the timing of tests, which could be given on weekly, monthly or irregular bases depending on class conditions. This would be an important move away from the standardization of the past.

M: 뉴질랜드 어린이들을 대상으로 한 새로운 초등학교 시험 제도에 관한 시범 프로그램이 진행 중입니다. 이렇게 되면 내년부터 이(초등) 학교 수준에서는 학생들의 시험 스트레스를 줄일 수도 있습니다. 정부는 교사들의 재량시험을 보다 중요시함으로써 시험을 좀 더 융통성 있게 만들고 학생들이 받는 압박을 줄이는 방법을 모색하고 있습니다. 이 새로운 시스템 하에서 교사들은 각 학급이나 학생들에게 어떤 시험이 알맞은지 판단할 수 있습니다. 교사들은 또한 시험 시간도 결정할 수 있습니다. 학급 상태에 따라 주간이 될 수도, 월간이 될 수도, 또는 불규칙적으로 적용될 수도 있습니다. 이는 과거의 표준화에 비할 때 의미 있는 행보가 될 것입니다.

Q What is the main idea of the news report?

(a) New Zealand teachers have been given greater powers.

(b) Standards have dropped in New Zealand elementary schools.

(c) Changes are being adopted in elementary school testing.

(d) New Zealand schools offer greater flexibility to each student.

이 뉴스 보도의 요지는?

(a) 뉴질랜드 교사들은 대단한 영향력(권력)을 부여받았다.

(b) 뉴질랜드 초등학교 내 기준이 떨어졌다.

(c) 초등학교 시험에 변화가 적용되었다.

(d) 뉴질랜드 학교들은 각 학생에게 보다 많은 융통성을 제공한다.

해설 뉴질랜드의 한 초등학교에서 학생들의 스트레스를 줄일 수 있는 보다 탄력적인 시험 제도를 운영한다는 내용의 뉴스이다. 따라서 학교 시험에 변화를 접목했다는 내용의 (c)가 정답이 된다.

함정 새로운 시스템을 위해 교사의 재량권을 중요하게 생각한다고 했다는 언급은 있으나 이로써 교사들에게 막대한 영향권을 행사하도록 했다(a)고 볼 수는 없다. (d)는 각 학생마다에게 적용되는 flexibility라는 내용은 없기 때문에 뉴스 내용의 범위를 벗어난다.

어휘 **pilot program** (정규 프로그램 편성 전에) 시험용으로 제작된 견본용 프로그램 **in progress** 진행 중인

---

flexible 융통성 있는, 탄력적인

discretion 선택의 자유, (자유) 재량, 결정권 move 조치, 수단

standardization 표준화

9

W: How's your aunt doing?

M: Well, she's not well after her stroke.

W: Why? What's happened?

M: She faints if she tries to get out of bed. She's not even able to go to the bathroom.

W: Is she that bad?

M: Yeah, the other day she tried getting out of bed, but fell down and sprained her ankle.

W: Oh, that sounds awful. How's she managing now?

M: We've appointed a nurse to look after her.

W: That's good. I hope she gets better soon.

W: 이모는 잘 계시니?

M: 뇌졸중 이후로 건강이 안 좋으셔.

W: 왜? 무슨 일이야?

M: 침대에서 일어나려고 하면 쓰러지셔. 화장실조차 가지 못하셔.

W: 그렇게 안 좋으시니?

M: 응, 며칠 전에 일어나려고 하셨다가 넘어져서 발목을 삐셨어.

W: 이런, 큰일이네. 지금은 어떻게 지내시니?

M: 그녀를 돌봐줄 간병인을 정했어.

W: 잘했구나. 빨리 나아지시길 바래.

Q What are the man and woman mainly discussing?

(a) how the man's aunt had a stroke

(b) problems the man has had since falling down

(c) difficulties the man's aunt has had since a stroke

(d) how the man's aunt fell down while getting out of bed

남자와 여자는 주로 무슨 이야기를 하고 있는가?

(a) 남자의 이모에게 어떻게 뇌졸중이 일어났는지

(b) 남자가 쓰러진 이후로 갖게 된 문제들

(c) 남자의 이모가 뇌졸중 이후로 갖게 된 어려움들

(d) 남자의 이모가 일어나려고 했을 때 어떻게 넘어졌는지

해설 남자의 이모에 대한 대화이다. 남자의 이모는 뇌졸중에 걸린 후부터 자리에서 일어나려고 하면 쓰러져서 화장실도 못 가고 있으며, 일전에는 넘어져서 발목까지 삐었고, 지금은 간병인을 지정했다고 한다. 따라서 두 사람은 지금 이모가 뇌졸중 이후로 겪고 있는 힘든 상황에 대해 이야기하

고 있으므로, 정답은 (c)이다.

어휘 stroke 뇌졸중 | faint 기절하다, 졸도하다 |
get out of bed 잠자리에서 일어나다 |
the other day 일전에, 며칠 전에 | fall down 넘어지다, 쓰러지다 |
sprain ~을 삐다 | ankle 발목 |
manage 이럭저럭 해나가다, 꾸려나가다 |
appoint 지명(임명)하다, 정하다 | nurse 간호사, 간병인 |
look after ~을 돌보다, 보살피다 |
get better (병, 상황 등이) 좋아지다, 호전되다

(c) 잘못 계획된 브라질의 수도

(d) 브라질리아의 실패 후 복귀 방법

해설 브라질의 수도 브라질리아의 평판에 대한 내용의 강의이다. 브라질리
아의 나쁜 명성과 그 배경에 대한 설명이다. 따라서 정답은 (c)가 된다.

어휘 reputation 명성, 평판 | urban planning 도시 계획 |
conceive 생각하다, 계획하다 | tremendous 굉장한, 거대한 |
be made up of ~으로 구성되다, 이루어지다 |
civil servant 공무원, 문관

10

W: You must have heard of Brasilia, the capital of Brazil, and its reputation as an example of poor urban planning. The <u>city was conceived and built</u> just over 50 years ago, but is often criticized. <u>It cannot be denied</u> that the growth of the city <u>has been tremendous</u>, but this growth has been almost entirely made up of civil servants who have been "forced" to move there. Brasilia is certainly not a human-friendly city. Even worse, the modern city <u>failed to impress the middle and upper classes</u> of Brazil, which would have been necessary <u>to draw them and their wealth</u> to Brasilia. Instead, they prefer the exciting cultural attractions of coastal cities like Rio, where most of them remain.

W: 여러분들은 틀림없이 브라질의 수도 브라질리아에 대해 들어보셨을
겁니다. 또한 브라질리아가 잘못된 도시 계획의 한 예로서 명성을 얻고 있
다는 사실도요. 이 도시는 겨우 50년 전에 계획되어 세워졌지만, 종종 비
난을 받고 있습니다. 대단히 괄목할 만한 도시 성장을 이루었다는 것을 부
정할 수는 없지만, 이러한 성장은 거의 대부분 '강제로' 그곳으로 이사한
공무원들에 의해 이루어진 것입니다. 브라질리아는 분명 사람들에게 친화
적인 도시는 아닙니다. 더 심각한 것은 이 현대 도시가 브라질의 중산층과
상류층에게 강한 인상을 심어주는 데 실패했다는 것입니다. 이들 중산층과
상류층을 그들의 부와 함께 브라질리아로 끌어들이는 일이 절대적인데 말
입니다. 그 대신 그들 대부분은 리오 같은 해변 도시의 흥미진진한 문화적
매력을 더 선호합니다. 그래서 그들 대부분은 아직 그곳에 남아 있습니다.

Q What is the main topic of the lecture?

(a) Brazil's changing growth patterns

(b) the significance of Brasilia as a capital city

(c) **the unsuccessfully planned capital city of Brazil**

(d) the way Brasilia made a comeback after failure

이 강의의 주요 화제는?
(a) 브라질의 변화하는 발달 패턴
(b) 수도로서의 브라질리아의 중요성

LISTENING REVIEW

A

1. reputation	2. conceive
3. faint	4. sprain
5. appoint	6. discretion
7. perspective	8. emerge
9. spell	10. bachelor
11. treacherous	12. reserve
13. extinction	14. postulate
15. prospect	16. rationale

1. the general estimation in which a person is held by the public

2. to think of a plan or idea and work out how it can be done

3. to lose consciousness for a short time

4. to accidentally damage your ankle or wrist by twisting it or bending it violently

5. to formally choose someone for a job or official position

6. the freedom and authority to decide what to do

7. a way of thinking about something, especially one that is influenced by your beliefs or experiences

8. to come out from an enclosed or dark space such as a room or a vehicle, or from a position where you could not be seen

9. a form of words supposed to have magic power

10. a man who has never married.

11. very dangerous and unpredictable

12. to arrange for a table, ticket, or magazine to be kept specially for you

13. the death of all living members of species of animal or plant

14. to suggest something as the basis for a theory, argument, or calculation, or assume that it is the basis

15. something that you expect or know is going to happen

16. the set of reasons on which a course of action, practice, or belief is based

B

1. b   **2.** b   **3.** a   **4.** a   **5.** a

1. 전기회로에 문제가 있는 것 같군요.

    (a) The electrical circuits have been the problem with it.

    (b) There might be some problem with its electrical circuits.

2. 저희가 수리해서 돌려 드릴까요?

    (a) Do you want to repair it and get it back to us?

    (b) Do you want us to repair it and give it back to you?

3. 저를 태우러 와서 무역 세계 센터까지 데려다 줄 수 있나요?

    (a) Can somebody pick me up and drop me by the Trade Globe Center?

    (b) Can somebody come to the Trade Globe Center and pick me up?

4. 짧은 거리라면 차를 타고 가기보다는 걸어가는 것을 택할 수 있습니다.

    (a) People can choose to walk short distances rather than to take cars.

    (b) People can choose to take a short walk instead of taking your car.

5. 요루바족의 집 밖에서 야생 토끼털을 발견하는 것은 아주 흔한 일입니다.

    (a) It is very common to find wild rabbit fur outside Yoruba houses.

    (b) Wild rabbit fur is usually kept outside Yoruba houses.

C

1. I can have some time to grab a sandwich.

2. People who have busy weekdays should try to be active.

3. There might be no logical rationale behind the practice.

4. The Yoruba people retain their belief that they do.

5. You will have to have the receipt with you.

1. some time / to grab a sandwich / I can have

2. who have busy weekdays / should try to be active / people

3. behind the practice / no logical rationale / there might be

4. the Yoruba people / that they do / retain their belief

5. have the receipt / you will have to / with you

D

1. b   **2.** b   **3.** a   **4.** a   **5.** b

1. Have you found anything you would like to get?

    (a) Would you like to get what you have found?

    (b) Did you find something you want to buy?

2. I'm so worried that he won't recognize me.

    (a) He didn't recognize me being so worried about me.

    (b) That he might not remember me concerns me very much.

3. The dolphin population here has increased by 12% over the past 18 years.

    (a) The number of dolphins has increased more than 12% in 18 years.

    (b) 12% of the dolphin population has grown over the past 18 years.

4. What is the number of people required for the trip?

    (a) How many people does the trip require?

    (b) What amount of people requested the trip?

5. The south may also experience rain mixed with ice.

    (a) Rain will be mixed with ice as you may have experienced in the south.

    (b) It may be raining with ice in the south.

VOCABULARY PREVIEW

01. subordinate *n.* 부하직원

02. release 풀어 주다, 석방하다

03. fraud 사기, 기만

04. pretext 구실, 핑계

05. in bondage 감금되어, 노예가 되어

06. sanction 재가, 인가, 제재, 처벌

07. measures 수단, 조치

08. fairground 광장, 박람회장

09. contestant 경쟁자, 경기 참가자

10. fundraising 기금 모금

11. revenue 수익, 세입

12. doze 꾸벅꾸벅 졸다

13. immature 미숙한, 미완성의

14. compliment 칭찬하다

15. maintenance 유지, 보수, 관리, 정비

16. laminated 코팅된

17. resistant 저항력이 있는, 저항하는

18. grease 기름, 유지

19. vapor 증기

20. entry form 참가신청서, 응모신청서

21. manure 비료, 거름

22. the former 전자

23. stringent (규칙 등이) 엄격한, 강제적인

24. allege 주장하다, 진술하다

GUIDED LISTENING

1 1. b　2. c　**2** 1. a　2. c

3 1. c　2. d　**4** 1. d　2. a

1 Conversation

M: I'm excited. I got an offer from a marketing company!

W: That's really good. So when are you joining them?

M: Actually, they want me to join immediately. But I've requested to delay it a week.

W: Do you have some work going on at your current company?

M: Not exactly, but I've got to hand over my responsibilities to my subordinate. I'll need some time to train her.

W: Okay. Have you informed your boss that you're leaving?

M: Yes. He wasn't very happy about it.

W: Poor guy! He was so dependent on you.

M: 나 너무 신나. 마케팅 회사에서 제의를 받았어!

W: 정말 잘됐구나. 언제 입사하게 돼?

M: 실은, 당장 오기를 원하나봐. 하지만 일주일 연기해 달라고 요청했어.

W: 지금 회사에서 진행하고 있는 일이 있는 거야?

M: 꼭 그런 것은 아니고, 부하직원에게 내 일을 인수인계해야 하거든. 그 사람을 교육시키는 데에 시간이 좀 걸릴 거야.

W: 그래. 그만두겠다고 상사에게는 알렸어?

M: 응. 좋아하지 않으시더라.

W: 안됐구나! 그 분은 너한테 의존을 많이 했잖아.

Comprehension

1 Which is correct according to the conversation?

(a) The woman is searching for a job in a marketing company.

(b) The man is switching to a new job.

(c) The man's boss has offered him a pay raise.

(d) The man is preparing a new worker to be his subordinate.

이 대화에 의하면 사실인 것은 무엇인가?

(a) 여자는 마케팅 회사에 직장을 구하고 있다.

(b) 남자는 새로운 직장으로 옮길 것이다.

(c) 남자의 상사는 남자에게 월급 인상을 제의했다.

(d) 남자는 새로운 사원을 그의 부하직원이 되도록 준비시키고 있다.

해설 새로운 회사에서 제안을 받은 남자와의 대화이다. 인수인계를 위해 시간이 좀 걸릴 것이지만, 남자는 직장을 옮길 것임을 알 수 있다. 그러므로 (b)가 정답이다.

함정 (a)와 (c)는 언급되지 않았다. (d)는 새로운 사원을 부하직원으로 준비시키는 것이 아니라 인수인계를 위해 부하직원을 교육시키는 것이므로 답이 아니다.

Detail

2 Why did he request to delay joining the company?

(a) He has a project going on.

(b) He wants to take time off.

(c) He has to train his subordinate.

(d) He has not talked to his boss.

남자가 그 회사에 입사 연기를 요청한 이유는?

(a) 진행 중인 프로젝트가 있다.

(b) 좀 쉬고 싶어 한다.

(c) 부하직원을 훈련시켜야 한다.

(d) 상사에게 말하지 않았다.

해설 그 회사로의 입사를 왜 미루었느냐는 여자의 질문에 대한 남자의 대답 I've got to hand over my responsibilities to my subordinate.에서 부하직원에게 인수인계해야 하기 때문임을 알 수 있다.

어휘 offer 제의, 제안 delay 연기하다, 늦추다
hand over 건네주다, 양도하다 subordinate 부하직원
dependent on ~에 의존하고 있는, 의지하는
switch 바꾸다, 교환하다 pay raise 월급 인상

2 Conversation

M: What happened? Why did the boss call you?

W: You won't believe what happened! Someone told the boss that I'm quitting. Now, he's quite upset with me.

M: Hey, it was me! But aren't you really quitting?

W: No. Who told you I was?

M: I heard you discussing that with your sister yesterday. Isn't it true?

W: You got confused! It's my sister who is quitting her job, not me!

M: I'm really sorry for this. I misunderstood the whole thing.

W: Please tell the boss that, too!

M: 무슨 일이 있었어요? 상사가 당신에게 왜 전화를 한 거죠?

W: 무슨 일이 있었는지 믿지 못할 거예요! 누군가가 내가 그만둘 거라고 그분에게 말했나 봐요. 지금, 그는 나한테 엄청 화가 나 있어요.

M: 있잖아요, 그거 나였어요! 하지만 정말 관둘 거 아닌가요?

W: 아니요. 내가 그럴 거라고 누가 말했어요?

M: 어제 당신 여동생과 얘기하고 있는 것을 들었는데요. 사실이 아닌가요?

W: 혼동하신 거예요! 직장을 그만두는 것은 제가 아니라 내 여동생이에요!

M: 정말 미안해요. 완전히 착각했었네요.

W: 제 상사께도 그렇게 말해 주세요!

Comprehension

1 Which is correct according to the conversation?

(a) The man said something incorrect about the woman.

(b) The woman made her sister quit her job.

(c) The woman was planning to quit some time later.

(d) The man criticized the woman in front of the boss.

이 대화에 의하면 사실인 것은?

(a) 남자가 여자에 대해 잘못된 것을 말했다.

(b) 여자가 그녀의 여동생이 직장을 그만두게 만들었다.

(c) 여자는 나중에 일을 그만둘 예정이었다.

(d) 남자는 상사 앞에서 여자를 비난했다.

해설 상사에게 여자에 대해 잘못된 정보를 전달한 남자가 사과하게 되는 대화이다. 남자의 I'm really sorry for this.라는 말 앞의 내용으로 보아, 남자가 상사에게 여자에 대해 잘못된 정보를 전달해서 미안해하고 있다.

함정 상사 앞에서 여자를 비난한 것이 아니라, 여자도 대해 잘못된 정보를 전한 것이므로, (d)는 오답이다.

Detail

2 Why was the boss upset?

(a) Because he thought the man told him a lie.

(b) Because the man told him that he would quit.

(c) Because he thought the woman was going to quit.

(d) Because the woman gave him some wrong information.

상사가 화난 이유는?

(a) 남자가 그에게 거짓말을 했다고 생각했기 때문이다.

(b) 남자가 그만둘 것이라고 말했기 때문이다.

(c) 여자가 그만둘 것이라고 생각했기 때문이다.

(d) 여자가 그에게 잘못된 정보를 주었기 때문이다.

해설 여자의 첫 번째 말 Someone told the boss that I'm quitting. Now, he's quite upset with me.에 답이 있다. 누군가 여자가 그만둘 것이라고 상사에게 말해서 상사가 화가 난 것이므로 (c)가 정답이다.

어휘 quit 그만두다 ㅣ misunderstand 잘못 생각하다, 오해하다 criticize 비난하다 ㅣ in front of ~ 앞에서

3 Monologue

M: Many approaches <u>are being undertaken to end slavery</u> in Sudan. Some of the most recent attempts have been taken by Christian organizations. These organizations purchase hundreds of slaves from slave traders and then release them. The move was started in good faith; however, it has been learned that <u>a great deal of fraud has been taking place</u> under the pretext of freeing slaves. For instance, some slave traders sell <u>mass quantities of slaves</u> that are only <u>pretending to be in bondage</u>. Other groups or nations <u>have applied sanctions on</u> the Sudanese government to help free the slaves; sanctions were also put on a Chinese oil company that operated in Sudan. Despite the many measures taken, none of them have been effective enough in stopping the slave trade to date.

M: 수단에서는 노예제도를 종식시키기 위해 많은 방법들이 수행되고 있습니다. 가장 최근의 시도는 기독교 단체에 의한 것이었습니다. 이 단체들은 노예상인들에게서 수백 명의 노예들을 사들여서 풀어 주었습니다. 이런 조처는 좋은 신념으로 시작되었지만, 노예를 풀어 준다는 구실 아래 상당한 부정이 있었다는 것이 알려졌습니다. 예를 들면, 몇몇 노예상인들은 노예인 척만 하는 노예들을 대량으로 팔아 넘겼습니다. 다른 단체들과 국가들은 노예들을 자유롭게 하는 것을 돕기 위해서 수단 정부에 제재를 가했습니다. 제재는 수단에서 운영하고 있는 중국 석유 회사에도 가해졌습니다. 많은 조치들이 취해지고 있는데도 불구하고, 그것들 중 어느 것도 지금까지는 노예 거래를 그만두게 할 만큼 충분히 효과적이지 못했습니다.

Comprehension

1 Which is correct according to the news report?

(a) Christian organizations purchase Sudanese slaves for labor.

(b) A Chinese company owns many slaves that it brings to China.

(c) **Various attempts to end slavery have not been successful.**

(d) Slave traders refuse to release slaves under any circumstances.

이 뉴스 기사에 따르면 옳은 것은?

(a) 기독교 단체들은 노동을 위해 수단 노예들을 사들인다.

(b) 중국 회사는 중국으로 데려올 많은 노예들을 소유하고 있다.

(c) 노예제도를 종식시키기 위한 다양한 시도들은 성공적이지 못했다.

(d) 노예상인들은 어떤 상황에서도 노예들을 풀어 주려고 하지 않는다.

해설 수단의 노예제도를 종식시키기 위해 많은 방법들이 동원되었지만, 그리 성공적이지 못하다는 기사이다. 그러므로 (c)가 옳다.

함정 (a) 기독교 단체들은 노동을 위해서가 아니라, 자유롭게 풀어 주려고 노예들을 샀다. (b)는 알 수 없는 내용이며, (d)는 언급되지 않은 내용이다.

Detail

2 What do Christian organizations do to end slavery?

(a) They sell their property in exchange of their slaves.

(b) They fight against companies hiring many slaves.

(c) They persuade slave traders to free their slaves.

(d) **They buy slaves from traders and free them.**

노예제도를 종식시키기 위해서 기독교 단체는 무엇을 하고 있는가?

(a) 그들의 재산을 팔아서 노예와 교환한다.

(b) 많은 노예들을 고용하는 회사에 반대하여 싸운다.

(c) 노예를 풀어 주라고 노예상인들을 설득한다.

(d) 상인들로부터 노예를 사서 풀어 준다.

해설 앞부분의 These organizations purchase hundreds of slaves from slave traders and then release them.에서, 기독 단체들이 노예제도의 종식을 위해서 노예를 사서 풀어 주고 있다는 것을 알 수 있다. 그러므로 정답은 (d)이다.

어휘 approach 접근, 해결 방법 ㅣ slavery 노예제도 attempt 시도 ㅣ release 풀어 주다, 석방하다 a great deal of 상당량의 ㅣ fraud 사기, 기만 take place 발생하다, 일어나다 ㅣ pretext 구실, 핑계 mass quantities of 대량의 in bondage 감금되어, 노예가 되어 sanction 재가, 인가, 제재, 처벌 ㅣ despite ~에도 불구하고 measures 수단, 조치 ㅣ to date 현재까지는 under any circumstances 어떠한 사정에서도

4 Monologue

W: An important announcement — the Happy Street <u>coloring contest</u> will be held on Friday morning at the Wonder Center Fairgrounds. The event <u>is co-sponsored</u>

by Denver TV. The winners of the contest will be awarded free tickets to attend a live recording of a TV program as members of the audience! The recording is scheduled for Saturday, June 30th, at the Brown Center. Children interested in the contest should be older than 4 years of age. Contestants are required to fill out a contest registration form with personal details such as name, age, parents' names, address and contact number. All necessary supplies will be provided. Contestants must send the form by May 21st.

W: 중요한 안내방송입니다. Happy Street 컬러링 콘테스트가 금요일 아침에 원더센터광장에서 열릴 것입니다. 그 행사는 덴버 TV가 공동 후원합니다. 콘테스트 입상자들에게는 TV 프로그램 생중계 녹화에 방청객으로서 참여할 수 있는 무료 티켓이 수여될 것입니다! 녹화 일정은 6월 30일 토요일에 브라운센터에서입니다. 콘테스트에 관심이 있는 어린이들은 4세 이상이어야 합니다. 참가자들은 콘테스트 등록 신청서에 이름, 나이, 부모님 성함, 주소와 연락 번호 같은 개인 상세 정보를 기입해야 합니다. 필요한 모든 물품은 제공될 것입니다. 참가자들은 5월 21일까지는 신청서를 보내야 합니다.

Comprehension

1 Which is correct according to the announcement?

(a) Anyone can just walk in and attend the contest on that day.

(b) Anyone in any age group can participate in the contest.

(c) Participants must bring necessary supplies to the contest.

(d) Contestants must provide personal information before the contest.

이 안내방송에 따르면, 다음 중 옳은 것은?

(a) 그날 누구든지 들어와서 콘테스트에 참여할 수 있다.
(b) 어느 연령대의 사람이든지 콘테스트에 참가할 수 있다.
(c) 참가자들은 콘테스트에 필요한 물품을 가져와야 한다.
(d) 참가자들은 콘테스트 전에 개인 정보를 제출해야 한다.

해설 콘테스트 안내 방송이다. Contestants are required to fill out a contest registration form with personal details(참가자들은 콘테스트 등록 신청서에 개인 상세 정보를 기입해야 합니다.) 이하에서 (d)의 내용을 알 수 있다.

합정 (a) 당일에 그냥 참여할 수 있는 것이 아니라, 사전에 등록해야 한다. (b) 4세 이상이어야 한다. (c) 필요한 물품은 모두 제공될 것이라고 했다.

Main Topic

2 What is the announcement about?

(a) a contest to get a free ticket to a TV program

(b) free coloring classes for children on TV

(c) art skills for children older than 4 years of age

(d) the grand opening of a bookstore

이 안내방송은 무엇에 관한 것인가?

(a) TV 프로그램에 참여할 수 있는 무료 티켓을 얻는 콘테스트
(b) TV에서 하는 어린이들을 위한 무료 컬러링 수업
(c) 4살 이상의 어린이들을 위한 예술적 기술
(d) 서점의 성대한 개업식

해설 앞으로 있을 콘테스트에 관한 정보를 제공하는 안내방송이다. 컬러링 콘테스트인데, 입상자에게는 TV 프로그램 녹화에 참여할 수 있는 티켓이 상으로 주어진다는 내용이므로, 정답은 (a)이다.

합정 참여할 수 있는 TV 프로그램이 무료 컬러링 수업이라는 내용은 언급되지 않았으므로, (b)를 정답으로 해서는 안 된다.

어휘 announcement 안내방송, 발표, 공고
fairground 광장, 박람회장   co-sponsor 공동 후원하다
audience 관중   contestant 경쟁자, 경기 참가자
fill out 기입하다, 써넣다   registration form 등록 신청서
grand 거대한, 성대한

PRACTICAL LISTENING

1. c	2. a	3. d	4. d	5. a
6. d	7. d	8. a	9. c	10. c

1 Comprehension

M: Driver, get me downtown — quickly!

W: Sure. Where exactly do you want to go, sir?

M: Le Meridian Hotel on Silverstone Street. I will have to pick up my client there at 4:00. How long it will take?

W: It won't take longer than 30 minutes from here if the traffic allows.

M: Sounds good. I believe it takes one hour by shuttle bus.

W: Yeah, the shuttle takes longer than a taxi.

M: Well, I will have to grab another cab back to my office after picking up my client. Do you think you can wait outside?

W: If you don't take too long.

M: I won't. And <u>how much do you think it'll be</u>?

W: Not more than $35, I would estimate.

M: 기사님, 시내로 데려다 주세요, 빨리요!

W: 알겠습니다. 정확히 어디로 가시나요?

M: 실버스톤 가의 르메리디안 호텔입니다. 4시에 거기서 고객을 픽업해야 해요. 얼마나 오래 걸릴까요?

W: 교통이 괜찮으면, 여기서 30분도 걸리지 않을 거예요.

M: 잘됐군요. 셔틀버스로는 1시간 걸릴 텐데 말이죠.

W: 네, 셔틀버스가 택시보다 더 오래 걸리죠.

M: 음, 고객을 픽업한 후 사무실로 다시 돌아오려면 다른 택시를 잡아야 할 거예요. 밖에서 기다려 줄 수 있을까요?

W: 오래 걸리지 않는다면요.

M: 그렇지는 않을 거예요. 그리고 요금은 얼마나 나올까요?

W: 어림잡아 35달러 아래일 거예요.

Q Which is correct according to the conversation?

(a) The man is going to have a meeting at the hotel.

(b) The woman will take the man's client to the hotel.

(c) The woman is going to take the man to the office.

(d) The man is going to arrive at the hotel after 4 o'clock.

대화에 의하면 옳은 것은?

ⓐ 남자는 호텔에서 회의를 할 것이다.

ⓑ 여자는 남자의 고객을 호텔로 데려다 줄 것이다.

ⓒ 여자는 남자를 사무실로 데려다 줄 것이다.

ⓓ 남자는 4시 이후에 호텔에 도착할 것이다.

해설 택시 기사와 손님과의 대화 내용이다. 남자는 4시까지 호텔로 고객을 데리러 가야 한다. 고객을 데리고 다시 사무실로 갈 수 있도록 택시가 기다려주기로 한 상황이다. 정답은 (c)가 된다.

합정 (d) 30분도 채 안 걸린다는 기사의 말에 Sounds good.이라고 대답하는 것으로 보아 4시 이전에 호텔에 도착하게 될 것임을 알 수 있다.

어휘 **downtown** 번화가(중심지)에 **exactly** 정확히
grab (택시 따위를) 잡다
not more than ~보다 많지 않은, 많아야
estimate ~을 어림하다, 견적하다, 평가하다

2

W: I'd like to emphasize here that <u>running a fundraising event</u> is very similar to running a company. Both demand the same planning, time and <u>capabilities to set targets and achieve financial goals</u>. A company has a revenue or profit target, and a fundraising event sets a target of how much money it wants to raise. Thus, both require good leadership, and are chiefly concerned with making money. Both organizations must also <u>employ capable managers</u>, staff and organizational techniques to meet their goals. So use the same strategies for fundraising as a business owner would and see how well you succeed. In particular, <u>be certain to make use of benchmarking techniques</u> on a regular basis, so you can see how close to your financial goals you are as you would in a company.

W: 이제 여기서, 모금 행사를 벌이는 것은 회사를 경영하는 것과 대단히 유사하다는 점을 강조하고 싶습니다. 둘 다 목표를 설정하고 재정 목표를 달성하기 위해서는 계획, 시간과, 수완이 필요합니다. 회사는 총수입 또는 이익에 대한 목표가 있고, 모금 행사는 얼마나 많은 금액을 모금할 것인가에 대해 목표를 세웁니다. 따라서 둘 다 훌륭한 지도력이 필요하며, 주로 돈을 모으는 것과 관련이 있습니다. 이러한 목표를 달성하려면, 양쪽 조직 모두 능력 있는 경영자와 직원, 그리고 관리상의 전문 기술을 갖추어야 합니다. 그러니 경영주가 하는 것과 같은 방식으로 모금 전략을 세워 보십시오. 그리고 당신이 얼마나 성공하는지 보십시오. 특히 정기적으로 반드시 벤치마킹 기술을 사용하십시오. 그러면 당신은 회사에서와 마찬가지로 당신이 정한 재정 목표에 얼마나 근접해 있는지를 알 수 있습니다.

Q What is the speaker's main point about fundraising?

(a) It needs to be run as if it were a business.

(b) Its primary aim is to raise money.

(c) Special skill is required to succeed at it.

(d) Corporate experience is essential for it.

기금 모금에 대해 화자가 주로 말하는 것은?

ⓐ 사업처럼 운영될 필요가 있다.

ⓑ 최고의 목표는 돈을 모금하는 것이다.

ⓒ 기금 모금에 성공하려면 특별한 기술이 요구된다.

ⓓ 회사 경험이 필수적이다.

해설 기금 모금을 회사 경영에 견주어 설명하고 있다. 회사 경영 방식과 같은 전략을 사용하면 성공할 수 있다고 했으므로 정답은 (a)가 된다.

합정 최상의 목표가 돈이라든가(b), 회사 경험이 필수적이다(d) 등은 화자가 말한 내용의 범주에 있지 않다. 회사 경영 방식을 쫓으면 성공할 것이라는 암시는 있었으나, 특별한 성공 기술을 언급하지 않았으므로 (c) 역시 정답이 될 수 없다.

어휘 **fundraising** 기금 모금 **planning** 계획, 기획
financial 재정의 **revenue** 수익, 세입
benchmarking 벤치마킹(자신의 제품이나 제조 방법의 향상을 위해 성공적인 또는 다른 회사와 비교하여 참고하는 것)
on a regular basis 정기적으로

3

W: Did you like the movie?

M: It wasn't that bad.

W: Really? Come on. I saw you <u>dozing in the middle</u>.

M: You noticed that, huh? Well, <u>I couldn't stand the second half</u>.

W: I guess <u>there wasn't much the director could do</u> as the storyline was quite weak.

M: True, <u>there were so many illogical and unnecessary scenes</u>.

W: The actors were immature <u>when it came to acting</u>.

M: Except for the actor who played the grandfather. He did very well.

W: That's right. He was the only one who seemed to have any real talent in the movie.

W: 영화 좋았어?

M: 그렇게 나쁘지는 않았어.

W: 정말? 솔직히 말해봐. 중간에 네가 조는 걸 봤는데.

M: 알고 있었구나? 음, 후반부에 못 참겠더라고.

W: 줄거리가 너무 빈약해서 감독이 할 수 있는 게 별로 없었나봐.

M: 맞아. 비논리적이고 불필요한 장면들이 너무 많았어.

W: 배우들의 연기도 미숙했고.

M: 할아버지 역을 맡은 배우만 빼고 말이야. 그는 아주 잘 했어.

W: 맞아. 그는 그 영화에서 진짜 재능을 가진 것 같은 유일한 사람이었어.

Q What is the man's opinion of the movie?

(a) He did not like the action scenes.

(b) He found the story interesting.

(c) He thought it was saved by its good actors.

(d) He felt most of the actors weren't talented.

영화에 대한 남자의 견해는?

(a) 액션신이 마음에 들지 않았다.

(b) 줄거리가 흥미로웠다.

(c) 훌륭한 연기자들 때문에 영화가 그나마 괜찮았다고 생각했다.

(d) 대부분의 배우들이 재능이 없다고 느꼈다.

[해설] 같이 본 영화에 대한 남녀의 대화이다. 두 사람은 할아버지 연기를 한 배우를 제외하고는, 줄거리가 빈약하고 쓸데없는 장면들이 너무 많으며, 배우들의 연기마저 너무 미숙했다는 점을 들면서 영화에 대한 불만을 토로하고 있다. 따라서 영화에 대한 남자의 견해는 (d)가 된다. 나머지 (a)는 언급되지 않았으며, (b)와 (c)는 틀린 설명이다.

[어휘] doze 꾸벅꾸벅 졸다 second half 후반전, 후반부
director 감독, 연출가 storyline 줄거리, 구상

illogical 비논리적인, 불합리한 unnecessary 불필요한
scene 장면 immature 미숙한, 미완성의 acting 연기
except for ~을 제외하고 play ~의 역을 맡다
talent 재주, 재능, 인재 save ~을 구하다, 구조하다, 지키다

4

M: Are you ready <u>for the curtain to go up</u>?

W: Yes, but I'm nervous. I've never performed in front of an audience.

M: You're an excellent dancer and <u>you've practiced your steps so well</u>.

W: That's true, but <u>what if I forget my steps</u>?

M: I'm sure that won't happen. Even if it did, <u>you'd know how to cover it up with other steps</u>, right?

W: Yes. But still, <u>I'm afraid that I might screw up</u>.

M: Relax! Your performance will be excellent.

W: I'm glad you're here to support me.

M: 막을 올릴 준비 됐니?

W: 응, 하지만 너무 긴장돼. 관객들 앞에서 공연한 적이 한 번도 없거든.

M: 너는 훌륭한 댄서고, 스텝 연습도 너무나 잘 해냈어.

W: 그건 그렇지만. 스텝을 잊어버리면 어떡하지?

M: 그럴 일은 분명히 없을 거야. 그런 일이 있다고 해도, 다른 스텝으로 커버하는 법을 알고 있잖아, 그렇지?

W: 응. 하지만 실수로 엉망이 될까봐 여전히 두려워.

M: 긴장을 풀어! 네 공연은 훌륭할 거야.

W: 네가 옆에서 응원해 줘서 기뻐.

Q What is the man trying to do in the conversation?

(a) to help the woman practice dancing

(b) to compliment the woman on her performance

(c) to tell the woman where the curtain is

(d) to comfort the woman ahead of her performance

이 대화에서 남자는 무엇을 하고 있는가?

(a) 여자의 춤 연습을 도와 주기

(b) 공연에 대해서 여자를 칭찬하기

(c) 여자에게 커튼이 어디 있는지 알려 주기

(d) 공연 전에 여자를 안심시키기

[해설] 댄스 공연의 막이 오르기 전에 나누는 남녀의 대화이다. 무대 경험이 없는 여자가 무척 긴장을 하자, 남자는 여자에게 훌륭한 댄서이며, 스텝 연습을 훌륭히 잘 소화해냈으니까 걱정하지 말라고 격려한다. 여자가 또 스텝을 잊어버릴까 걱정을 하자, 다른 스텝으로 잘 마무리할 수 있을 거라고

말해주면서 여자의 긴장을 계속 풀어주고 있다. 따라서 대화에서 남자가
하고 있는 것은 (d)가 된다.

5 Comprehension

W: The kitchen is where the most work is done in any household. Not only is it the place where we cook, it is also <u>a place that needs regular intensive cleaning</u>. Tonight's program focuses on choosing <u>a low-maintenance kitchen</u> so you can minimize the time that you have to spend there. The most important thing is <u>to select surfaces that are easy to clean</u>. You don't want kitchen surfaces that need intensive scrubbing. Remember that while natural wood looks great, it needs a lot of maintenance. <u>A laminated surface</u>, however, doesn't. Also, make sure that your kitchen walls are <u>resistant to the grease, vapor and moisture</u> from your cooking.

W: 어느 집이나 가장 많은 집안일을 하는 곳이 바로 부엌입니다. 부엌은 요리를 하는 장소일 뿐만 아니라, 정기적으로 집중적인 청소를 해야 하는 곳이기도 합니다. 오늘 프로에서는 관리가 덜 필요한 부엌을 선별하는 데 초점을 맞추었습니다. 그래서 여러분이 부엌에서 보내는 시간을 최소화할 수 있도록 말입니다. 가장 중요한 것은 청소하기 용이한 외관(자재)을 고르는 것입니다. 아마 여러분들도 힘들여 빡빡 문질러야 하는 그런 부엌을 원하지는 않으실 테지요. 천연 나무 소재가 보기에는 아주 좋아보여도 그 상태를 유지하려면 많은 노력이 필요하다는 점을 명심하시기 바랍니다. 하지만 코팅 처리된 표면은 그렇지 않습니다. 또한 부엌 벽면이 음식을 할 때 발생하는 유분이나 증기, 그리고 습기에 저항력이 있는 것인지 확인하세요.

Q Which is correct according to the radio program?

(a) Laminated surfaces need less maintenance.

(b) Kitchen walls must absorb moisture efficiently.

(c) Natural wood surfaces are ideal for kitchens.

(d) Mess is unavoidable while cooking.

이 라디오 프로그램에 따르면 사실인 것은?

(a) 코팅된 표면은 유지(관리) 노력이 덜 든다.

(b) 부엌 벽면은 습기를 충분히 빨아들여야 한다.

(c) 천연 나무 소재 표면이 부엌에 이상적이다.

(d) 요리할 때 어질러지는 것은 피할 수 없다.

6

M: Would you like to have dinner with me tonight?

W: Um, I'll have to <u>check with my cousin</u>. I'm supposed to go out with her for dinner.

M: Oh, is she the one you were talking about before?

W: Right. She's here for a business meeting, so we thought <u>we'd catch up on each other over dinner</u>. You want to join?

M: If that is okay with your cousin, <u>I don't see any reason to refuse</u>.

W: Like I said, I will check with my cousin.

M: You do that. And <u>if she wouldn't be comfortable</u>, I can meet you tomorrow.

W: I'll let you know by 4 o'clock. Is that too late for you?

M: Not at all. If I can see you tonight, I'll pick you up at 8:00 p.m. then.

M: 오늘 밤에 저녁 식사 같이 할래?

W: 음, 내 사촌한테 물어 봐야 할 거야. 오늘 그녀와 나가서 저녁 식사를 하기로 했거든.

M: 아, 전에 네가 이야기했던 그 사람?

W: 응, 업무상 회의로 이곳에 와있어. 그래서 저녁식사를 하면서 그 동안 못다 한 얘기를 하려고 했거든. 너도 함께 할래?

M: 너네 사촌이 괜찮다면, 거절할 이유가 없지.

W: 내 말이 그 말이야. 사촌에게 물어 볼게.

M: 그래. 그녀가 불편하다면, 나랑은 내일 만나도 돼.

W: 4시까지는 알려 줄게. 너무 늦나?

M: 전혀. 오늘 밤에 볼 수 있으면, 8시에 데리러 갈게.

Q What is the conversation mainly about?

(a) deciding on a restaurant to dine at

(b) how to arrange a meeting with the woman's cousin

(c) whether the cousin can join the dinner or not

(d) making an appointment for dinner

이 대화는 주로 무엇에 관한 것인가?

(a) 식사할 식당 결정하기

(b) 여자의 사촌과 만남을 어떻게 준비해야 하는지

(c) 사촌이 저녁 식사에 합류할지 말지

(d) 저녁 식사 약속 정하기

해설 남자는 여자에게 오늘밤에 같이 저녁 식사를 하자고 권했지만 여자는 회의 차 이곳에 온 사촌과 이미 저녁 약속을 해 둔 상태이다. 여자는 사촌과의 저녁 식사에 합류하라고 제안했고, 사촌에게 괜찮은지 물어 보고 알려 주기로 했다. 오늘 안 된다면, 내일 만나도 된다는 남자의 말로 보아, (d) 저녁 식사 약속 정하기에 관한 대화임을 알 수 있다.

어휘 check with ~와 상담하다, ~에게 문의하다 cousin 사촌
business meeting 업무상 모임, 회의
catch up on 그동안 못했던 것을 하다
pick up ~을 데리러/태우러 가다
decide on ~을 결정하다, ~로 정하다 dine 식사하다
arrange 준비하다, 주선하다

7 Comprehension

M: You've been waiting for it all summer, and now it's here! <u>The 10th annual</u> Walcott Home and Garden Festival will be the best place to get quality goods at low prices from all over the province! This will be an event that you just won't want to miss. To take advantage of it, be at the Walcott Grounds on Sunday, <u>May 12th between 9:00 a.m. and 6:00 p.m.</u> This is your opportunity to buy or just look over quality items <u>from over 137 vendor stalls.</u> Visitors can also win <u>a 1,000 dollar gift coupon</u> for furniture and garden supplies. Pick up your entry forms <u>at any of the participating shops or stalls,</u> fill it out and hand it in at any of the exits.

M: 여름 내내 기다렸던 축제가 이제 시작됩니다. 10번째 맞이하는 '월코트 홈 앤 가든 페스티벌'은 전국 각지의 고품질 물품들을 저가에 구입할 수 있는 최적의 장소입니다! 여러분들이 놓치고 싶지 않은 이벤트일 것입니다. 이 기회를 잡으시려면 5월 12일 일요일 오전 9시에서 오후 6시 사이에 이곳 월코트 그라운드로 오십시오. 137개 노점에서 내놓은 품질 좋은 물품들을 구입하고 둘러볼 수 있는 기회입니다. 방문객들은 또한 1,000달러 상당의 가구 및 가든 장비 경품권에 당첨되실 수 있습니다. 참가 상점 또는 노점에서 응모신청서를 받아 작성하신 후, 나가실 때 아무 출구에나 제출하시면 됩니다.

Q Which is correct according to the announcement?

(a) The festival is held every Sunday during the month

of May.

(b) Purchases can be made from the festival's website.

(c) All shops offer gift certificates as prizes.

(d) Visitors can submit entry forms when leaving the festival.

이 안내방송에 따르면 옳은 것은?

(a) 이 축제는 5월 한 달 간 매주 일요일에 열린다.

(b) 이 축제의 (해당) 웹사이트에서 물품을 구입할 수 있다.

(c) 모든 상점에서 상품권을 상으로 제공한다.

(d) 방문객들은 축제에서 돌아갈 때 참가신청서를 제출할 수 있다.

해설 10번째 맞이하는 월코트 홈 앤 가든 페스티벌을 알리는 안내방송이다. 방문하는 모든 고객들은 1,000달러에 상당하는 경품에 응모할 수 있으며 응모신청서는 나갈 때 제출하면 된다고 했으므로 정답은 (d)이다.

함정 'annual event'라고 했으므로 일 년에 한 번 개최되는 축제임을 알 수 있다. 또한 참가업체로부터 경품 응모신청서를 받을 수 있다고 했지 각 업체가 직접 상품권을 제공하는 것은 아니다.

어휘 annual 해마다의, 연간의
province 지역, (행정 구역으로서의) 주(州), 성(省), 현(縣), 도(道)
take advantage of ~를 이용하다 vendor 행상인
stall 매장, 노점 entry form 참가신청서, 응모신청서
participate 참여하다, 참가하다 hand in ~을 제출하다
exit 출구 gift certificate 상품권 submit 제출하다

8

W: There's another important aspect of teaching. I'd like to discuss today, <u>classroom organization</u>. This involves organizing the placement of desks, bookcases, file cabinets and so on. This does not involve just "making the room look nice." Classroom organization is in fact an important part of the entire learning experience and also <u>reflects the attitude of the teacher</u>. Since your classroom indicates your style, <u>go ahead and add</u> a few personal touches like plants, art displays, colorful rugs or even cushions for the reading corner. <u>Bright colors motivate students</u>, particularly young ones, to do their best in the class. At the same time, you need to make sure that students <u>have easy access to all materials</u> so that they can work quickly and efficiently.

W: 교육에는 또 다른 중요한 측면이 있습니다. 오늘 논의코자 하는 부분은 교실 정돈입니다. 교실 정돈에는 책상, 책장, 파일함 등을 배치하는 것이 포함됩니다. 이는 단순히 '교실을 좋아 보이도록 만드는' 것을 의미하지 않습니다. 교실 정돈은 사실 전체 학습 경험의 중요한 부분이며 또한 교사의 태

도를 반영하기도 하지요. 교실의 모습이 여러분의 스타일을 나타내는 것이므로 화분이나 진열품, 색색깔의 깔개, 심지어는 독서 코너에 쿠션을 놓는 등, 여러분의 개인적인 손길을 더해 보세요. 밝은 색상은 학생들이 수업 중에 최선을 다할 수 있도록 해 줍니다. 특히 어린 학생들의 경우에는 말이죠. 동시에 학생들이 모든 자료들을 쉽게 이용할 수 있도록 하세요. 학생들이 빠르고 효과적으로 학습할 수 있도록 말입니다.

Q What is the talk mainly about?

(a) planning the layout of a classroom

(b) arranging activities for students

(c) making a classroom interesting

(d) choosing good course material

이 이야기는 주로 무엇에 관한 것인가?

(a) 교실 배치 계획하기

(b) 학생들을 위한 활동 준비하기

(c) 교실을 재미나게 꾸미기

(d) 좋은 교과 과정 자료 선정하기

해설 교실 구성의 전반적인 개념, 방법 등을 설명하는 강의이다. 도입부의 I'd like to discuss today, classroom organization. 부분을 통해 강의의 주제가 (a)임을 알 수 있다.

함정 (c)는 classroom organization의 일부 측면에 불과하다. (b), (d)는 구체적인 언급이 없다.

어휘 aspect 관점, 양상, 국면 organization 조직, 구성, 편성 reflect 반영하다, 나타내다 indicate 가리키다, 나타내다 touch 손길, 특색 motivate 자극하다, 동기를 주다 have access to ~에 접근할 수 있다. (자료 등을) 이용할 수 있다 efficiently 능률적으로 layout 배치

9 Comprehension

M: Where did you get these seeds? Are you trying to learn <u>about gardening</u>?

W: Well, my friend <u>gave me some seeds</u>, I thought I <u>ought to try to grow</u> them.

M: Have you ever done this before?

W: Why do you think I have <u>so many pots</u>?

M: What happened to plants you used to grow?

W: Don't ask. <u>I didn't have much success.</u> But this time I'll make sure that I do.

M: Well, why don't you try putting some manure in the soil?

W: That's a good idea. Where could I get it?

M: In any home and garden store.

M: 이 씨앗들을 어디에서 얻었어? 원예를 배우려고 하는 거야?

W: 음. 친구가 씨앗을 좀 줘서, 그것들을 길러봐야 할 것 같았거든.

M: 전에 해 본 적은 있어?

W: 이렇게 많은 화분을 내가 왜 가지고 있는 것 같아?

M: 네가 키웠던 식물들은 어떻게 됐는데?

W: 묻지 마. 그다지 성공적이지 않았어. 하지만 이번에는 기필코 잘 해볼 거야.

M: 흙에 비료를 좀 줘보는 게 어떨까?

W: 좋은 생각이야. 어디서 구하지?

M: 가정원예용품 가게에서.

Q Which is correct according to the conversation?

(a) The man offered to buy manure for the woman.

(b) The woman bought a lot of seeds from a store.

(c) The woman bought garden pots before.

(d) The man is going to help the woman grow plants.

이 대화에 의하면 옳은 것은?

(a) 남자는 여자에게 비료를 사 주겠다고 제안했다.

(b) 여자는 가게에서 씨앗을 많이 샀다.

(c) 여자는 이전에 원예 화분을 샀다.

(d) 남자는 여자가 식물 키우는 것을 도울 것이다.

해설 여자가 친구에게서 얻은 씨앗을 길러 보려 한다는 내용이다. 길러 본 적이 있느냐는 남자의 말에 자기에게 왜 이렇게 많은 화분이 있는 것 같냐고 반문하는 것으로 보아, 예전부터 화분을 가지고 있었음을 알 수 있다. 그러므로 (c)가 정답이다.

함정 (b)는 씨앗을 가게에서 산 게 아니라, 친구로부터 받은 것이라서 옳은 설명이 아니다. 남자는 여자에게 흙에 비료를 주라고 제안하고 있는 것이지, 여자가 식물을 키우고 있는 것을 직접 도와 줄 것이라거나 비료를 사 주겠다는 내용은 아니므로 (a)와 (d)도 오답이다.

어휘 seed 씨앗 gardening 원예, 조경 가꾸기 ought to ~해야 하다 grow 기르다, 재배하다 (=garden) pot 단지, 항아리, 화분 make sure 확실히 ~하다 try -ing ~해보다, 시도하다 manure 비료, 거름 soil 흙, 토양 buy+목+for 사람 ~에게 …을 사주다 plant 식물

10

W: There are generally two types of books on weight loss in stores today: <u>those concerning diet</u> and those concerning exercise. As we know, <u>the former far outsell the latter</u>. On today's show we will speak with Dr. Matt Durant, <u>known for his stringent criticism of the diet</u> and weight-loss industry in North America, and the books, videos and other programs that promote those diets.

Dr. Durant alleges that most weight-loss regimens unfairly exploit customers' desire for quick weight reduction through dieting and charge vast sums of money. He argues that these programs are not really faster or better than regular exercise and healthy eating, both of which can be practiced by anybody with more sustained results.

regimen (식사, 운동 등에 의한) 섭생, 처방 계획
exploit 착취하다, 부당하게 이용하다 vast 막대한
sustained 일관된, 지속적인 persuade 설득하다

W: 요즘 서점에는 체중 감량에 관해 일반적으로 두 가지 종류의 책들이 있습니다. 식이요법에 관한 것과 운동에 관한 것입니다. 우리도 알다시피 판매량에 있어 전자가 후자를 훨씬 앞지릅니다. 오늘 방송에서는 북미 식이요법 및 체중 감량 업계와 이들 식이요법을 광고하는 서적, 비디오, 기타 프로그램에 대해 지독히 비판적이라고 알려진 Matt Durant 박사와 말씀을 나눠 보겠습니다. Durant 박사는 대부분의 체중 감량법은 식이요법을 통해 급속하게 체중을 감량하려는 소비자들의 욕망을 악용하여 거액을 지불케 하는 부당한 행위라고 강력히 주장합니다. Durant 박사는 이들 (식이요법) 프로그램이 규칙적으로 운동하고 건강한 식생활을 하는 것보다 정말로 더 빠르거나 효과적인 것은 아니라고 주장합니다. 이 두 방법 (규칙적 운동과 건강한 식생활)은 누구나 실천할 수 있으며 보다 안정적인 결과를 도출할 수 있다고 합니다.

Q Which statement would Dr. Durant more likely agree with?

(a) Most people decide to follow efficient diet programs.

(b) People are willing to pay for a diet if it is effective.

(c) Diet weight-loss regimens do not have long-lasting results.

(d) People should be persuaded to buy special diet programs.

다음 중 Durant 박사가 가장 동의할 것 같은 내용은?
(a) 대부분의 사람들이 효과적인 식이요법 프로그램을 따르려고 한다.
(b) 식이요법이 효과적이라면 사람들이 기꺼이 (그 방법에 대해) 비용을 지불할 것이다.
(c) 식이요법 체중 감량법은 장기적인 효과가 없다.
(d) 사람들은 특별 식이요법 프로그램을 구매하도록 설득당해야 한다.

해설 식이요법을 통한 체중 감량에 비판적인 Durant 박사와의 담화 프로그램을 광고하는 내용이다. Durant 박사는 운동과 건강한 식생활을 통해 체중감량을 하는 것이 더 안정적인 효과를 볼 수 있다고 주장하고 있으므로 이를 통해 (c)를 유추할 수 있다.

함정 (a)와 (b)는 틀린 내용이라기보다는 Durant 박사가 동의할 것 같은 내용이 아니라는 점에 유의하여 답을 골라야 한다.

어휘 weight loss 체중 감량 concerning ~에 관하여
the former 전자 (↔ the latter)
stringent (규칙 등이) 엄격한, 강제적인 allege 주장하다, 진술하다

A

1. subordinate	2. criticize
3. pretext	4. measures
5. contestant	6. fundraising
7. benchmarking	8. revenue
9. doze	10. immature
11. compliment	12. maintenance
13. vapor	14. allege
15. submit	16. motivate

1. someone with a less important position than you in the organization that you both work for

2. to express your disapproval of someone or something by saying what you think is wrong with them

3. a reason which you pretend has caused you to do something

4. particular actions that someone, usually a government or other authority, takes in order to achieve a particular result

5. a person who takes part in a competition or quiz

6. the activity of collecting money to support a charity or political campaign or organization

7. a process in which a company compares its products and methods with those of the most successful companies in its field, in order to try to improve its own performance

8. money that a company, organization, or government receives from people

9. to sleep lightly or for a short period, especially during the daytime

10. not yet completely grown or fully developed

11. to say something to someone that expresses praise

12. the process of keeping a building, vehicle, road, or machine in good condition by regularly checking it and repairing it

13. tiny drops of water or other liquids in the air, which appear as mist

14. to assert without proof

15. to formally send a proposal, report, or request to someone so that they can consider it or decide about it

16. to make someone feel determined to do something

B

1. a   **2.** a   **3.** b   **4.** b   **5.** a

1. 서점에는 체중 감량에 관해 일반적으로 두 가지 종류의 책들이 있습니다.

   (a) There are generally two types of books on weight loss in stores.

   (b) There are two general ways to loss weight in many books in stores.

2. 그것들을 길러봐야 할 것 같았거든.

   (a) I thought I ought to try to grow them.

   (b) I thought I have to see how I can grow them.

3. 이것은 책상, 책장, 파일함 등을 배치하는 것이 포함됩니다.

   (a) Desks, bookcases, file cabinets should be included when organizing.

   (b) This involves organizing the placement of desks, bookcases, file cabinets and so on.

4. 밝은 색상은 학생들이 수업 중에 최선을 다할 수 있도록 해 줍니다.

   (a) Bright colors work best when students do their best in the class.

   (b) Bright colors motivate students to do their best in the class.

5. 어느 집이나 가장 많은 집안일을 하는 곳이 바로 부엌입니다.

   (a) The kitchen is where the most work is done in any household.

   (b) The most households have a kitchen where the most work is done.

C

1. I'm supposed to go out with her for dinner.

2. The festival will be the best place to get quality goods.

3. Pick up your entry forms at any of the participating shops.

4. These programs are not really faster or better than regular exercise.

5. You'd know how to cover it up with other steps.

1. go out / I'm supposed to / with her for dinner

2. to get quality goods / the best place / the festival will be

3. pick up / at any of the participating shops / your entry forms

4. these programs / than regular exercise / are not really faster or better

5. how to cover it up / with other steps / you'd know

D

1. b   **2.** a   **3.** b   **4.** b   **5.** b

1. A fundraising leader sets a target of how much money it wants to raise.

   (a) A goal of fundraising is to raise as much money as possible.

   (b) The amount of money it targets to raise is set by a fundraising leader.

2. Be certain to make use of benchmarking techniques on a regular basis.

   (a) It is important that benchmarking techniques are used regularly.

   (b) Benchmarking techniques are regularly used to make things certain.

3. You can see how close to your financial goals you are.

   (a) You can get closer to the financial goals you've set.

   (b) You may know how much of your financial goals have been accomplished.

4. There wasn't much the director could do as the storyline was quite weak.

   (a) The director couldn't do much about the storyline that was quite weak.

   (b) The director couldn't do much since the storyline wasn't great.

5. He was the only one who seemed to have any real talent in the movie.

(a) It seemed that he showed his real talent only in the movie.

(b) All the actors and actresses except him were poor in the movie.

VOCABULARY PREVIEW

01. disaster 재해

02. death toll 사망(희생)자 수

03. attribute ~의 탓으로 돌리다

04. rebuke 비난하다, 꾸짖다

05. vast 막대한, 광대한

06. deforestation 산림 벌채

07. lessen 줄이다, 적게 하다

08. momentum 운동량, 여세, 힘

09. dwelling 집, 거주

10. aftermath 여파, 영향

11. destructive 파괴적인

12. landslide 산사태

13. debris 부스러기, 파편, 잔해

14. spoil 상하다, 썩다

15. ban n. 금지하다

16. phenomenon 현상

17. anonymously 익명으로

18. insulting 모욕적인

19. trait 특징

20. encounter n. 만남, 조우

21. stimulus 자극, 격려

22. civility 정중함, 공손함

23. discreet 분별 있는, 신중한

24. proactive 전향적인, 미리 대책을 강구하는

GUIDED LISTENING

| **1** | 1. b | 2. b | **2** | 1. c | 2. c |
| **3** | 1. c | 2. b | **4** | 1. a | 2. a |

1 Conversation

M: Hi, I'm Jeffrey Peterson.

W: I'm Lillian Brook. Welcome to the Connecticut office. I guess you've just been transferred from New York.

M: Yes. I joined the office yesterday.

W: How do you like it here so far?

M: Well, it's chillier than I thought. Winters are cold in New York, too. But it feels like it's much colder here.

W: I think you're right. And summer is hot and humid throughout the state, but not as much as in New York, I guess.

M: But things are calmer here. I mean, people are more relaxed and gentle.

W: Right. I was in New York for one year. I couldn't believe how fast-paced things were there.

M: 안녕하세요. 저는 Jeffrey Peterson입니다.

W: 저는 Lillian Brook이에요. 코네티컷 사무실로 오신 것을 환영해요. 뉴욕에서 이제 막 전근오신 분이시군요.

M: 네, 어제 이 사무실로 왔어요.

W: 지금까지는 어떠셨어요?

M: 생각했던 것보다 춥네요. 음, 뉴욕도 겨울은 춥지만, 여기가 훨씬 더 추운 것 같아요.

W: 맞아요. 그리고 여름은 주 전체가 뜨겁고 습기가 많지만, 아마 뉴욕만 큼은 그렇지 않을 거예요.

M: 하지만 여기가 더 조용해요. 그러니까, 사람들이 더 느긋하고 여유 있 는 것 같아요.

W: 맞아요. 1년 동안 뉴욕에 있어 봤는데, 거기는 어찌나 빠른지 믿을 수 가 없었어요.

Relationship of Ideas

1 What comparison do the speakers make between New

York and Connecticut?

(a) working environment and condition

(b) climate and pace of life

(c) weather and prices of commodities

(d) temperature and personality

대화자들이 뉴욕과 코네티컷 사이에서 비교하고 있는 것은?

(a) 근무 환경과 조건

(b) 날씨와 생활의 속도

(c) 날씨와 일상용품의 가격

(d) 기온과 개성

해설 코네티컷으로 이제 막 전근 온 남자와의 대화이다. 둘 다 뉴욕에서 산 적이 있어서, 날씨와 생활의 속도에 대해 대화를 나누고 있다. 겨울에는 코네티컷이 더 춥고, 여름에는 뉴욕이 더 덥고 습하다. 그리고 코네티컷의 생활이 좀더 여유 있고 느긋하다고 말하고 있다.

Comprehension

2   Which is correct about the man and woman?

(a) The man wants to return to New York.

(b) They both have been to New York.

(c) The woman thinks it is hotter in Connecticut.

(d) They both like Connecticut better.

남자와 여자에 대해 옳은 것은?

(a) 남자는 뉴욕으로 돌아가고 싶어 한다.

(b) 그들은 둘 다 뉴욕에서 산 적이 있다.

(c) 여자는 코네티컷이 더 덥다고 생각한다.

(d) 그들은 둘 다 코네티컷을 더 좋아한다.

해설 뉴욕에서 코네티컷 사무실로 전근 온 남자와 인사하는 내용이다. 여자의 마지막 말 I was in New York for one year.로 보아, 둘 다 뉴욕에서 산 적이 있음을 알 수 있다.

함정 (a)와 (d)는 언급된 바가 없으며, 여자는 뉴욕이 더 덥고 습하다고 생각하므로 (c)는 오답이다.

어휘 transfer 옮기다, 전임시키다 humid 습한 relaxed 느긋한 fast-paced 속도가 빠른 commodity 일상용품

2 Conversation

W: Excuse me. I'm new to this town. <u>Could you tell me the way to the public library</u>?

M: Sure. Which one are you looking for? There are a lot of public libraries here.

W: I just need to get there <u>as fast as I can</u>.

M: Okay. Just go straight from here and then <u>take a right at the traffic light</u>. You'll see a coffee shop there. There is a library on the same side as the coffee shop. It is the Gordon Library. It is a little small and they don't have many books there.

W: Hmm, is there another library nearby?

M: Actually, if you <u>walk several blocks from here</u>, you'll see the City Library right next to a department store. It's about a 30 minute walk, but there are more books and <u>it's huge</u>.

W: 실례합니다. 저는 이 도시에 처음인데요. 공공도서관으로 가는 길을 가르쳐 주시겠습니까?

M: 물론이죠. 어느 도서관을 찾고 계시죠? 여기는 공공도서관이 많이 있거든요.

W: 될 수 있는 한 빨리 가야 해요.

M: 좋아요. 여기서 곧장 가다가 교통 신호등에서 오른쪽으로 가세요. 그러면 커피숍이 보일 거에요. 그 커피숍 쪽으로 도서관이 하나 있어요. 그게 Gordon 도서관이에요. 좀 작은 도서관이라, 책이 많지는 않아요.

W: 흠, 근처에 다른 도서관이 있나요?

M: 사실, 여기서 몇 블록 걸어가면, 백화점 바로 옆에 City 도서관이 있어요. 걸어서 30분 정도 걸리지만, 거기에는 책이 더 많고 아주 커요.

Relationship of Ideas

1   Which best explains the difference between the Gordon and City Library?

(a) One is neat but has less books; the other is messy but has more books.

(b) One is close but has old books; the other is far but has new books.

(c) One is near but has less books; the other is far but has more books.

(d) One is small but has more books; the other is big but has less books.

Gordon 도서관과 City 도서관 사이의 차이점을 가장 잘 설명한 것은?

(a) 하나는 깨끗하지만 책이 더 적고, 다른 하나는 지저분하지만 책이 더 많다.

(b) 하나는 가깝지만 책이 오래 되었고, 다른 하나는 멀지만 책이 새 것이다.

(c) 하나는 가깝지만 책이 더 적고, 다른 하나는 멀지만 책이 더 많다.

(d) 하나는 작지만 책이 더 많고, 다른 하나는 크지만 책이 더 적다.

해설 급하게 도서관을 찾고 있는 여자에게 길을 알려 주고 있는 남자와의 대화이다. 가까운 Gordon 도서관은 작아서 책이 많지 않지만, 좀 더 먼 걸어서 30분 거리에 있는 City 도서관에는 책이 더 많다고 말하고 있으므

로, (c)가 정답이다.

Comprehension

2 Which is correct according to the conversation?

(a) There is a library across from the coffee shop.

(b) It is too far to walk to the City Library.

(c) The woman is urgently looking for a library.

(d) The man was heading for the department store.

이 대화에 따르면 옳은 것은?

(a) 커피숍 건너편에 도서관이 있다.

(b) City 도서관은 너무 멀어서 걸어갈 수 없다.

(c) 여자는 도서관을 급히 찾고 있다.

(d) 남자는 백화점으로 가는 길이었다.

해설 앞부분에 있는 여자의 I just need to get there as fast as I can.이라는 말에서 (c)의 내용을 알 수 있다.

함정 (a) 커피숍과 같은 편에 도서관이 있으며, (b) City 도서관은 걸어서 30분 거리이다. (d) 남자는 백화점으로 가는 길이 아니라, 백화점 옆에 City 도서관이 있다.

어휘 look for ~을 찾다 as fast as I can 될 수 있는 한 빨리 take a right 우회전하다 nearby 근처에

3 Monologue

W: The Yangtze and Yellow Rivers are <u>reported to be overflowing their banks</u>. As a result, the northwest area of China, which is usually dry during these months, has been flooded. This is considered the worst natural disaster of the century, <u>as the death toll has risen to</u> several hundred, with hundreds more still missing. The flood conditions are not expected to change for another week <u>as there is a likelihood of heavy rains</u> for the next few days. The Chinese government <u>attributes the floods to seasonal changes</u>, an unavoidable part of the natural cycle. However, international organizations have <u>rebuked China for vast deforestation</u> that may have contributed to the flooding.

W: 양쯔강과 황화강의 강둑이 범람되고 있다는 보고입니다. 그 결과, 지금 같은 달 동안에는 대개 건조한 지역인 중국의 북서 지역이 침수되고 있습니다. 이것은 세기 최악의 자연 재해로 여겨지는데, 사망자 수가 수백에 이르고 있고 수백이 더 아직 실종 상태입니다. 홍수 상황은 앞으로 몇 주간 변화가 없을 것으로 예상되는데, 다음 며칠 동안 폭우가 내릴 가능성이 있기 때문입니다. 중국 정부는 이번 홍수를 계절 변화, 즉 자연 순환의 피할 수 없는 부분이 그 원인이라고 생각하고 있습니다. 하지만 국제기구는 홍수의 원인일 수 있는 막대한 산림 벌채에 대해 중국을 비난하고 있습니다.

Relationship of Ideas

1 What comparison does the speaker make between the Chinese government and international organizations?

(a) what damages they think the flood had caused

(b) what measures they think are the best to prevent floods

(c) what they think are the causes for the flood

(d) how long the disaster would last this time

중국 정부와 국제기구에 대해 화자가 비교하고 있는 것은?

(a) 홍수가 일으킨 피해가 무엇이라고 생각하는지

(b) 홍수를 막기 위한 최상의 조치가 무엇이라고 생각하는지

(c) 홍수의 원인이 무엇이라고 생각하는지

(d) 이번에는 재해가 얼마나 오랫동안 지속될 것이라고 생각하는지

해설 중국에서 일어나고 있는 홍수에 대한 뉴스이다. 중국 정부는 이번 홍수를 계절 변화, 즉 자연 재해라고 생각하고 있지만, 국제기구는 막대한 산림 벌채에 대해 중국을 비난하고 있다고 했으므로, (c)가 정답이다.

Comprehension

2 Which is correct about the current flooding in China?

(a) It is beneficial for areas which are usually dry.

(b) It has left hundreds of people dead.

(c) It has contributed to deforestation.

(d) It will lessen in a few days.

중국에서 발생하고 있는 현재의 홍수에 대해 옳은 것은?

(a) 일반적으로 건조한 지역에 유익하다.

(b) 는 수백 명의 사람들을 죽게 했다.

(c) 산림 벌채에 기여했다.

(d) 며칠 안에 줄어들 것이다.

해설 그 홍수로 인해 수백 명이 실종 또는 사망했고 앞으로 몇 주 더 계속될 수 있다고 전망했다. 그러므로 (b)가 옳다.

함정 (a) 홍수가 건조한 지역에 유익하다는 내용은 없다. 홍수가 산림 벌채에 기여한 것이 아니고, 산림 벌채가 홍수를 일으킨 것이므로, (c)는 오답이다.

어휘 overflow 넘쳐흐르다 bank 강둑 disaster 재해 death toll 사망(희생)자 수 likelihood 가능성 attribute ~의 탓으로 돌리다 rebuke 비난하다, 꾸짖다 vast 막대한, 광대한 deforestation 산림 벌채 beneficial 유익한, 이익이 되는 lessen 줄이다, 적게 하다

4 Monologue

W: Earthquakes are a form of natural disaster that

have the potential to cause damage <u>on a mass scale</u>. Earthquakes <u>have a direct impact on tidal waves</u>. Tidal waves can gain momentum and travel at very high speeds <u>covering large distances</u>. These waves may destroy human dwellings near coastal areas and also sweep away <u>people who are caught unaware</u>. The aftermath of an earthquake is equally destructive. After an earthquake, an area may be hit hard by landslides and underwater slides, the consequences of which are horrific. Many people may become <u>buried by the debris</u> formed due to landslides and the collapse of buildings. Buildings and other structures weakened by earthquakes may collapse even weeks after an earthquake has occurred.

W: 지진은 대규모로 피해를 일으킬 가능성이 있는 자연재해의 한 형태입니다. 지진은 해일에 직접적인 영향을 미칩니다. 해일은 여세를 몰아 매우 빠른 속도로 먼 거리까지 이동할 수 있습니다. 이러한 해일은 해안 지역에서 가까운 사람들의 거주지를 파괴할 수 있고, 인식하지 못하고 있는 사람들을 휩쓸어갈 수 있습니다. 지진의 여파도 똑같이 파괴적입니다. 지진이 있은 후에, 그 지역에는 그 무시무시한 결과인 땅위와 수중 산사태로 타격을 입을 수 있습니다. 많은 사람들이 산사태와 건물의 붕괴 때문에 생긴 잔해들에 묻힐 수 있습니다. 지진으로 인해 약해진 빌딩이나 다른 건물들은 지진이 지나가고 몇 주 후에 붕괴될 수도 있습니다.

Relationship of Ideas

1 How does the speaker categorize the effects of earthquakes?

(a) the first effects and the secondary effects

(b) the major effects and the minor effects

(c) the effects on humans and the environment

(d) the effects on the earth and the ocean

화자는 지진의 영향을 어떻게 분류하고 있는가?

(a) 직접적인 영향과 파급 영향

(b) 주요 영향과 사소한 영향

(c) 인간과 환경에 대한 영향

(d) 땅과 바다에 대한 영향

해설 지진에 관한 내용이다. 앞부분에서는 직접적인 영향을, 뒷부분에서는 지진이 지난 간 다음의 여파에 대해 이야기하고 있으므로, (a)가 정답이다.

함정 (b) 직접적인 영향과 파급 영향 모두 파괴적이고 위험하다고 했으므로, 주요 영향과 사소한 영향으로 나눈 것은 아니다.

Inference II

2 What can be inferred from the talk?

(a) The amount of damage may increase as time passes.

(b) Tidal waves generate earthquakes.

(c) Strong buildings may remain unaffected by earthquakes.

(d) Landslides occur only in coastal areas.

이 이야기에서 추론할 수 있는 것은 무엇인가?

(a) 피해의 규모는 시간이 지남에 따라 커질 수 있다.

(b) 해일이 지진을 일으킨다.

(c) 튼튼한 건물은 지진의 영향을 받지 않을 수 있다.

(d) 산사태는 해안지역에서만 발생한다.

해설 지진의 파괴적인 피해에 관한 언급이다. 지진으로 인한 직접적인 피해도 굉장히 크지만, 지진의 여파도 똑같이 파괴적이라고 말하고 있다. 갈수록 피해가 커질 수 있다는 것이므로, 정답은 (a)이다.

함정 해일이 지진을 일으키는 것이 아니라, 지진이 해일에 직접적인 영향을 미친다고 했다(Earthquakes have a direct impact on tidal waves.)는 데에 주의한다. 그러므로 (b)는 오답이다.

어휘 disaster 재해, 재난 potential 가능성, 잠재력
on a mass scale 대규모로 tidal wave 해일
momentum 운동량, 여세, 힘 dwelling 집, 거주
aftermath 여파, 영향 destructive 파괴적인 landslide 산사태
consequences 결과 debris 부스러기, 파편, 잔해
collapse 붕괴, 무너짐, 붕괴하다

PRACTICAL LISTENING

1. a	2. c	3. b	4. c	5. b
6. c	7. a	8. a	9. a	10. c

1

M: <u>The pearl necklace you're wearing</u> is very beautiful.

W: Thank you. I also like it.

M: <u>Where did you buy it from</u>?

W: Well, my friend gave it to me as a gift for my birthday. She got it from the Jewel House in City Center Mall.

M: Actually, <u>my sister is turning 20 tomorrow</u>. I'm sure <u>she'd like something like this</u>.

W: In that case, I can <u>help you choose something nice</u>

for your sister.

M: Thank you. My sister will be very happy.

M: 지금 하고 있는 진주 목걸이 정말 예쁘다.

W: 고마워. 나도 마음에 들어.

M: 어디서 샀니?

W: 친구가 생일 선물로 준 건데, 시티센터몰에 있는 주얼 하우스에서 샀대.

M: 실은 내 여동생이 내일 스무 살이 되거든. 걔가 이런 걸 분명히 좋아할 것 같아서 말이야.

W: 그렇다면 내가 여동생에게 줄 걸 고르는 걸 도와줄게.

M: 고마워. 동생이 진짜 기뻐할 거야.

Q What can be inferred from the conversation?

(a) **The man will buy something similar to the woman's necklace.**

(b) The woman usually shops at City Center Mall.

(c) The woman does not have much experience in buying jewelry.

(d) The woman is now turning 20.

이 대화를 통해 추측할 수 있는 것은?

(a) 남자는 여자의 목걸이와 비슷한 무언가를 살 것이다.

(b) 여자는 주로 시티센터몰에서 쇼핑을 한다.

(c) 여자는 보석 사는 데 경험이 별로 없다.

(d) 여자는 이제 스무 살이 된다.

해설 여자가 하고 있는 진주목걸이에 대한 남자의 질문으로 대화가 시작된다. 남자는 여동생의 스무 번째 생일 선물로 여자가 하고 있는 목걸이가 같은 것을 선물해 주고 싶어 한다. 그러자 여자는 목걸이 고르는 것을 도와 주겠다고 한다. 따라서 정답은 (a)이다.

함정 여자의 친구가 그 목걸이를 시티센터몰에서 사줬다고 해서, 여자가 거기서 주로 쇼핑을 한다는 것을 뜻하는 것이 아니므로 (b)는 오답이다. 여자가 선뜻 남자에게 목걸이 고르는 것을 도와 주겠다는 것으로 보아, 여자가 보석 사는 데 경험이 별로 없다고 단정지을 수도 없으며, 대화의 어디에도 여자가 보석 구입에 대한 경험이 별로 없다고 언급된 부분은 없다. 따라서 (c)는 정답으로 타당하지 못하다.

어휘 pearl 진주 | necklace 목걸이 |
wear 입고 있다, 몸에 걸치고 있다 | jewel 보석, 액세서리 |
actually 실제로, 사실은 | turn ~이 되다, ~로 변하다 |
in that case 그 경우에는, 그렇다면 | similar 비슷한, 유사한 |
jewelry 보석류

2 Relationship of Ideas

M: Are you aware that almost all foods are now genetically modified?

W: Yes, I know and I'm quite concerned about the consequences.

M: Well, I've eaten quite a lot of them, but I don't see any side effects.

W: They may not be evident for many years. Why can't we just stick to naturally-grown food?

M: Actually they spoil very easily, and you can't enjoy as many varieties with them.

W: At least you'd be protected from the harmful effects of genetically modified food, though.

M: I agree with you. We had better ban those foods.

M: 지금 거의 모든 식품들이 유전자 변형인 거 알고 있니?

W: 응, 알아. 그리고 그 결과가 너무 걱정스러워.

M: 나는 유전자 변형 식품들을 꽤 많이 먹었지만, 어떤 부작용도 보이지는 않아.

W: 수년 동안 분명하게 나타나지 않을지도 몰라. 우리는 왜 천연 재배식품들을 고수할 수 없는 걸까?

M: 사실 그것들은 아주 쉽게 상해서 다양한 변화를 즐길 수가 없어.

W: 하지만 적어도 유전자 변형 식품의 해로운 영향으로부터는 보호받을 거 아니야.

M: 동감이야. 그런 식품들은 금지하는 게 낫겠다.

Q What comparison do the speakers make between genetically modified and naturally-grown foods?

(a) the quality and nutrition

(b) the length of cultivation and diversity

(c) **the convenience and health issue**

(d) the cost and taste

화자들이 유전자 변형 식품과 천연 재배식품 간에 비교하고 있는 것은?

(a) 품질과 영양

(b) 재배 기간과 다양성

(c) 편리함과 건강 문제

(d) 가격과 맛

해설 유전자 변형 식품에 대한 남녀의 대화이다. 거의 모든 식품들이 유전자 변형이이어서 그 결과로 인해 나타날지도 모를 부작용과 피해를 걱정하고 있다. 또한 천연 재배식품은 쉽게 상해서 다양함을 즐길 수 없을 것이라는 내용도 있다. 그러므로 남자와 여자가 비교하고 있는 것은 유전자 변형 식품이 편리하기는 하지만, 건강에 해로울 수 있다는 것이다.

함정 영양, 재배 기간, 가격에 대한 언급은 이루어지지 않았다.

어휘 genetically 유전학적으로, 유전적으로 |
modify 변경(수정)하다, 변화시키다

be concerned about ~에 대해 걱정하다
consequence 결과 side effect 부작용
evident 명백한, 분명한
stick to ~을 고수(고집)하다, 끝까지 해내다
naturally-grown 자연적으로 자란, 천연 재배된
spoil 상하다, 썩다 variety 변화, 다양성

3 Relationship of Ideas

W: Psychologists are taking interest in the new phenomenon of "flaming," where individuals <u>anonymously post</u> insulting messages on the Internet. This behavior is directed as much by individual personality traits as by the way the human brain <u>is conditioned for interaction</u>. <u>Face-to-face encounters</u> provide a wide range of stimuli like voice tone and facial expression, which guide human responses and serve to <u>keep them within limits of civility</u>. These are absent in online, <u>text-only communications</u>. So when the brain doesn't receive such direct information, <u>responses are likely to be less discreet</u>.

W: 심리학자들은 '플레이밍' 이라는 새로운 현상에 관심을 갖게 되었는데, 이 현상에서는 사람들이 인터넷에 익명으로 모욕적인 글을 올립니다. 이러한 행동은 개인의 성격적인 특징에 의해 영향을 받는 만큼이나, 인간의 뇌가 상호작용을 위해 반응하는 방식에 의해서도 영향을 받습니다. 직접적인 만남에는 어조나 얼굴 표정과 같은 다양한 자극이 있는데, 그것들이 사람의 반응을 통제하고 정중하게 행동하게 하는 것입니다. 글자로만 의사소통을 하는 온라인에서는 이런 것들이 결여되어 있습니다. 따라서 뇌가 그러한 직접적인 정보를 받지 못하게 되어, 반응이 덜 신중하게 되는 것 같습니다.

Q Which best explains the relationship between stimuli and civility?

(a) Less stimuli cause better civility.

(b) More stimuli cause better civility.

(c) Better stimuli cause better civility.

(d) Worse stimuli cause worse civility.

자극과 예의바름의 관계를 가장 잘 설명한 것은?
(a) 더 적은 자극이 더 예의바르게 한다.
(b) 더 많은 자극이 더 예의바르게 한다.
(c) 더 좋은 자극이 더 예의바르게 한다.
(d) 더 나쁜 자극이 덜 예의바르게 한다.

해설 "플레이밍" 이라는 새로운 현상에 대한 강의이다. 이것은 인터넷에 모욕적인 글을 올리는 현상인데, 그 이유로는 두 가지를 들고 있다. 첫째는 개인의 성격, 둘째는 직접 대면하지 않고 글로만 상대를 대하기 때문이라

는 설명이다. 말하는 어조를 듣거나 얼굴 표정을 보게 되면 좀 더 신중하게 행동을 하게 되는데, 인터넷에서는 그렇지 않기 때문에 이러한 현상이 생겨난다는 내용이다. 그러므로 자극이 많을수록 더 예의바르게 된다는 (b)가 정답이다.

함정 더 좋거나 나쁜 자극에 대한 언급은 나타나 있지 않다.

어휘 psychologist 심리학자 phenomenon 현상
flaming 플레이밍(불특정 타인이나 무관심한 주제에 대하여 적대성을 표현하는 반사회적인 행동들로서 과거 오프라인에서는 경험하지 못한 소비자들의 새로운 행동들) anonymously 익명으로
insulting 모욕적인 personality 개성, 성격 trait 특징
face-to-face 정면으로 마주보는, 직접적인 range 범위, 한계
stimulus 자극, 격려 (pl. stimuli) civility 정중함, 공손함
text-only 글자로만 discreet 분별 있는, 신중한

4

W: Big businesses are beginning <u>to pay greater attention to</u> the good health of their employees. <u>This is a proactive step</u> suggested by experts to reduce spending on future employee health problems. This trend is not just about the bottom line, according to health economist Robin Boon, but a move <u>with a political motive</u>. He says that if employees are not treated well, companies could <u>come under greater government control</u> and be forced to <u>comply with stricter guidelines</u>. Big businesses would certainly not like this to happen.

W: 대기업들이 직원들의 건강에 더 많은 관심을 기울이기 시작하고 있습니다. 이것은 나중에 직원 건강 문제로 지출하는 비용을 줄이기 위해 전문가들이 제안한 전향적인 조치입니다. 이러한 경향은 보건 경제학자인 로빈 분에 따르면 최저선일 뿐만 아니라, 정치적 동기가 있는 움직임입니다. 그는 직원들을 잘 대우하지 않으면, 회사가 정부의 통제 하에 들어가서 더 엄격한 규제를 따를 수 밖에 없다고 말합니다. 대기업들은 분명히 이런 일이 일어나는 것을 바라지 않습니다.

Q What is implied about big businesses according to the news report?

(a) Their employees are given inadequate health facilities.

(b) Their workers are responsible for their own health care.

(c) Their aim is to avoid government interference.

(d) They spend generously on worker health insurance.

이 뉴스 기사에 따르면 대기업에 대해 짐작할 수 있는 것은 무엇인가?
(a) 대기업의 직원들이 부적절한 의료 혜택을 받고 있다.

해설 대기업들이 직원들의 건강 문제에 대해 관심을 갖게 되었다는 기사이다. 그 이유로는 나중에 비용이 더 많이 들 것을 피하기 위해서라는 것과, 그렇지 않으면 정부의 규제를 받게 될 것이기 때문이라는 전문가의 설명이 나오고 있다. 그러므로 대기업에 대해 짐작할 수 있는 것은 (c)라고 할 수 있다.

함정 (a) 현재 대기업의 직원들이 부적절한 의료 혜택을 받고 있는 것은 아니라는 것에 주의한다.

어휘 pay attention to ~에 주의를 기울이다
proactive 전향적인, 미리 대책을 강구하는   expert 전문가
comply with ~에 따르다   strict 엄격한   inadequate 부적절한
facilities 편의시설   interference 간섭, 중재
generously 후하게, 관대하게

5 Relationship of Ideas

M: Did you like <u>the art exhibition</u>?

W: Well, the paintings were excellent. How did you like it?

M: When I first went in, I thought the place was really quiet and neat.

W: Yes, it was. <u>I like the lighting there</u>. It was really something.

M: Right. But as more people came in, I <u>started to feel the place was a little small</u>. And then, the museum became too crowded as more time passed.

W: I know. The Art Hall at the City Center would have been <u>more appropriate</u>. The rooms in this museum are very small and can't even accommodate ten people.

M: And with this crowd, it's too noisy.

W: True. But it was surprising <u>to meet the artists on the way out</u>. They were shaking hands with all the visitors who were leaving the exhibition.

M: I thought that was very impressive, too.

M: 이 미술전시회 마음에 들었니?

W: 음, 그림들은 훌륭하네. 너는 어땠어?

M: 처음에 들어갔을 때, 정말 조용하고 깨끗하다고 생각했어.

W: 응, 그랬지. 거기 조명이 좋더라. 정말 뭔가 달라 보였어.

M: 맞아. 하지만 더 사람들이 오니까, 장소가 너무 협소하게 느껴지기 시작하더라. 그리고 미술관은 시간이 지남에 따라 너무 북적거렸잖아.

W: 그래. 시티 센터에 있는 아트홀이 좀 더 적합했을 텐데. 이 미술관의

전시실들은 너무 협소해서 10명의 인원도 수용하지 못할 거야.

M: 그리고 이렇게 북적대니까 너무 시끄러워.

W: 맞아. 하지만 출구에서 예술가들을 만날 수 있다는 것은 정말 놀라웠어. 그들은 전시회에서 나가는 모든 방문자들과 악수를 하고 있었잖아.

M: 그건 정말 나에게도 인상적이었어.

Q In what order, do the speakers explain the exhibition?

(a) from the most impressive thing to the least impressive thing

(b) from the first impression to the last impression

(c) from the exterior to the interior of the museum

(d) from the worst experience to the best experience

해설 미술 전시회에 대한 남녀의 대화이다. 두 사람은 전시회의 그림들은 훌륭하지만, 전시관이 너무 협소하고 시끄러워서 제대로 그림을 감상할 수 없다고 불평하다가, 마지막에 나올 때 예술가들과 만날 수 있었던 것은 정말 인상적이었다는 내용으로 진행되고 있으므로 정답은 (b)이다.

어휘 art exhibition 미술전시회   lighting 조명, 채광
crowded 혼잡한, 붐비는, 만원인
appropriate 적당한, 어울리는, 알맞은
accommodate 수용하다, 숙박시키다
crowd 군중, 관객, 많은 사람들   impressive 인상적인
exterior 외부, 외관 (↔ interior)

6

M: Let me now introduce you to gastropods. Gastropods are of two basic types, snails and slugs. Now, you might think the two <u>look very different</u> since <u>the snail has a shell</u> and the slug has only a thin mantle. However, <u>the two share one common feature</u> which puts them into the same family despite their external differences: in both creatures <u>the feet help to digest food</u>. Actually, the term "gastropod" comes from this feature: it <u>literally means</u> "stomach feet."

M: 복족류(gastropod)에 대해 말씀드리겠습니다. 복족류는 기본적으로 두 가지 형태가 있는데, 달팽이와 민달팽이가 있습니다. 이제, 여러분은 아마 달팽이는 달팽이집을 가지고 있고, 민달팽이는 얇은 외투막만을 가지고 있기 때문에 서로 다르게 생긴 것이라고 생각할지 모릅니다. 하지만 그 둘

은 모습의 차이에도 불구하고 같은 과(科)에 속하게 하는 공통적인 특징을 갖고 있습니다. 두 생물 모두 다리가 음식을 소화하도록 돕게 되어 있습니다. 사실, "gastropod"라는 용어가 이러한 특징에서 나온 말입니다. 그것은 글자 그대로 "위-다리"를 의미합니다.

Q What is mainly being discussed about snails and slugs?

(a) what their shells are made of

(b) how they are different from each other

(c) why they are grouped together

(d) how their stomachs help them move

달팽이와 민달팽이에 관해 주로 언급되고 있는 것은 무엇인가?

(a) 그것들의 껍질이 무엇으로 만들어져 있는지

(b) 그것들이 서로 어떻게 다른지

(c) 그것들이 왜 함께 분류되는지

(d) 그것들의 위가 어떻게 그것들이 움직이도록 돕고 있는지

해설 복족류인 달팽이와 민달팽이에 대한 강의이다. 두 생물은 서로 모습이 많이 다른데도 다리가 소화를 돕는다는 공통점이 있고, 그런 이유로 두 생물을 같은 과로 분류한다는 내용이므로 (c)가 정답이다.

함정 처음에 서로 다른 점이 언급되었다고, 끝까지 듣지 않고 (b)를 정답으로 오해해서는 안 된다.

어휘 **gastropod** 복족류(腹足類) (달팽이 따위) **snail** 달팽이
slug 민달팽이 **shell** 껍질, 조가비
mantle (연체동물의) 외투막(膜) **share** 공유하다 **feature** 특징
family (생물) 과(科) **despite** ~에도 불구하고
external 외부의, 겉의 **digest** 소화시키다 **term** 용어, 어휘
literally 글자 그대로 **stomach** 위, 복부

한 몇 가지 정보를 드리겠습니다. 대부분 놀라시겠지만, 체로키어가 문자화된 것은 다소 최근의 일입니다. 이렇게 된 것은 체로키 인디언 전사인 Chekoya의 공로입니다. 그는 1809년 체로키어 알파벳 86개를 만들기 시작했습니다. 그는 영문법책을 이용하여 영어 기호들을 접했으며, 이 기호들이 체로키어의 소리를 표현하는 데 쓰였습니다. Chekoya의 작업은 1821년에 마무리되어, 사람들이 처음으로 체로키어를 읽고 쓸 수 있게 되었습니다.

Q What does the lecture mainly focus on?

(a) Chekoya's system of writing the Cherokee language

(b) Chekoya's compilation of ancient Cherokee writing

(c) learning to speak and write Cherokee

(d) Chekoya's Cherokee language book

이 강의가 주로 다루는 것은 무엇인가?

(a) 체코야의 체로키 언어 쓰기 체계

(b) 체코야의 고대 체로키 문서 편찬

(c) 체로키 언어 말하기와 쓰기 배우기

(d) 체코야의 체로키 언어 교재

해설 체로키 언어의 문자가 만들어진 배경을 설명하고 있다. 다소 최근에 Chekoya가 영문법책을 이용하여 영어 기호로 체로키 언어의 알파벳을 만들었다는 내용이다. 이 강의의 주제는 첫 문장인 Let me give you some information about ~에 잘 나와 있다.

함정 체로키 언어가 문자화된 것이 최근이므로 (b)에서 ancient Cherokee writing은 맞지 않다. ancient라는 말을 놓치면 정답이라고 착각하기 쉽다.

어휘 **credit** 공로, 공적 **warrior** 전사, 용사 **adapt** 적합하게 하다
capture 붙잡다, 손에 넣다 **compilation** 편찬

7

M: Let me give you some information about the writing system in the Cherokee language, <u>before going into the opening</u> chapter of our Cherokee language book. Most of <u>you will be surprised</u> to know that the written Cherokee language was developed rather recently. <u>The credit for this</u> goes to Cherokee Indian warrior Chekoya. He began creating the 86 letters of the Cherokee alphabet in 1809. He used an English grammar book to access English symbols <u>which were then adapted to capture sounds</u> in the Cherokee language. Chekoya's work <u>was completed in 1821</u>, making it possible for people to read and write Cherokee for the first time.

M: 체로키어 교재의 첫 챕터를 시작하기 전에 체로키어의 쓰기 체계에 관

8

M: Oh, I feel so good traveling by train.

W: Really? <u>Any specific reason for that</u>?

M: One is that you don't have <u>traffic congestion</u>.

W: You don't have that traveling by air. And it's faster.

M: But <u>I find trains to be more relaxing</u>. You have all the time to do whatever you want.

W: That's true. But I just want to get there as fast as I can.

M: Well, usually, airports are very far from cities and <u>it takes time to get to the airport</u>. And <u>you wait until boarding</u>, too. And trains are less expensive than planes.

W: I don't know. I still think we should take an airplane.

M: 와, 나는 기차여행이 너무 좋아.

W: 정말? 무슨 특별한 이유라도 있어?

M: 첫째로 교통체증이 없지.

W: 비행기 여행도 교통체증은 없어. 게다가 더 빠르잖아.

M: 하지만 난 기차가 마음이 더 편해. 그 시간에 하고 싶은 걸 다 할 수 있 거든.

W: 그건 맞아. 하지만 가능하면 더 빨리 거기 도착하고 싶어.

M: 음. 일반적으로 공항은 도시에서 너무 멀리 떨어져 있어서 공항까지 가는 데에 시간이 걸리지. 그리고 탑승할 때까지도 기다려야 해. 게다 가 기차가 비행기보다 덜 비싸잖아.

W: 잘 모르겠다. 그래도 우리가 비행기를 타고 가야 한다고 생각해.

Q What are the speakers mainly talking about?

(a) the types of transportation that they prefer

(b) the benefits of traveling by trains

(c) the cost of a train and a plane

(d) how to avoid traffic congestion

화자들은 주로 무엇에 대해 이야기하고 있는가?

(a) 그들이 선호하는 교통수단

(b) 기차로 여행하는 것의 장점

(c) 기차와 비행기 비용

(d) 교통체증을 피하는 방법

해설 남자가 기차로 여행하는 것이 너무 좋다고 하고, 여자는 빨리 가고 싶 기 때문에 비행기를 선호한다. 남자의 여러 설명에도 불구하고 여자는 여 전히 비행기를 타고 가고 싶다고 말하고 있다. 그러므로 이 대화는 남자와 여자가 선호하는 교통수단에 대한 것이다.

함정 (b), (c), (d)는 모두 선호하는 교통수단을 설명하기 위한 것으로 제 시되었을 뿐이다.

어휘 specific 특별한, 분명한, 구체적인
traffic congestion 교통체증, 교통혼잡
relaxing 긴장을 풀어주는, 마음을 가라앉혀 주는
boarding 탑승, 승선 | expensive 비싼 | still 아직도, 여전히

9 Relationship of Ideas

W: Books can't be called expensive, when you seriously consider them. In Boston you'd have to pay 9 dollars for a movie. A first-run showing of a major play would cost 300 dollars while front-row tickets to concerts or sports events cost about 150 dollars. Consider, however, that all these give only about 2-4 hours of entertainment. A good book, on the other hand, provides ten times as much. A single large, interesting book can take anywhere from 2 weeks to a month to read. Moreover, you can lend it to friends, thereby doubling or tripling its enjoyment. You can even sell it later, or give it to charity; things impossible to do with a movie or play. So, spending 25 dollars on a book seems pretty reasonable!

W: 책에 대해 진지하게 생각해 본다면 책값을 결코 비싸다고 할 수 없을 겁니다. 보스턴에서는 영화 값으로 9달러를 지불합니다. 일류 연극의 첫 무대 공연료는 300달러가 들 것이며 콘서트나 스포츠 경기의 제일 앞자리 티켓 가격은 150달러 정도 될 것입니다. 그러나 이 모든 것들이 고작 2~4시간의 여흥을 준다는 점을 생각해 보세요. 반면에 좋은 책은 그 열 배의 즐거움을 제공합니다. 두툼하고 재미있는 책 한 권은 어디라도 들고 다닐 수 있으며 읽는 데 2주 내지 한 달 가까이 걸립니다. 게다가 친구에게 도 빌려줄 수 있어서, (책 읽는) 즐거움을 두 배 또는 세 배로 늘릴 수 있습 니다. 나중에 팔 수도 있고 자선단체에 기부할 수도 있고 말이죠. 영화나 연극에서는 불가능한 일입니다. 그러니까 책 한 권에 25달러를 들이는 것 은 아주 합리적인 가격으로 보입니다.

Q What comparison does the speaker make between books and movies or plays?

(a) the price and the duration of enjoyment

(b) their cost and their convenience

(c) the benefits earned from reading or watching

(d) the amount of money that can be saved

화자가 책과 영화나 연극을 비교하는 것은 무엇인가?

(a) 가격과 즐거움의 기간

(b) 비용과 편리성

(c) 읽거나 보는 것에서 얻을 수 있는 장점

(d) 저축할 수 있는 금액

해설 영화나 연극에 비해 책에 들이는 돈이 더 합리적이라는 내용이다. 그 러므로 (a)가 정답이다.

어휘 major 주요한, 일류의 | showing (연극, 공연의) 상연 |
front-row 앞줄의, 앞좌석의 | entertainment 오락, 여흥 |
double 두 배로 하다, 배로 늘리다 | triple 세 배로 하다 |
charity 자선단체 | reasonable 적당한, 비싸지 않은

10

W: I heard you're planning a vacation to Australia. Have you reserved the tickets?

M: No, I tried doing so, but all the travel agencies were too expensive.

W: Why don't you try Premier Travel? They <u>offer many affordable packages</u>.

M: Are you sure? I've never heard of them.

W: I always get my travel booked through them.

M: Well, I'll check with them. Could you <u>give me their address</u>?

W: Sure, <u>it's here on this card</u>.

W: 네가 호주로 휴가 갈 계획이라고 들었는데. 표는 예약했니?

M: 아니. 하려고 했는데, 여행사들이 모두 너무 비쌌어.

W: 프리미어 트래블에서 해봐. 알맞은 가격의 여행상품을 많이 제공해 줘.

M: 정말? 들어 본 적 없는데.

W: 나는 항상 거기서 여행을 예약하거든.

M: 문의해 봐야겠다. 주소 좀 줄래?

W: 응, 이 카드에 적혀 있어.

Q What can be inferred from the conversation?

(a) The man will go to Australia with the woman.

(b) The woman does not like Premier Travel.

(c) The man is looking for an inexpensive ticket.

(d) The woman works overseas.

이 대화를 통해 유추할 수 있는 것은?

(a) 남자는 여자와 함께 호주에 갈 것이다.

(b) 여자는 프리미어 트래블을 좋아하지 않는다.

(c) 남자는 저렴한 티켓을 찾고 있다.

(d) 여자는 해외에서 일한다.

해설 남자는 휴가 때 호주로 여행갈 계획이지만, 여행사들이 제시하는 비행기표가 너무 비싸서 아직 예약하지 못했다. 이에 여자는 자신이 늘 저렴하게 이용하는 여행사를 소개시켜 주고 있는 장면이다. 따라서 남자는 저렴한 티켓을 찾고 있는 것이므로 정답은 (c)가 된다.

함정 남자는 여자가 말해주기 전까지 프리미어 트래블에 대해 전혀 몰랐으며, 여자의 소개로 그 여행사에 티켓을 문의해 보겠다고 하고 있는 것으로 보아, 여자가 프리미어 트래블을 싫어한다는 근거는 어디에도 없다. 따라서 (b)는 정답이 될 수 없다.

어휘 **reserve** 예약하다, 확보해 두다
travel agency 여행대리점, 여행사
affordable (가격 등이) 알맞은, 감당할 수 있는
inexpensive 값싼, 저렴한 **overseas** 해외에서, 외국으로

LISTENING REVIEW

A

1. disaster	2. rebuke
3. potential	4. aftermath
5. collapse	6. destructive
7. landslide	8. debris
9. modify	10. evident
11. ban	12. phenomenon
13. anonymous	14. insulting
15. discreet	16. interference

1. a very bad accident such as an earthquake or a plane crash, especially one in which a lot of people are killed

2. to speak severely to someone because they have said or done something that you do not approve of

3. the necessary abilities or qualities to become successful or useful in the future

4. the situation that results from an important event, especially a harmful one

5. to fall down very suddenly

6. being capable of causing great damage, harm, or injury

7. a large amount of earth and rocks falling down a cliff or the side of a mountain

8. pieces from something that has been destroyed or pieces of rubbish or unwanted material that are spread around

9. to change something slightly, usually in order to improve it

10. easily or clearly noticeable

11. to state officially that it must not be done, shown, or used

12. something that is observed to happen or exist

13. not letting people know that you were the person who did something

14. rude or offensive

15. polite and careful in what you do or say, because you want to avoid embarrassing or offending someone

16. unwanted or unnecessary involvement in something by a person or group

B

1. b   **2.** a   **3.** b   **4.** a   **5.** b

1. 그것은 친구가 생일 선물로 준 거예요.

   (a) It is my friend that gave me the gift for my birthday.

   (b) **My friend gave it to me as a gift for my birthday.**

2. 부작용들이 수년 동안 분명하게 드러나지 않을지도 몰라.

   (a) **Side effects may not be evident for many years.**

   (b) I'm not sure if any side effects are evident or not.

3. 직접적인 만남은 다양한 자극을 제공한다.

   (a) A variety of stimuli can cause face-to-face encounters.

   (b) **Face-to-face encounters provide a wide range of stimuli.**

4. 글자로만 의사소통을 하는 온라인에서는 이런 것들이 결여되어 있다.

   (a) **These are absent in online, text-only communications.**

   (b) Text-only communications are absent in online communication.

5. 이것은 전문가들이 제안한 전향적인 조치입니다.

   (a) This is the proactive step that experts take as suggested.

   (b) **This is a proactive step suggested by experts.**

C

1. Companies could be forced to comply with stricter guidelines.
2. Big businesses would certainly not like this to happen.
3. It was surprising to meet the artists on the way out.
4. I thought that it was very impressive.
5. The two share one common feature which puts them into the same family.

1. could be forced / companies / to comply with stricter guidelines

2. this to happen / would certainly not like / big businesses

3. to meet the artists / on the way out / it was surprising

4. it was / very impressive / I thought that

5. the same family / which puts them into / the two share one common feature

D

1. b   **2.** b   **3.** a   **4.** a   **5.** b

1. He used an English grammar book to access English symbols.

   (a) English symbols were used by him to access an English grammar book.

   (b) **He learned English symbols from an English grammar book.**

2. I still think we should have taken an airplane.

   (a) We might have to take an airplane next time.

   (b) **An airplane would have been a better choice.**

3. Consider that all these give only about 2-4 hours of entertainment.

   (a) **You should consider that you can only enjoy these for only 2-4 hours.**

   (b) You should consider these within only 2-4 hours of entertainment.

4. You can lend it to friends, thereby doubling or tripling its enjoyment.

   (a) **The enjoyment can be doubled or tripled by lending it to your friends.**

   (b) Your friends can enjoy it even more when you lend it to them.

5. They offer many affordable packages.

   (a) The package is more affordable than those they usually offer.

   (b) **The prices of the many packages they offer are cheap.**

VOCABULARY PREVIEW

01. bridegroom 신랑

02. innate 타고난, 선천적인

03. portray 묘사하다

04. homebound 집에 틀어박혀 있는

05. exotic 이국적인

06. accompany ~와 동행하다, 따라가다

07. frustration 좌절

08. abandon 그만두다, 단념하다

09. detection 발견, 간파

10. upcoming 다가오는, 이번의

11. generate 낳다, 생성하다

12. contractual 계약상의

13. obligation 의무, 책임

14. legendary 전설적인

15. captivate ~의 마음을 사로잡다

16. complication (의학) 합병증

17. avid 탐내는, 갈망하는

18. rub 바르다, 문지르다

19. remedy 치료, 치료법

20. restorative 회복시키는, 강장제의

21. bizarre 괴상한, 이상한

22. suspend 미루다, 일시 정지하다

23. inevitable 피할 수 없는, 당연한

24. recession 불황, 경기침체

GUIDED LISTENING

1 1. a 2. a   **2** 1. c 2. b
3 1. c 2. c   **4** 1. a 2. c

1 Conversation

W: I heard that you were in the hospital for a week. What happened?

M: Well, I was down with the flu.

W: Oh, how are you feeling now?

M: Much better, but I'm more worried about the chemistry classes I missed.

W: Don't worry. I'm sure you can quickly catch up. You can borrow my notes if you want.

M: Really? Well, I'd be very grateful to you if you lent them to me. Can I get them today?

W: Sure, but remember to give them back next week. We have a test coming up.

M: Okay, I won't forget.

W: 네가 일주일 동안 병원에 있었다고 들었어. 무슨 일이야?

M: 음, 독감에 걸렸었거든.

W: 아, 지금은 어때?

M: 훨씬 나아졌지만, 화학 수업 빼먹은 게 더 걱정이야.

W: 걱정하지 마. 금방 따라잡을 수 있을 거야. 원한다면 내 노트를 빌려 줄게.

M: 정말? 음, 네가 빌려 준다면 정말 고맙겠다. 오늘 줄 수 있어?

W: 물론이지, 하지만 다음 주에는 돌려줘야 한다는 걸 기억해 줘. 곧 시험이 있잖아.

M: 그래, 잊지 않을게.

Inference I

1 What can be inferred about the woman?

(a) She is taking the same class as the man.

(b) She took chemistry last semester.

(c) She doesn't need her notes for a test.

(d) She doesn't want the man to borrow her notes.

여자에 대해 추론할 수 있는 것은?

(a) 남자와 같은 수업을 듣는다.

(b) 지난 학기에 화학을 수강했다.

(c) 시험을 위해 노트가 필요하지 않다.

(d) 남자가 자기 노트를 빌려가기를 원하지 않는다.

해설 아파서 화학 수업에 빠졌던 남자에게 여자가 노트를 빌려주겠다는 대화이다. 시험이 있으므로 다음 주에는 돌려달라고 당부하고 있으므로, 여자와 남자와 같은 화학 수업을 듣는다는 것을 알 수 있다.

Comprehension

2 Which is correct according to the conversation?

(a) The man had an illness.

(b) The woman wants her notes back today.

(c) The woman has recently passed a test.

(d) The man does not like chemistry.

이 대화에 의하면 옳은 것은 무엇인가?

(a) 남자는 병이 났었다.

(b) 여자는 오늘 노트를 돌려받고 싶어 한다.

(c) 최근에 여자는 시험에 합격했다.

(d) 남자는 화학을 좋아하지 않는다.

해설 남자는 감기에 걸려 수업에 빠졌던 것이었으므로, (a)의 내용을 알 수 있다.

함정 여자는 다음 주에 노트를 돌려달라고 했으므로 (b)는 오답이며, (c)와 (d)는 언급되지 않은 내용이다.

어휘 down with 병으로 누워 있는 | chemistry class 화학 수업 | miss 빠뜨리다, 빼먹다 | catch up 따라잡다 | borrow 빌리다, 차용하다 | grateful 감사하고 있는, 고마워하는

2 Conversation

W: This is a no-parking zone. <u>You can't park here</u>.

M: I didn't know that. Is it <u>written anywhere</u>?

W: It's on the board. Can't you read it?

M: I'm sorry, but I have to park my car here. I'm waiting for a bridegroom.

W: This is against traffic rules, so please <u>drive off</u>.

M: Well, I can't go without taking the bridegroom. We're already late for his wedding.

W: <u>That can't be helped</u>. If you don't move on, I'll have <u>to write you a ticket</u>.

M: Okay, I'm going. I need to find another parking space, I guess.

W: 여기는 주차금지 구역입니다. 여기 주차하면 안 됩니다.

M: 몰랐네요. 어디에라도 쓰여 있나요?

W: 저기 게시판에요. 읽지 못하나요?

M: 죄송하지만, 저는 여기에 주차해야 해요. 신랑을 기다리고 있거든요.

W: 교통 규칙에 위배되는 것이니까, 차를 빼 주세요.

M: 음, 신랑을 태우지 않으면 갈 수 없어요. 벌써 결혼식에 늦었거든요.

W: 어쩔 수 없어요. 옮기지 않으면, 교통 딱지를 떼야 합니다.

M: 알겠어요, 갈게요. 다른 주차 공간을 찾아봐야겠군요.

Inference I

1 What can be inferred about the man?

(a) He will not move his car until his friend comes.

(b) He is getting married today.

(c) He didn't see the no-parking sign before he parked.

(d) He got a ticket at the same place before.

남자에 대해 추론할 수 있는 것은?

(a) 친구가 올 때까지 차를 움직이지 않을 것이다.

(b) 오늘 결혼할 것이다.

(c) 주차하기 전에 주차 금지 표지판을 보지 못했다.

(d) 전에 같은 장소에서 딱지를 떼었다.

해설 주차단속원인 여자와 불법 주차를 하고 있는 남자와의 대화이다. 남자의 Is it written anywhere?라는 질문에 여자가 Can't you read it?라고 대답하는 것으로 보아, 남자가 주차하기 전에 주차 금지 표시를 보지 못했다는 것을 알 수 있다.

함정 (a) 교통 딱지를 떼겠다고 하자, 차를 빼겠다고 말했다. (b) 남자가 아니라 남자의 친구가 오늘 결혼할 것이다.

Detail

2 What is the man's problem?

(a) His car won't work.

(b) He is late for a wedding.

(c) He doesn't know how to drive.

(d) He failed to pay a ticket.

남자의 문제는 무엇인가?

(a) 차가 작동하지 않는다.

(b) 결혼식에 늦었다.

(c) 운전할 줄 모른다.

(d) 범칙금을 내지 못했다.

해설 차를 옮겨달라는 여자의 말에 남자는 결혼식에 데려갈 신랑을 기다리고 있는데 이미 늦었다고 답하고 있으므로, 남자의 문제는 (b)임을 알 수 있다.

어휘 no-parking zone 주차금지 구역 | park 주차하다 | bridegroom 신랑 | drive off (차 따위가) 떠나버리다 | write a ticket 교통 위반 딱지를 떼다

3 Monologue

W: Everyone has <u>an innate talent that needs to be recognized</u> and given enough room for growth. Henry James, the famous novelist who portrayed the upper class of American society, is the best example in this context. He might have never imagined that he could become <u>famous enough to be counted among the best-known figures</u> of the 19th century. Henry James was always <u>overshadowed by his brother</u> William James, who was more educated than him and was a professor of law at Harvard University. As a result, he was never recognized by others early in his life. He also <u>suffered from ill health</u>, making him homebound most of the time. This gave him <u>an opportunity to direct all his energy into writing</u>. Gradually his works gained popularity and he gained recognition as a great writer.

W: 모든 사람은 타고난 재능이 있으므로 이를 인정받으며 성장할 수 있도록 충분한 기회를 받아야 합니다. 미국 사회의 상류 계층을 묘사했던 유명한 소설가인 Henry James는 이런 상황의 가장 좋은 본보기입니다. 그는 자신이 19세기의 가장 잘 알려진 인물들에 속할 만큼 충분히 유명해지리라고 결코 상상하지 못했을 것입니다. Henry James는 항상 그의 형인 William James의 그늘에 가려져 있었는데, William James는 Henry James보다 더 많은 교육을 받았고 하버드 법대의 교수였습니다. 그 결과, 그는 그의 생애 초기에는 다른 사람들의 인정을 받지 못했습니다. 그는 또한 좋지 않은 건강 때문에 고생했는데, 그로 인해 대부분의 시간 동안 집에 묶여 있어야 했습니다. 이것은 그의 모든 에너지를 글쓰기에 몰두하게 하는 기회를 주었습니다. 점차적으로 그의 작품은 인기를 얻게 되었고, 그는 위대한 작가로 인정을 받게 되었습니다.

Inference I

1   What can be inferred about Henry James?

(a) He didn't like his brother when he was young.

(b) He enjoyed staying home rather than going outside.

(c) He became recognized slowly over a long period of time.

(d) He wanted to study at Harvard University.

해설 모든 사람에게는 타고난 재능이 있다는 것이 주제이며, Henry James를 예로 들어 설명하고 있다. Henry James는 똑똑한 형 때문에 어렸을 때는 주목을 받지 못했다. 건강이 좋지 않아 집에 있는 시간이 많아서 글쓰기에 몰두하여, 나중에는 위대한 작가로서 인정을 받게 되었다는 내용이다. 그러므로 (c)가 정답이다.

합정 (a) 형보다 못했지만, 그가 형을 좋아하지 않았는지는 알 수 없다. (b) 건강이 좋지 않아 집에 있는 시간이 많았다는 내용이지 그걸 좋아했는지는 알 수 없다. (d) 형이 하버드 대학의 교수였다는 내용만 있다.

Comprehension

2   Which is correct according to the lecture?

(a) Some people are just born more talented.

(b) Henry James didn't receive proper education.

(c) Henry James spent a lot of time at home.

(d) People started to recognize him when he went to Harvard.

해설 건강이 좋지 않아 집에 있는 시간이 많아서 글쓰기에 몰두하여, 나중에는 위대한 작가로서 인정을 받게 되었다는 내용이다. 그러므로 (c)가 옳다.

합정 (a) 누구나 재능을 가지고 태어난다고 되어 있다. (b) Henry James의 교육에 관한 언급은 없다. (d) Henry James는 나중에 위대한 작가로 인정되었다.

어휘 innate 타고난, 선천적인 | room 여지, 기회 | novelist 소설가 | portray 묘사하다 | upper 상위의 | context 문맥, 상황, 사정 | count ~의 축에 들다, ~으로 간주하다 | figure 인물 | overshadow 그늘지게 하다, 어둡게 하다 | suffer from ~으로 고생하다 | homebound 집에 틀어박혀 있는 | recognition 인지, 인정

4 Monologue

M: Good evening, ladies and gentlemen. Welcome to Shop Town! Hope you are having a good time <u>shopping with our bargain prices</u>! Hurry up, because today is the last day of our Thanksgiving Day sale! Our prices have never been as attractive: you can <u>get 20 to 60% off on all goods</u>, from clothing to footwear and from pots to exotic gift sets. Don't delay, because <u>supplies are limited and are running out quickly</u>. For kids, we have an exciting discount on a variety of toys, books and kids' wear. Attention, Shop Town Card Members! With your membership you can <u>receive an extra 15% off</u> in addition to the already existing discounted prices.

M: 신사숙녀 여러분, 안녕하십니까. Shop Town에 오신 것을 환영합니다! 할인 판매가로 쇼핑하시면서 즐거운 시간이 되기를 바랍니다! 서두르십시오, 오늘이 추수감사절 할인행사의 마지막 날이기 때문입니다! 가격이 이렇게 매력적이었던 때는 없었습니다. 의류에서 신발까지, 그릇에서 이국적인 선물 세트에 이르기까지의 모든 물건을 20에서 60%까지 할인하여 구입할 수 있습니다. 지체하지 마십시오, 물품이 한정되어 있고 금방 바닥날 것이기 때문입니다. 아이들을 위해서는, 다양한 장난감, 서적과 아동 의류에 있어서 신나는 할인행사를 합니다. Shop Town 카드 회원님들은 주목해 주세요! 회원일 경우에는, 기존의 할인가에서 15% 추가 할인을 받으실 수 있습니다.

Inference I

1 What can be inferred about Shop Town?

(a) They are providing discounts for limited time.

(b) They ran out of most of their supplies.

(c) They don't offer any discounts for non-members.

(d) They are closing the store after this sale.

Shop Town에 대해서 추론할 수 있는 것은 무엇인가?

(a) 한정된 기간 동안 할인 판매가 진행 중이다.

(b) 대부분의 물품이 바닥났다.

(c) 비회원에게는 할인이 되지 않는다.

(d) 이번 세일 후에는 가게 문을 닫는다.

해설 추수감사절 할인행사에 대한 안내방송이다. 오늘이 할인 마지막 날이며, 얼마나 할인되는지, 회원일 경우에는 어떻게 되는지에 대한 언급이 있다. 그러므로 (a)가 정답이다.

함정 (b) 곧 바닥날 수 있다고 했지, 이미 그렇다는 내용은 아니다. (c) 누구에게나 할인이 되며, 회원을 위한 추가 할인이 언급되어 있다.

Detail

2 What is the maximum discount the members can get?

(a) 60 %

(b) 80 %

(c) 75 %

(d) 70 %

회원이 받을 수 있는 최대 할인은 얼마인가?

(a) 60 %

(b) 80 %

(c) 75 %

(d) 70 %

해설 누구에게나 20에서 60%까지 할인이 제공되며, 회원에게는 15% 추가 할인이 된다고 했으므로, 최대 할인은 75%일 것이다.

어휘 **Thanksgiving Day** 추수감사절
attractive 매력적인, 마음을 끄는   **footwear** 신발류   **pot** 그릇
exotic 이국적인   **delay** 지체하다   **run out** 바닥이 나다
a variety of 다양한   **extra** 추가의

PRACTICAL LISTENING

1. c	2. b	3. b	4. b	5. a
6. d	7. d	8. a	9. c	10. c

1

W: I heard that the new shopping mall is very big. <u>Have you been there</u>?

M: No. How about you?

W: No, <u>I haven't been there either</u>. But I'm planning to go there this weekend.

M: Would you mind <u>if I accompanied you</u>? I need to do some shopping.

W: Not at all, <u>provided you don't mind meeting my friends</u>.

M: Are you going along with them?

W: Yeah, we've had this plan for the last two weeks.

W: 새로 생긴 쇼핑몰이 굉장히 크다던데, 가 본 적 있니?

M: 아니, 넌?

W: 나도 안 가 봤어. 근데 이번 주말에 가 볼 계획이야.

M: 나도 같이 가도 될까? 쇼핑할 게 있어서.

W: 물론이지, 내 친구들과 만나는 걸 싫어하지 않다면 말이야.

M: 친구들과 같이 갈 거야?

W: 응, 2주 전부터 계획한 거야.

Q Which is correct according to the conversation?

(a) The man usually goes to the shopping mall.

(b) The woman has been to the shopping mall once.

(c) The woman and her friends are going to the mall.

(d) The man does not want to meet the woman's friends.

대화에 의하면 옳은 것은?

(a) 남자는 주로 그 쇼핑몰에 간다.

(b) 여자는 그 쇼핑몰에 한 번 가 봤다.

(c) 여자와 친구들은 쇼핑몰에 갈 것이다.

(d) 남자는 여자의 친구들을 만나고 싶어 하지 않는다.

해설 새로 생긴 대형 쇼핑몰에 관한 대화이다. 둘 다 아직 가 본 적이 없으며, 여자는 이번 주말에 친구들과 함께 그곳에 갈 계획이다. 남자가 같이 가도 되냐고 묻자, 이에 여자는 친구들과 같이 가는 것이 괜찮다면, 같이 가도 좋다고 답하고 있다. 따라서 (c)가 정답이다. 나머지 (a)와 (b)는 오답이며, (d)는 언급되지 않았다.

어휘 either (부정문에서) ~도 또한 plan to ~할 작정이다

would you mind if ~해도 괜찮겠습니까?

accompany ~와 동행하다, ~을 따라가다

do some shopping 쇼핑하다, 장보다

not at all 천만에, 그렇지 않다 provided 만약 ~라면

mind -ing ~을 싫어하다, 꺼리다 along with ~와 함께, 같이

2

W: I'm going to start this talk on dyslexia by referring to dyslexic children and <u>their feelings of hopelessness and frustration at school</u>. They typically <u>blame themselves for doing badly</u>. In extreme cases, dyslexia can cause a child to eventually get into criminal trouble, as he or she abandons school for "street" activities. While early detection of dyslexia is one of the main ways to resolve it, another method is to get schools and teachers to <u>change their attitudes towards children with regards to this problem</u>. It's important to remember that children with dyslexia are not people who can't or don't want to learn, they merely do so differently from others. Also, it's often the negative treatment they receive that turns them off of learning.

W: 독서 장애가 있는 아이들, 그들이 학교에서 느끼는 절망감과 좌절에 대해 얘기하는 것으로 난독증에 관한 강의를 시작할까 합니다. 독서 장애를 가진 아이들은 일반적으로 자신이 글을 잘 읽지 못하는 것에 대해 스스로를 탓합니다. 극단적인 경우에는 난독증이 있는 아이들은 학교를 포기하고 '거리'에서 생활하여 결국 범죄 문제에 연루되는 원인이 되기도 합니다. 이 문제를 해결하는 주요 방법 중의 하나는 초기 발견입니다만, 또 다른 방법은 학교나 교사들이 이런 문제를 지닌 아이들을 대하는 태도를 바꾸는 것입니다. 난독증이 있는 아이들이 학습을 할 수 없거나 학습하기를

싫어하는 아이들이 아니라, 단지 다른 아이들과 다를 뿐이라는 점을 인식하는 것이 중요합니다. 또한 이들을 학습으로부터 멀어지게 하는 것도 이런 부정적인 취급을 받기 때문인 경우가 종종 있습니다.

Q Which is correct about children with dyslexia according to the talk?

(a) They must be taught in special schools.

(b) They are students who learn differently.

(c) They need to stop engaging in crime.

(d) They tend to lag behind at school even with extra help.

이 이야기에 따르면 난독증이 있는 아이들에 관해 사실인 것은?

(a) 그들은 특수학교에서 교육받아야 한다.

(b) 그들은 다른 방식으로 학습하는 학생들이다.

(c) 그들은 범죄 가담을 중단해야 한다.

(d) 그들은 특별 도움을 받고도 학교에서 뒤처지는 경향이 있다.

해설 난독증 증세가 있는 아이들에 대해 설명하고 있다. 난독증을 겪는 아이들은 학습 능력이 없거나 학습 의사가 없는 것이 아니라 다른 아이들과 학습 방법이 다르므로 이들에 대한 부정적인 태도를 바꿀 필요가 있음을 주지시키고 있다. 따라서 정답은 (b)이다.

함정 일부의 경우에 범죄에 가담하는 경우가 있다는 사실적 언급은 있었으나, 그 사실에 대한 강사의 견해는 나타나 있지 않으며, 이들의 학습 성과와 특별 교육에 관한 언급도 없으므로 (c)나 (d)는 답이 될 수 없다.

어휘 dyslexia 난독증 refer to ~을 언급하다

dyslexic 독서 장애의, 독서 장애자

hopelessness 가망 없음, 절망 frustration 좌절

blame A for B B에 대해 A를 비난하다

abandon 그만두다, 단념하다 detection 발견, 간파

resolve 해결하다 merely 단지, 다만 engage in ~에 가담하다

lag behind 뒤지다, 뒤떨어지다

3 Inference I

(Telephone rings.)

W: Hello, Sam. This is Lucy here.

M: Hi Lucy. What's up?

W: Well, <u>I've prepared a new Italian dish</u>. Would you like to <u>try it out</u>?

M: Thanks, Lucy. But I <u>need to work on some urgent papers</u>. I can't come over now.

W: Then let me bring it to your place.

M: That'd be great. Are you sure it would be no problem?

W: I'm just two doors from you. I could walk it over. You could take a break from your studies while we eat.

M: Sounds like a plan! I'll be waiting for you.

- -

(전화벨이 울린다.)

W: 안녕, 샘. 나 루시야.

M: 안녕, 루시. 웬일이야?

W: 음, 이탈리아 요리를 준비했는데, 한번 먹어 볼래?

M: 고마워, 루시. 근데 급한 보고서를 써야 해서, 지금 갈 수가 없어.

W: 그럼 내가 네네 집으로 가져다줄게.

M: 너무 좋지. 그렇게 해 줄 수 있겠어?

W: 두 집 건너인데 뭘. 걸어갈 수 있어. 먹는 동안 일에서 잠깐 쉴 수 있잖아.

M: 좋은 생각이야! 기다릴게.

Q What can be inferred about the woman?

(a) She likes cooking some Italian food.

(b) She doesn't want the man to miss her food.

(c) She will wait until the man finishes the papers.

(d) She wants the man to finish his papers early.

- -

여자에 대해 추론할 수 있는 것은?

(a) 이탈리아 음식을 요리하는 것을 좋아한다.

(b) 남자가 자신의 음식을 먹지 못하게 되는 것을 원하지 않는다.

(c) 남자가 보고서를 끝낼 때까지 기다릴 것이다.

(d) 남자가 보고서를 빨리 끝내기를 바란다.

해설 이웃에 살고 있는 남녀의 대화이다. 남자는 급한 보고서 때문에 여자가 만든 이탈리아 요리를 가서 먹을 수 없다고 하자, 여자가 직접 음식을 가지고 가겠다(let me bring it to your place)고 말하고 있다. 남자가 그 음식을 꼭 먹기를 바라는 여자의 마음을 알 수 있으므로 정답은 (b)가 된다.

함정 이탈리아 음식을 요리했지만, 여자가 요리하는 것을 즐기는지는 알 수 없으므로 (a)는 정답이 아니다.

어휘 prepare (요리 등을) 준비하다, 차리다 ┃ dish 접시, 요리 ┃ try out 시험하다 ┃ urgent 긴급한 ┃ paper 서류, 문서, (연구)논문, 보고서 ┃ take a break 잠시 휴식을 취하다 ┃ while ~하는 동안 ┃ wait for ~을 기다리다

4

W: How do you commute to the office?

M: By subway. It saves a lot of time.

W: I've found it crowded most of the time. Do you always get a seat?

M: Yes. I usually never have problems doing that. However, when I do, I have to stand for one and a half hours.

W: One and half hours is quite long! What do you do during that time?

M: I usually read books. I'm an avid reader.

W: That's a good way to kill time.

M: Yeah, I've actually started loving the ride because I get so much time to myself.

- -

W: 회사에 어떻게 통근하니?

M: 지하철로. 시간이 많이 절약돼.

W: 지하철은 대개 붐비던데. 항상 자리에 앉니?

M: 응. 보통 앉는 데는 전혀 문제가 없어. 하지만 못 앉으면 한 시간 반 동안이나 서서 와야 돼.

W: 한 시간 반이면 꽤 긴 시간이네! 그 동안 뭐 하니?

M: 주로 책을 읽어. 난 열렬한 독서가거든.

W: 시간 보내기엔 좋은 방법이지.

M: 응. 실은 내 자신을 위한 시간을 많이 가질 수 있어서 지하철 타는 것이 좋아지기 시작했어.

Q What is the main topic of the conversation?

(a) what books the man reads while commuting

(b) the man's commute to work by subway

(c) how the man gets a seat on the subway

(d) the man's opinion about subway services

- -

대화의 주요 화제는?

(a) 통근시간에 남자가 무슨 책을 읽는지

(b) 남자의 지하철 통근

(c) 지하철에서 남자가 어떻게 자리에 앉는지

(d) 지하철 서비스에 대한 남자의 견해

해설 남자의 통근수단에 관한 대화이다. 남자는 한 시간 반 동안 지하철을 타고 출퇴근하고 있으며, 그 시간 동안 주로 독서를 한다. 그는 지하철을 타는 동안에 자기 자신을 위한 시간을 보낼 수 있어서 지하철 통근을 좋아하기 시작했다. 따라서 대화의 주된 화제는 (b)이다.

함정 통근시간에 남자는 주로 책을 읽지만, 무슨 책을 읽는지는 언급되지 않았으므로 (a)는 오답이다. 또한 남자는 주로 지하철에서 자리에 앉는 편이지만, 어떻게 자리를 구해서 앉는지에 대한 언급은 없다. 따라서 (c)도 오답이다. (d)는 언급되지 않았다.

어휘 commute 통근하다, 통학하다 ┃ crowded 혼잡한, 붐비는 ┃ most of 대부분의 ┃ avid 열심인, 열광적인 ┃ kill time 시간을 보내다, 소일하다 ┃ ride (탈 것에) 타기, 타고 가기, 타고 있는 시간

5 Inference I

M: I have a few concerns about our upcoming business deal with Olsons Inc. We need to rethink our position <u>before signing any contract with</u> that company. Olsons is a great potential customer that may be able to generate millions of dollars worth of revenue each year for us. <u>That is the upside</u>. However, we also know that our company does not currently have <u>enough capital to complete major orders</u> for them. We <u>lack the machinery</u> to create enough goods to meet their demand. This means that we would need to borrow heavily in order to meet our contractual obligations with Olsons. There are <u>big risks involved</u>, as you know, and I'm seriously worried about them.

M: Olsons 사와의 이번 사업 거래와 관련하여 몇 가지 염려되는 점이 있습니다. Olsons 사와 어떤 계약을 하기에 앞서, 우리(회사)의 입지에 대해 재고할 필요가 있습니다. Olsons 사는 자사를 위해 매년 수백만 달러의 수익을 창출해낼 수 있는 대단히 잠재력 있는 고객입니다. 그 점이 좋은 측면입니다. 그러나 우리는 또한 현재 자사가 그들의 대형 주문을 충족시킬 만한 충분한 자본이 없다는 것을 알고 있습니다. 우리는 그들의 수요를 충족시킬 만큼의 충분한 물자를 만들어낼 기계가 부족합니다. 이는 우리가 Olsons과의 계약 의무를 실행키 위해서는 상당한 비용을 차용해야 한다는 것을 의미합니다. 아시다시피 여기에는 큰 위험이 따르고, 저는 이 점이 심히 염려되는 바입니다.

Q What can be inferred about the speaker?

(a) The speaker has doubts about taking out loans.

(b) The speaker considers the terms of the contract unfair.

(c) The speaker objects to Olsons' high demands.

(d) The speaker is worried over the company's reduced revenues.

화자에 대해 추론할 수 있는 것은?

(a) 대출을 받는 것에 관해 회의적이다.

(b) 계약 조항들이 불공평하다고 생각한다.

(c) Olsons 사의 높은 요구사항에 반대한다.

(d) 자사의 자산 축소에 대해 걱정하고 있다.

해설 Olsons 사와의 큰 거래 계약을 앞두고 회사의 현재 위치에 관해 재고해야 함을 주장하고 있는 내용이다. Olsons 사의 높은 수요를 충족시키려면 외부로부터 자금을 들여와야 하는데, 이 점이 염려된다고 밝히고 있다. 따라서 정답은 (a)이다.

함정 화자는 Olsons 사의 물량 주문 자체에 반대하는 것이 아니라, 물량 수요를 맞추기에는 역부족인 여러 가지 문제점들을 제기하고 있다. 따라서 (c)는 화자의 요지를 벗어난 잘못된 추측이 된다.

어휘 upcoming 다가오는, 이번의 │ sign a contract 계약하다 │ potential 가능성이 있는, 잠재하는 │ generate 낳다, 생성하다 │ revenue 수익, 총수입 │ upside 위쪽, (가격 등의) 상승 경향 │ capital 자본, 자산 │ contractual 계약상의 │ obligation 의무, 책임 │ involved 포함된

6

M: Inkahta Music Company today announced <u>the death of legendary</u> Swahili singer Nelson Arutha, <u>following a long illness</u>. Arutha was the lead singer in the 1970s group "The African Tigers" which first introduced Swahili music to the world. The Swahili rhythms <u>captivated listeners</u> around the world, from London to Beijing, and even <u>breathed new life into the study</u> of Swahili culture, history and language. Indeed, Swahili emerged as one of the few African languages that Westerners have at least <u>a passing knowledge about</u>. Known for his gravelly voice, he was a popular figure among the old and young alike. Arutha was famed for going into the audience and encouraging people to dance, from kids to grandmothers. His death is said to be from complications due to lung disease.

M: Inkahta 음악 회사는 오늘 스와힐리 출신의 전설적인 가수 Nelson Arutha가 오랜 투병 끝에 사망했다는 소식을 전했습니다. Arutha는 1970년대 스와힐리 음악을 세계에 처음으로 소개한 "아프리칸 타이거"라는 그룹의 리드싱어였습니다. 스와힐리 리듬은 영국 런던에서 중국 베이징에 이르기까지 전 세계 청중들을 사로잡았고, 스와힐리 문화, 역사, 언어 연구에 새로운 숨결을 불어넣었습니다. 실제, 스와힐리어는 서양인들이 적어도 한 번쯤 알게 되는 몇 안 되는 아프리카 언어 중의 하나로 부상했습니다. 귀에 거슬리는 듯한 목소리로 잘 알려진 그는 젊은이나 나이 많은 청중들에게도 인기 있는 가수였습니다. Arutha는 청중에게 직접 다가가 아이들에서부터 할머니에 이르기까지 (공연 도중) 춤을 추도록 이끌었던 가수로 유명했습니다. 그의 죽음은 폐질환에 따른 합병증인 것으로 밝혀졌습니다.

Q Which is correct according to the talk?

(a) His music company will re-launch his music.

(b) His style of music is no longer popular in Africa.

(c) His songs described Africa's traditional legends.

(d) His band made Swahili music known internationally.

이 이야기에 따르면 옳은 것은?

(a) 그의 음악 회사는 그의 음악을 재발매할 것이다.

(b) 그의 음악 스타일은 아프리카에서 더 이상 대중적이지 않다.

(c) 그의 노래는 아프리카의 전통적인 전설을 묘사했다.

(d) 그의 밴드는 스와힐리 음악을 세계적으로 유명하게 만들었다.

해설 스와힐리 출신의 전설적인 가수가 폐질환으로 사망한 소식을 전하는 뉴스이다. Arutha가 속한 그룹이 스와힐리 음악을 세계에 처음 소개함으로써 스와힐리 음악 뿐 아니라, 언어와 문화를 알리는 데 공헌했다고 설명하고 있으므로 (d)가 정답이다.

함정 (c)는 legendary(전설적인, 대단히 유명한)와 legend(전설)의 유사한 발음을 빌미로 제시된 보기이다. 정확한 발음을 캐치하지 못했다 하더라도 문맥상 스와힐리 전설에 대한 이야기가 아니라는 정도는 이해할 수 있어야 한다.

어휘 legendary 전설적인 ‖ Swahili 스와힐리 사람
captivate ~의 마음을 사로잡다 ‖
breathe (생기·생명·영혼 따위를) 불어넣다 ‖
emerge 나타나다, 알려지다 ‖ passing 지나가는, 접하게 되는 ‖
gravelly 목소리가 귀에 거슬리는 ‖ figure 인물, 거물 ‖
complication 합병증 ‖ lung disease 폐질환

7

M: Cosmetics, as I have mentioned, date back to ancient Egypt. Cosmetics do not refer simply to items such as lipstick or coloring nor do they <u>have to do solely</u> with women. Men have also been <u>avid users</u> of cosmetics to improve their appearance, in particular their hair. Since ancient times, <u>men have tried many solutions to the problem of hair loss</u>. The ancient Egyptians rubbed animal fat over their bald spots, in the hope that it would cause hair to re-grow. In ancient Rome, Julius Caesar wore his characteristic laurel wreath low in order to hide <u>a receding hairline</u>. No doubt these sound silly to us today, but modern remedies ranging from hair restorative lotions to toupees are <u>equally bizarre and certainly just as ineffective</u>.

M: 말씀드렸다시피 화장품(의 기원)은 고대 이집트 시대로 거슬러 올라갑니다. 화장품이라고 해서 단순히 립스틱이나 색조 화장품 같은 것을 의미하지는 않습니다. 또한 단지 여성용만도 아니지요. 남성들 역시 외모를 개선하기 위해, 특히 머리카락과 관련하여 화장품 사용에 열성적이었습니다. 고대 시대부터 남성들은 탈모증 문제를 해결하기 위해 여러 해결책들을 시도해왔습니다. 고대 이집트인들은 머리가 빠진 부분에 동물성 기름을 문질렀습니다. 머리카락이 다시 자라게 될 것이라는 희망을 가지고서 말입니다. 고대 로마 시대에 줄리어스 시저는 앞 머리카락이 자꾸 빠지는 것(앞머리가 빠져 앞쪽 머리선이 뒤로 밀려나는 모양)을 감추려고 특별한 월계관을 아래쪽으로 내려썼습니다. 요즘에는 이런 일들이 분명 어리석게 보입니다만 머리카락 회생용 로션부터 부분 가발에 이르는 현대 치료법들도 마찬가지로 괴상하고 효과 없기는 마찬가지입니다.

Q Which is correct about hair loss according to the talk?

(a) Hair loss has increased since Ancient Egyptian times.

(b) Ancient Egyptian cosmetics were usually derived from laurels.

(c) Julius Caesar is believed to have used animal fat for hair-styling.

(d) Modern means to fight hair loss are no better than ancient ones.

강의에 따르면 탈모와 관련하여 사실인 것은?

(a) 고대 이집트 시대 이후 탈모는 계속 증가했다.

(b) 고대 이집트 화장품은 주로 월계수에서 얻어낸 것들이다.

(c) 줄리어스 시저는 헤어 스타일링을 위해 동물성 지방을 사용했던 것으로 생각된다.

(d) 탈모 방지를 위한 현대적 수단들도 고대의 방법들보다 나을 것이 없다.

해설 남성 탈모증 해결을 위해 사용된 화장 방법에 대한 강의이다. 고대로부터 화장품은 여성용만이 아닌 남성용으로도 사용되어 왔으며, 특히 남성 탈모증을 감추기(치료하기) 위한 하나의 방법으로 사용되어 왔음을 명시하고 있다. 마지막 문장에서 현대적 방법들도 고대의 방법과 마찬가지로 괴상하고 비효과적이라고 했으므로 정답은 (d)이다.

함정 (c) 동물성 지방은 시저가 아니라 고대 이집트인들이 사용했던 방법이다.

어휘 cosmetics 화장품 ‖ have to do with ~와 관련이 있다 ‖
avid 탐내는, 갈망하는 ‖ appearance 외모, 모양 ‖ hair loss 탈모 ‖
rub 바르다, 문지르다 ‖ fat 지방 ‖ laurel wreath 월계관 ‖
in order to ~하기 위해서 ‖ recede 물러나다, 멀어지다 ‖
remedy 치료, 치료법 ‖ restorative 회복시키는, 강장제의 ‖
toupee (남자용) 부분 가발 ‖ bizarre 괴상한, 이상한

---

8 Inference I

(Telephone rings.)

M: Hello, this is Steven from Trix Supermarket.

W: Hi, I saw <u>your job advertisement</u>. I need some more details about it.

M: Okay, what would you like to know?

W: Well, what's the salary for this job?

M: <u>Minimum wage</u> would be the starting pay.

W: Are you sure? Is there <u>anything extra for experienced applicants</u>?

M: Well, it's <u>the standard rate</u> for everybody <u>seeking this position</u>.

（전화벨이 울린다.）

M: 안녕하세요. 트릭스 슈퍼마켓의 스티븐입니다.

W: 안녕하세요. 구인광고를 봤는데, 상세한 정보가 더 필요해서요.

M: 네, 무엇을 알고 싶으세요?

W: 음. 급여가 얼마인가요?

M: 처음에는 최저임금일 겁니다.

W: 정말이요? 경력자 특별 수당 같은 건 없나요?

M: 음, 그게 일자리를 구하는 모든 사람들의 표준임금입니다.

Q What can be inferred about the speakers?

(a) The woman thinks the pay is low.

(b) The man is irritated by the woman.

(c) The man is considering more pay for experienced workers.

(d) The woman doesn't like shopping.

화자들에 대해 추측할 수 있는 것은?

(a) 여자는 급여가 적다고 생각한다.

(b) 남자는 여자 때문에 짜증이 난다.

(c) 남자는 경력자에게 좀 더 많은 급여를 고려하고 있다.

(d) 여자는 쇼핑을 좋아하지 않는다.

해설 여자가 슈퍼마켓의 구인광고를 보고 전화를 걸어서 급여에 관해 물어보는 장면이다. 남자가 표준임금에 따라 초기의 최저임금을 제시하자, 여자는 정말이냐면서 경력자 추가수당 같은 건 없는지 재차 확인하고 있다. 여기서 여자가 제시된 급여를 만족스러워 하지 않음을 알 수 있다. 따라서 정답은 (a)이다.

함정 남자가 여자 때문에 짜증낼 만한 장면은 전혀 없으므로 (b)는 오답이다. 급여가 적다고 여긴 여자가 경력자 추가 수당을 물어 보지만, 남자는 초기에 최저임금을 주는 것이 표준임금이라고 일축해 버린다. 즉, 경력자를 위해 더 높은 급여를 고려하고 있는 것이 아니므로 (c)는 오답이다.

어휘 job advertisement 구인 광고   details 상세한 설명
minimum wage 최저 임금   starting pay 초봉
extra 추가의, 여분의, 특별한, 별도의   experienced 경험이 있는
applicant 지원자, 신청자   standard 표준의, 기준이 되는
rate 요금, 임금   irritate ~을 짜증나게 하다, 화나게 하다

9

M: There's a rumor going around the office that our bonuses have been temporarily suspended.

W: Yeah, I've heard that. It was inevitable.

M: Why do you say so?

W: The market is experiencing an economic recession and every company has to take measures to cut expenses and maintain stability.

M: Aren't there other ways of doing that?

W: Yes, there are. Our benefits could be reduced, working hours increased or employees told to leave.

M: I do understand. Those would all be unpleasant. Even so, suspending the bonuses is very unfair.

M: 보너스 지급이 일시 중단됐다는 소문이 사무실에 떠돌고 있어.

W: 응, 나도 들었어. 피할 수 없는 일이야.

M: 왜 그렇게 말하는 거야?

W: 시장이 경제 불황을 맞고 있어서, 모든 회사들이 경비를 줄이고 안정을 유지하기 위한 조치를 취해야만 해.

M: 다른 방법은 없을까?

W: 아니. 있어. 우리의 이익을 줄일 수 있고, 근무시간을 늘리거나 직원을 해고할 수도 있지.

M: 이해해. 전부 다 불쾌한 것들이지. 그렇다고 해도 보너스를 중지하는 건 너무 부당해.

Q What is the conversation mainly about?

(a) methods for improving productivity

(b) schedules for bonus payments

(c) the company's new policy and the reason behind it

(d) frustrations over the company's marketing strategies

대화의 주요 화제는?

(a) 생산성을 향상시킬 방법들

(b) 보너스 지급 일정

(c) 회사의 새로운 정책과 그 이유

(d) 마케팅 전략에 대한 실망감

해설 남자는 회사의 보너스 지급 중지에 대해 거론하며, 여자는 회사가 그럴 수 밖에 없는 이유에 대해 설명하고 있으므로 정답은 회사의 새로운 정책과 그 이유라고 말한 (c)이다.

함정 마케팅 전략에 대한 언급은 없으므로 (d)는 오답이다.

어휘 rumor 소문   temporarily 일시적으로
suspend 미루다, 일시 정지하다   inevitable 피할 수 없는, 당연한
recession 불황, 경기침체   take measures 조치를 취하다
expense 비용, 지출   maintain 유지하다, 지속하다
stability 안정(성)   benefit 수당, 보조금
employee 종업원, 직원   even so 그렇다 하더라도
unfair 불공평한, 부당한   strategy 전략
overcome 이겨내다, 극복하다   downturn 하강, 침체
frustration 좌절, 실망, 불만

10 Inference I

M: Good morning. We're meeting today to discuss CompuNext's <u>new product line</u>. Up to now, <u>we have had a large share of the computer market</u> for older professionals, the kinds of people we see <u>working on laptops</u> in cafes or in parks. I believe that we must <u>shift our new product line towards the youth market</u>. We can do that by making it possible for our users to express their individuality. In short, we need to provide more customization features. This should be our key strategy to attract young buyers <u>between 13 and 30 years of age</u>, both male and female, if we are to increase our market share.

M: 안녕하십니까. 오늘 우리는 콤퓨넥스트의 신제품 라인에 관해 토론하기 위해 모였습니다. 지금까지 우리 회사 컴퓨터 구매층의 상당 부분은 나이 많은 직업인들, 즉 카페나 공원에서 휴대용 노트북을 가지고 일하는 사람들이었습니다. 저는 우리 신제품 라인은 젊은 시장으로 옮겨가야 한다고 생각합니다. 우리 고객들로 하여금 자신의 개성을 표현할 수 있도록 만들어 준다면 가능합니다. 다시 말해, 우리는 보다 고객 취향적인 기능들을 공급할 필요가 있다는 겁니다. 우리가 시장 점유율을 높이려고 한다면, 13세에서 30세까지의 남녀 젊은 고객들을 끌어들이는 이 방법이 우리의 주된 전략이 되어야 합니다.

Q What can be inferred about CompuNext?

(a) It has experienced decreased sales recently.

(b) It is the most leading company in the market.

(c) Its products have not attracted young people.

(d) It has been customizing its products.

콤퓨넥스트에 대해 추론할 수 있는 것은?

(a) 최근 들어 판매 감소를 겪고 있다.

(b) 시장에서 가장 선두적인 회사이다.

(c) 회사의 제품이 젊은 사람들의 마음을 끌지 못하고 있다.

(d) 그들의 제품을 고객 취향에 맞추었다.

해설 화자는 기존의 나이든 직장인들이 주요 고객이었던 콤퓨넥스트가 신제품 출시를 기회로 젊은 고객층을 끌어들이기 위해 새 전략이 필요하다는 의견을 제기하고 있다. 따라서 아직은 그렇지 않다는 내용의 (c)가 정답이다.

활정 신제품의 타깃 고객층을 13세~30세 사이의 젊은 남녀를 대상으로 해야 한다는 것에 초점이 맞춰져 있다. (a)나 (b)는 주제에서 동떨어진 얘기이며, 고객 취향적 기능 탑재가 주요 성공 전략이라고 했으므로 (d)는 아직 알 수 없거나, 의도한 바와 다른 얘기이다.

어휘 **product line** 제품군, 제품 라인 | **share** 시장 점유율 | **shift** 옮기다, 바꾸다 | **customization** 주문에 응하여 만듦, 고객 취미에 맞게 설정함 |

attract ~의 마음을 끌다

LISTENING REVIEW

A

1. strategy	2. attract
3. rumor	4. inevitable
5. recession	6. suspend
7. rub	8. restorative
9. bizarre	10. remedy
11. gravelly	12. obligation
13. commute	14. avid
15. urgent	16. abandon

1. a general plan or set of plans intended to achieve something, especially over a long period

2. to cause people to like or admire particular qualities

3. a story or piece of information that may or may not be true, but that people are talking about

4. It is used to explain that it is certain to happen and cannot be prevented or avoided.

5. a period when the economy of a country is doing badly

6. to delay or stop something from happening for a while or until a decision is made about it

7. to move your hand or fingers forwards and backwards over a part of your body while pressing firmly

8. something that makes you feel healthier, stronger, or more cheerful after you have been feeling tired, weak, or miserable

9. very odd and strange

10. something that is intended to cure you when you are ill or in pain

11. It used to describe a voice that is low and rather rough and harsh.

12. a duty to do something

13. to travel a long distance every day between your home and your place of work

14. It is used to describe someone who is very enthusiastic about something that they do.

15. It is used to describe something that needs to be dealt with as soon as possible.

16. to stop doing an activity or piece of work before it is finished

B

1. b   **2. a**   **3. a**   **4. b**   **5. a**

1. 모든 사람은 인정받아야 할 타고난 재능이 있다.

   (a) Everyone should recognize their innate talent.

   (b) Everyone has an innate talent that needs to be recognized.

2. 이것이 그의 모든 에너지를 글쓰기에 몰두할 수 있는 기회를 주었다.

   (a) This gave him an opportunity to direct all his energy into writing.

   (b) Putting all his energy into writing gave him an opportunity.

3. 점차적으로 그의 작품은 인기를 얻게 되었고, 그는 인정을 받게 되었습니다.

   (a) Gradually his works gained popularity and he gained recognition.

   (b) His works became popular after he became recognized gradually.

4. 기존의 할인가에서 15% 추가 할인을 받으실 수 있습니다.

   (a) You can enjoy an extra discount in addition to 15% of discount on existing prices.

   (b) You can receive an extra 15% off in addition to the already existing discounted prices.

5. 전혀요, 내 친구들과 만나는 게 싫지 않다면요.

   (a) Not at all, provided you don't mind meeting my friends.

   (b) Not at all, if you don't want to meet my friends.

C

1. Children with dyslexia are not people who can't learn.

2. You could take a break from your studies while we eat.

3. I usually never have problems doing that.

4. I've actually started loving the ride because I get so much time to myself.

5. I have a few concerns about our upcoming business deal.

1. who can't learn / are not people / children with dyslexia

2. from your studies / you could take a break / while we eat

3. I usually / doing that / never have problems

4. because I get so much time to myself / loving the ride / I've actually started

5. I have / about our upcoming business deal / a few concerns

D

1. a   **2. b**   **3. a**   **4. a**   **5. a**

1. Olsons is a great potential customer that may be able to generate millions of dollars.

   (a) We can make millions of dollars from this potential customer, Olsons.

   (b) Olsons can raise millions of dollars as it has a great potential as a customer.

2. Our company does not currently have enough capital to complete major orders.

   (a) Our company does not have major orders to earn enough money currently.

   (b) Our company can't handle huge orders until we get enough money to complete them.

3. He was a popular figure among the old and young alike.

   (a) He became famous among not only old people, but young people.

   (b) He became famous appealing to the old, rather than the young.

4. Men have also been avid users of cosmetics to improve their appearance.

   (a) Men also used cosmetics often to look better.

   (b) Men who used cosmetics were also favored for their better appearance.

5. Is there anything extra for experienced applicants?

   (a) Can applicants with experience get paid more?

   (b) Is there any requirement for applicants with experience?

VOCABULARY PREVIEW

01. donate 기부하다

02. take ~ for granted ~을 당연하게 생각하다

03. agenda 안건

04. significant 중대한, 의미 있는

05. revise 개정하다, 수정하다

06. threat 위협

07. controversial 논쟁의, 논란의 대상이 되는

08. cite 인용하다

09. detrimental 유해한, 해가 되는

10. revive 부활시키다, 소생시키다

11. hustle and bustle 혼잡, 북새통

12. incapacitate 무능력하게 하다

13. incoherent 조리가 없는, 횡설수설하는

14. antibody 항체, 항독소

15. toxic 독성의

16. infectious 전염성의, 전염병의

17. uptight 초조한, 불안한

18. primitive 원시의, 미개발의

19. wondrous 불가사의한, 놀랄 만한

20. sophisticated 기교적인, 세련된

21. skeptical 회의적인

22. progressive 진보적인

23. innate 타고난

24. emergence 출현, 발생

GUIDED LISTENING

1 1. d 2. d   **2** 1. c 2. d

3 1. a 2. c   **4** 1. c 2. c

1 Conversation

M: Amy, what's the problem with Jane? You know what she did yesterday?

W: I guess <u>you both were supposed to meet</u> somewhere, right?

M: Yeah, but Jane didn't show up! I waited there <u>for a whole hour</u> for her.

W: Are you sure? She told me <u>that you made her wait</u> for more than an hour at Lee's cafe.

M: Is she crazy? We were supposed to meet at Presto's.

W: That means you both waited for each other <u>at different places</u>. Have you spoken to Jane since then?

M: No. <u>I'll do it right now and clear this up.</u>

W: You can use my phone if you want.

M: Amy. Jane에게 무슨 문제가 있니? 어제 Jane이 뭐 했는지 알아?

W: 너희 둘 어딘가에서 만나기로 했던 것으로 알고 있는데, 맞지?

M: 응, 그런데 Jane이 나타나지 않았어! 거기서 한 시간 내내 기다렸거든.

W: 정말이야? Jane의 말로는 네가 그녀를 Lee's 카페에서 한 시간 이상 기다리게 만들었다고 하던데.

M: 무슨 말이야? 우리는 Presto's에서 만나기로 했었는데.

W: 그러니까 너희 둘은 서로 다른 장소에서 서로를 기다린 거네. 그 이후에 Jane과 얘기해 봤어?

M: 아니. 지금 바로 얘기해서 해결해야겠다.

W: 원하면, 내 전화를 써도 돼.

Inference II

1 What can be inferred from the conversation?

(a) Amy will now call Jane to explain what happened.

(b) Jane totally forgot her appointment with the man.

(c) The man is much angrier than Amy and Jane.

(d) The man and Jane misunderstood each other.

이 대화에서 추론할 수 있는 것은 무엇인가?

(a) Amy는 지금 Jane에게 전화를 걸어 무슨 일이 있었는지 설명할 것이다.

(b) Jane은 남자와의 약속을 까맣게 잊고 있었다.

(c) 남자는 Amy와 Jane보다 훨씬 더 화가 나 있다.

(d) 남자와 Jane은 서로 오해하고 있었다.

해설 남자가 만나기로 했던 Jane과 만나지 못한 것에 대한 대화이다. 뒷부분의 '그러니까 너희 둘은 서로 다른 장소에서 서로를 기다린 거네.' 라는 것으로 보아, 남자와 Jane은 서로 다른 장소에서 기다렸다는 것을 알 수 있다.

함정 Amy가 아니라 남자가 Jane에게 전화할 것이므로 (a)는 오답이다.

Main Topic

2 What are the man and woman talking about?

(a) where to meet Amy next time

(b) a problem the man will have with Amy

(c) how to make an appointment

(d) why the appointment fell through

남자와 여자는 무엇에 대해 이야기하고 있는가?

(a) 다음에 Amy를 어디에서 만날지

(b) 남자가 Amy와 겪게 될 문제

(c) 약속을 하는 방법

(d) 약속이 왜 지켜지지 않았는지

해설 서로 다른 장소에서 서로를 기다리다가 만나지 못한 것에 대한 대화이므로 (d)가 정답이다.

어휘 be supposed to ~하기로 되어 있다

show up 나타나다, 나오다 since then 그때 이후로

clear ~ up (문제·의심 따위를) 풀다, 해결하다

fall through 수포로 돌아가다, 실패하다

2 Conversation

M: I heard the dean say that Mr. Barkley donated one million dollars to New Castle University instead of us here at Nevada University.

W: Are you sure? Mr. Barkley has been supporting Nevada University for a long time.

M: Yes, everybody at Nevada University was surprised to hear what he's done.

W: But why did he suddenly change his mind? He always really loved Nevada University.

M: That's right. I guess we were overconfident about ourselves. We never imagined he'd do this.

W: Why do you say so?

M: Actually, New Castle University asked him for donations, and we didn't. I guess we thought he'd always donate to us even if we didn't ask.

W: It is a lesson for us but we learned it the hard way!

M: 학장님이 말씀하시는 것을 들었는데, Barkley씨가 여기 우리 Nevada 대학 대신에 New Castle 대학에 백만 달러를 기부했대요.

W: 정말이에요? Barkley씨는 Nevada 대학을 오랫동안 후원해 왔잖아요.

M: 그래요, Nevada 대학의 모든 사람들이 그가 그랬다는 것을 듣고서 놀라워했어요.

W: 그런데 그는 왜 갑자기 마음을 바꿨을까요? 그는 언제나 Nevada 대학을 정말 좋아했는데요.

M: 맞아요. 나는 우리가 너무 자신만만했었다고 생각해요. 그가 이럴 거라고는 상상도 하지 못했잖아요.

W: 왜 그렇게 말씀하시는 거예요?

M: 사실, New Castle 대학은 그에게 기부를 요청했다고 하네요. 우리는 그러지 않았잖아요. 우리가 요청하지 않아도 그는 언제나 우리에게 기부할 거라고 생각했나 봐요.

W: 우리에게 교훈이 되긴 하지만, 힘들게 배우게 되었네요!

Inference II

1 Which best describes the lesson learned?

(a) Don't expect money from others.

(b) Don't trust anyone unconditionally.

(c) Don't take anything for granted.

(d) Don't accept gifts without knowing.

배우게 된 교훈을 가장 잘 묘사한 것은 무엇인가?

(a) 다른 사람들에게 돈을 기대하지 마라.

(b) 아무도 무조건 믿지 마라.

(c) 어떤 것도 당연하게 받아들이지 마라.

(d) 모르고서는 선물을 받지 마라.

해설 대학 후원자에 관한 대화이다. 당연하게 생각했던 후원자가 다른 대학을 후원하게 되었다는 대화 후, 교훈을 배우게 되었다는 내용이므로 그 교훈으로는 (c)가 가장 적절하다.

Comprehension

2 Which is correct about Mr. Barkley?

(a) He didn't want to donate to Nevada University.

(b) He had donated to New Castle for many years.

(c) He is not financially sound this year.

(d) He was asked for a donation by New Castle.

Barkley씨에 관해 다음 중 옳은 것은?

(a) Nevada 대학에 기부하기를 원하지 않았다.

(b) 몇 년 동안 New Castle에 기부해 왔다.

(c) 올해 재정적으로 탄탄하지 못하다.

(d) New Castle의 기부 요청을 받았다.

해설 오랫동안 Nevada 대학에 기부해 왔던 Barkley씨가 New Castle 대학의 요청에 따라 이번에는 Nevada 대학이 아니라 New Castle 대학에 기부를 한 상황이므로 (d)가 정답이다.

함정 Barkley씨가 Nevada 대학에 기부하기를 원하지 않았는지에 대한 언급은 없다.

어휘 donate 기부하다 | support 후원하다, 지지하다 | overconfident 자신만만한, 자부심이 강한 | even if ~할지라도 | take ~ for granted ~을 당연하게 생각하다

3 Monologue

M: The agenda of today's meeting is to modify our marketing plan <u>in light of new consumer survey results</u>. A survey conducted by our consumer research department indicates that teenagers <u>between the ages of 13 to 18 years</u> are the biggest drinkers of our cola. Another significant finding is that women over 35 years of age seldom drink our product. Therefore, I strongly feel that <u>we need to revise our marketing strategy</u>. We should <u>focus on getting teenagers to notice</u> our product and this can be done if we advertise our cola on the Internet and television. The advertisements must also cover schools and cafes, as these are <u>places most frequently visited</u> by this group.

M: 오늘 회의의 안건은 새로운 소비자 조사 결과에 비추어 우리의 마케팅 기획안을 수정하는 것입니다. 우리의 소비자 조사 부서에 의해 시행된 조사 결과, 13세에서 18세 연령층 사이의 10대들이 우리 콜라의 가장 큰 소비자라는 것이 나타났습니다. 또 다른 중대한 조사 결과는 35세 이상의 여성들은 우리 제품을 거의 마시지 않는다는 것입니다. 그래서 저는 우리의 마케팅 전략을 수정해야 한다고 강하게 느끼고 있습니다. 우리는 10대들이 우리 제품에 대해 알게 하는 데에 집중해야 하는데, 인터넷이나 텔레비전에 우리의 콜라를 광고하면 이렇게 될 수 있습니다. 광고는 또한 학교와 카페에도 되어야 하는데, 이런 곳들이 이 연령층이 가장 자주 방문하는 장소이기 때문입니다.

Inference II

1 What can be inferred from the talk?

(a) The previous marketing plan targeted a broader age range.

(b) Their marketing plan for their cola product has failed.

(c) Less teen consumers like cola drinks nowadays.

(d) Women over 35 years of age drink lighter drinks.

이 이야기에서 추론할 수 있는 것은 무엇인가?

(a) 이전의 마케팅은 더 넓은 연령층을 타깃으로 한 것이었다.

(b) 콜라 제품의 마케팅 계획은 실패했다.

(c) 요즘 10대 소비자들은 콜라 음료를 덜 좋아한다.

(d) 35세 이상의 여성들은 칼로리가 적은 음료를 마신다.

해설 회의의 안건을 소개하고, 조사 결과를 발표하면서 마케팅 기획안이 수정되어야 한다는 내용이다. 조사 결과 10대들이 가장 주요 고객이므로 10대를 타깃으로 해야 한다는 것이다. 그러므로 이전 마케팅은 모든 연령층을 대상으로 했었다는 점을 추론할 수 있다.

함정 (b) 마케팅 전략이 수정되어야 한다는 언급만으로 이전의 마케팅 계획은 실패했다고는 볼 수 없다.

Main Topic

2 What is mainly being discussed?

(a) new products to promote

(b) new consumers to target

(c) adjusting the age group to focus on

(d) problems with their products

주로 논의되고 있는 것은 무엇인가?

(a) 판매를 촉진할 새로운 상품

(b) 타깃이 되는 새로운 소비자들

(c) 타깃 연령층의 조정

(d) 새로운 제품이 지닌 문제점

해설 조사 결과 10대들이 가장 주요 고객이어서 10대를 마케팅 타깃으로 해야 하는데, 그 방안에 대한 것들이 주로 논의되고 있다. 그러므로 (c)가 정답이다.

어휘 agenda 안건 | modify 수정하다 | in light of ~에 비추어 | consumer 소비자 | indicate 표시하다, 지시하다 | significant 중대한, 의미 있는 | finding 발견, 조사 결과 | seldom 거의 ~하지 않다 | revise 개정하다, 수정하다 | strategy 전략 | focus on ~에 집중하다, 초점을 맞추다 | advertise 광고하다 | frequently 자주, 빈번하게

4 Monologue

W: <u>Use of threat in foreign policy</u> has been controversial from ancient days. Today, we will discuss its significance in relationships among countries. Many examples can be cited from history which describe the detrimental consequences of threatening a country with military force or using military force on a country. We use the term "target country" for one which is being threatened by another. Threats are likely to make the target country <u>fearful and anxious</u>, which may compel it to react with force itself. <u>The threatened country</u> tends to increase its military and <u>intelligence forces</u> and <u>ready itself for war</u>. Let's take a look at Germany prior to World War II. Germany revived its military force to counter Britain and France's threats in the late 1930s.

W: 외교 정책에서 위협을 사용하는 것은 고대로부터 논쟁의 대상이었습니다. 오늘 우리는 국가들 간의 관계에서 그 심각성을 논하고자 합니다. 무력으로 어떤 국가를 위협하거나 어떤 국가에 병력을 휘두르는 것이 해로운 결과를 가져온다는 많은 실례들이 역사에서 인용될 수 있습니다. 다른 나라로부터 위협을 받는 나라를 가리켜 "표적 국가" 라는 용어를 사용합니다. 위협은 표적 국가를 두려워하고 불안하게 할 수 있는데, 그것은 그 국가로 하여금 무력으로 대응할 수 밖에 없게 할 수 있습니다. 위협받는 국가는 병력과 정보력을 강화하여 전쟁에 대비하려는 경향이 있습니다. 제2차 세계대전 이전의 독일을 살펴보도록 하죠. 독일은 1930년대 후반에 영국과 프랑스의 위협에 맞서기 위해 병력을 부활시켰습니다.

Inference II

1 What can be inferred from the lecture?

(a) Germany is still threatened by Britain and France.

(b) World War II is to blame for much change in foreign policies.

(c) Threatening with military force may create resistance.

(d) Peace is more desirable than war.

이 강의에서 추론할 수 있는 것은?

(a) 독일은 아직도 영국과 프랑스의 위협을 받고 있다.

(b) 제2차 세계대전은 외교 정책의 많은 변화에 책임이 있다.

(c) 군사력으로 위협하는 것은 많은 저항을 일으킬 수 있다.

(d) 전쟁보다 평화가 더 바람직하다.

해설 이 강의는 어떤 국가를 무력으로 위협하는 것에 대한 심각성을 논하고 있다. 무력은 또 다른 무력을 낳는다는 것이다. 그러므로 이 강의의 주요 요점은 (c)이다.

오답 (a)와 (b)는 언급된 바가 없다. 그리고 (d)는 지나친 확대 해석으로,

이 강의에서는 전혀 언급되지 않았음에 유의한다.

Detail

2 Which country is mentioned as an example of a "target country"?

(a) France

(b) England

(c) Germany

(d) The United States

"표적 국가" 의 예로 언급된 것은 어느 국가인가?

(a) 프랑스

(b) 영국

(c) 독일

(d) 미국

해설 Let's take a look at Germany prior to World War II.(제2차 세계대전 이전의 독일을 살펴보도록 하죠.)라는 언급이 있고, 그 앞에 표적 국가가 보이는 경향이 나타나 있다. 그러므로 정답은 독일이다.

어휘 threat 위협 controversial 논쟁의, 논란의 대상이 되는
significance 심각성, 중대성 cite 인용하다
detrimental 유해한, 해가 되는 threaten 위협하다
military force 군세, 병력, 무력
compel ~ to ~로 하여금 …하지 않을 수 없게 하다, 강제로 시키다
tend to ~하는 경향이 있다 prior to ~이전의
revive 부활시키다, 소생시키다 resistance 저항
desirable 바람직한

PRACTICAL LISTENING

1. a	2. b	3. a	4. c	5. a
6. c	7. d	8. c	9. d	10. d

1 Inference II

M: So, Jennie, how did you like the food here?

W: I liked it very much. I think I want to bring my friends here next time.

M: By the way, <u>what do you think about having a blind date</u>?

W: <u>Blind date</u>? Well, I don't know. I mean I don't really like it. Why do you ask?

M: My cousin, George, is coming home from Paris for his vacation.

W: And you want me to go on a date with him?

M: Yes. You <u>saw him in the pictures</u> the other day, right? You told me he is cute.

W: Yeah, but I'm not sure if he would like to see me.

M: He knows that we are meeting today and he wanted me <u>to find out if you would be interested.</u>

W: Well, how does he know about me?

M: <u>I sent him some of my pictures</u> and he saw you there.

M: 그런데 Jennie. 여기 음식 어땠어?

W: 아주 좋았어. 다음에는 친구들을 데려와야겠어.

M: 그런데 소개팅하는 거 어떻게 생각해?

W: 소개팅? 음, 잘 모르겠는데. 진짜로 좋아하지는 않아. 왜 물어 보는 거야?

M: 내 사촌 George가 방학 때 파리에서 돌아오거든.

W: 내가 그 사람이랑 데이트하길 원하는 거야?

M: 응. 언젠가 사진에서 그 애를 본 적이 있잖아, 맞지? 귀엽다고 나한테 말했었는데.

W: 응, 하지만 이 애가 나를 만나고 싶어 할지 모르겠는걸.

M: 오늘 우리가 만난다는 걸 알고는 네가 관심이 있는지 물어 봐 달라고 했어.

W: 음. 그가 나를 어떻게 알아?

M: 내가 그에게 사진을 몇 장 보냈거든, 거기서 너를 봤지.

Q What can be inferred from the conversation?

(a) Both the woman and George are interested in each other.

(b) The man and the woman will meet George together.

(c) They are not interested in having a blind date.

(d) The man wants to go out with the woman.

이 대화에서 추론할 수 있는 것은?

(a) 여자와 George 둘 다 서로에게 관심이 있다.

(b) 남자와 여자는 함께 George를 만날 것이다.

(c) 그들은 소개팅하는 것에 관심이 없다.

(d) 남자는 여자와 사귀고 싶어 한다.

해설 소개팅(blind date)에 대한 남녀의 대화이다. 남자는 사촌 George 를 여자에게 소개시켜 주려고 한다. 여자와 George는 서로를 사진에서 본 적이 있고, 둘 다 관심 있어 하는 대화이므로 (a)가 정답이다.

함정 (b) 남자와 여자가 함께 George를 만날 것인지, 여자만 George를 만날 것인지에 관한 정보는 나와 있지 않다.

어휘 blind date 소개팅 go on a date with ~와 데이트하다
cute 귀여운 go out with ~와 사귀다

2

M: Are you tired of <u>the hustle and bustle</u> of city life? Here's your chance <u>to get away!</u> <u>Win a luxury vacation</u> at the Paradiso Island Resort in the Bahamas! Purchase <u>any item worth over $50</u> at a Top Mart store and you automatically enter our contest for an all-expenses-paid vacation for two, worth over $10,000. This includes your stay for seven nights and eight days at the Resort's <u>luxurious presidential suite</u>, with a personal assistant, a driver, and an 80-foot yacht at your service. Live like royalty during your vacation, having all your personal needs attended to. Don't miss this opportunity of a lifetime: enter the contest at any Top Mart store right away! <u>What have you got to lose</u>?

M: 복잡한 도시 생활에 지치셨나요? 멀리 떠날 수 있는 기회를 드리겠습니다! 바하마에 있는 파라디소 아일랜드 리조트의 호화로운 휴가 경품권을 획득하십시오! 탑 마트에서 50달러 이상의 물품을 구입하신 모든 분은 자동적으로 모든 비용을 책임지는 만 달러에 상당하는 2인용 휴가 경품권을 탈 수 있는 이번 행사에 참여하실 수 있습니다. 리조트 고급 귀빈실에서의 7박 8일 숙박권, 개인 비서, 운전사, 그리고 80피트 요트까지 포함됩니다. 여러분이 필요한 것이라면 뭐든지 시중받으면서 휴가 동안 왕족처럼 생활하십시오. 일생에 한 번 있을 이번 기회를 놓치지 마십시오. 지금 바로 탑 마트 매장에서 콘테스트에 참가하세요. 밑져야 본전 아닌가요?

Q Which is correct about the contest according to the advertisement?

(a) Two prizes will be given.

(b) It offers a prize of an eight-day luxury stay.

(c) Shoppers can submit only one entry each.

(d) Shoppers can win gifts worth over 100 dollars.

광고에 따르면 콘테스트에 관해 사실인 것은?

(a) 2개의 경품이 주어질 것이다.

(b) 8일 간의 고급 숙박권이 경품으로 제공된다.

(c) 구매자들은 각자 한 번의 참가만 가능하다.

(d) 구매자들은 100달러 상당의 선물을 받게 된다.

해설 상품 구매 시 추첨을 통해 주어지는 만 달러짜리 여행 경품권에 관한 광고이다. 리조트 고급 귀빈실에서의 7박 8일 숙박권, 개인 비서, 운전사, 요트까지 제공된다고 했으므로 정답은 (b)이다.

함정 (a) 2인용이라고 했지 2개의 경품이라고 하지 않았다. (c)는 언급되지 않았으며, (d) 100달러짜리 선물도 아니다.

어휘 hustle and bustle 혼잡, 북새통
luxury 호화로운, 사치스러운 automatically 자동적으로
all-expenses-paid 모든 경비가 지급되는
presidential suite (대통령, 귀빈 등이 묵는) 특별실, 귀빈실

royalty 왕족, 왕위   attend to (맡은 일 등을) 챙기다
lifetime 일생, 일생의

3

W: Why didn't you <u>turn up</u> last night? I'm sure I told you about the party we were having.

M: Actually <u>I was on my way to it</u>, but <u>got a call</u> from the hospital.

W: What happened? Anything serious?

M: Yes, there was an emergency. A person needed <u>immediate surgery</u>.

W: Oh, that's too bad. At least you could have informed me about that, though.

M: Yes, I meant to, but I became very caught up in the situation. I'll <u>make it up to you</u> some other time.

W: Okay, I'll look forward to that.

W: 어젯밤에 왜 안 왔어? 파티가 있다고 내가 분명히 말했는데.

M: 실은 파티에 가는 길이었는데, 병원에서 전화가 걸려 왔어.

W: 무슨 일 있었어? 심각한 거야?

M: 응, 비상사태였어. 응급수술이 필요한 사람이었어.

W: 그것 참 안됐다. 하지만 적어도 나한테 알려줄 수는 있었잖아.

M: 응, 그러려고 했는데, 상황이 너무 급박하게 돌아가서. 다음에 언제 보상할게.

W: 알았어. 기대할게.

Q Why didn't the man go to the party?

(a) He had to go to the hospital.

(b) He became sick on the way to the party.

(c) He was not informed of the party.

(d) He wants to meet the woman alone.

남자는 왜 파티에 가지 않았나?

(a) 병원에 가야만 했다.

(b) 파티에 가는 길에 아팠다.

(c) 파티에 대해 듣지 못했다.

(d) 여자만 만나기를 바란다.

[해설] 남자가 파티에 오지 못한 이유에 대해 이야기하는 대화이다. 여자가 이유를 묻자, 남자는 파티에 가는 길에 응급수술이 필요한 환자가 발생했다는 병원의 전화를 받고, 다시 병원으로 돌아가야만 했다고 여자에게 설명하고 있다. 따라서 정답은 (a)이다.

[함정] 병원에 가야 했다는 말만 듣고, 남자가 아팠다고 성급하게 판단해서는 안 된다.

[어휘] turn up 나타나다   on one's way to ~에 가는 길에
emergency 비상, 긴급 사태   immediate 즉시의, 즉각적인
at least 적어도, 최소한   though 그러나, 하지만
mean to ~을 의도하다, ~할 작정이다
be caught up in ~에 휘말려 들다, 열중하다, 몰두하다
make ~up (손해 등을) 보상하다   look forward to ~을 기대하다

4 Inference II

M: A fever may look quite frightening to ordinary people. This is especially so in the cases of extreme fever, where a patient may be truly incapacitated, <u>sweating and incoherent</u>. As medical students you need to remember that fever is not so much an illness as a symptom of one. It is generally the result of a sickness and is <u>a sign of the body's defense mechanism</u> working hard to produce <u>antibodies to get rid of toxic material</u>. A fever works with antibiotics <u>to shorten illness and make it less infectious</u>. In other words, fever is the body's way of trying to fight sickness and it is therefore <u>beneficial to let it run its course</u>.

M: 일반인들은 열이 나면 꽤나 겁을 먹을지도 모릅니다. 그러나 이는 극단적인 발열인 경우에만 그렇습니다. 환자가 완전히 무기력해지거나, 땀을 많이 흘리고 횡설수설하는 경우처럼 말입니다. 의학도로서 여러분들은 열은 병이라기보다는 병의 증상이라는 점을 기억해야 합니다. 열은 일반적으로 병의 결과이며 몸의 독소를 제거하는 항체 생성을 위해 신체 방위 기제가 열심히 작동 중이라는 신호입니다. 열은 항체와 작용하여 병을 줄이고 보다 감염성이 적어지도록 기능합니다. 다시 말해, 열은 병을 싸워 이기려는 신체의 노력의 하나이므로 열을 그대로 두는 것이 이롭습니다.

Q What can be inferred from the lecture?

(a) Several benefits are associated with fever.

(b) It is risky to leave a fever untreated.

(c) A fever should not be the target of treatment.

(d) A fever is frightening to ordinary people.

이 강의에서 추론할 수 있는 것은?

(a) 발열에는 몇 가지 이로운 점이 수반된다.

(b) 열이 나는 것을 치료하지 않으면 위험하다.

(c) 발열이 치료의 목표가 되어서는 안 된다.

(d) 열은 일반인들을 겁먹게 한다.

[해설] 의대생들에게 열(발열)에 대해 설명하는 강의이다. 열 그 자체는 병이 아니며, 병의 징후인 동시에 신체 방위 기제가 작동하고 있다는 신호라고 했다. 극단적인 발열이 아닐 경우에는, 열 자체를 치료하려고 하지 말라는 강의이므로 정답은 (c)이다.

어휘 fever 열, 열병 | frightening 겁나게 하는 | extreme 극단적인 |
incapacitate 무능력하게 하다 |
incoherent 조리가 없는, 횡설수설하는 |
defense mechanism 방위 기제 | antibody 항체, 항독소 |
get rid of ~을 제거하다 | toxic 독성의 |
infectious 전염성의, 전염병의

5

M: Sharon, I heard you've traveled a lot. Is that true?

W: Yeah, I've been to 22 different countries.

M: That's quite a lot! Have you been to Malaysia?

W: Yes, I've been there once with my parents.

M: Mmm, what about Indonesia?

W: Oh, it is a beautiful country. You definitely have to go there sometime.

M: One of my friends lives there and he's been telling me to come whenever I talk to him. What about Mauritius? Have you been there?

W: Well, no, but we're planning to go there this summer.

M: I heard that's a good place to go to for vacation.

W: Yes, it's famous for its beaches.

M: Sharon, 너 여행을 많이 했다고 들었는데, 사실이니?

W: 응, 22개국을 가 봤어.

M: 정말 많이 다녔구나. 말레이시아에는 가 봤니?

W: 응. 부모님과 같이 한번 가 봤어.

M: 음, 인도네시아는 어때?

W: 아, 아름다운 나라지. 너도 언젠가 꼭 가 봐야 할 거야.

M: 내 친구 중 한 명이 거기 사는데, 나랑 이야기할 때마다 오라고 하고 있어. 모리셔스는 어때? 거기도 가 봤어?

W: 음, 아니. 그런데 이번 여름에 갈 계획이야.

M: 휴가를 보내기 좋은 곳이라고 들었어.

W: 응, 그곳은 해변으로 유명하지.

Q What are the man and woman mainly talking about?

(a) countries the woman has visited

(b) vacations with parents

(c) places they want to visit for their vacation

(d) difficulties to face while traveling

남자와 여자는 주로 무슨 이야기를 하고 있는가?

(a) 여자가 방문한 나라들

(b) 부모님과의 휴가

(c) 휴가 때 가 보고 싶은 장소

(d) 여행할 때 직면하는 어려움들

해설 여자가 여행을 많이 했다는 말을 들은 남자가 여자에게 여러 나라들 에 대해 묻는 대화이다. 여자가 22개국을 여행했다고 하자, 남자는 말레이 시아와 인도네시아, 그리고 모리셔스를 가 본 적이 있냐고 다시 묻고 있고, 여자가 답하고 있는 장면이다. 따라서 두 사람은 주로 '여자가 방문한 나라 들'에 대해 이야기 하고 있으므로 정답은 (a)이다.

활정 여자는 이번 여름에 모리셔스를 갈 예정이지만, 이 대화가 (c) 휴가 때 가 보고 싶은 장소에 대한 것은 아님에 유의한다.

어휘 have been to ~에 가 본 적이 있다 |
definitely 확실히, 틀림없이 | be famous for ~로 유명하다 |
face ~에 직면하다, ~의 쪽을 향하다

6

M: Rose, I can't find my car keys. Have you seen them?

W: No, dear. Have you looked on the dresser?

M: Yeah, but they aren't there. I even searched for them in my bag.

W: Have you checked in your table drawers?

M: No. I'll look.

W: Are they there? You might have left them while you were taking out some bills.

M: You're right. The keys are right here.

W: Honey, you should calm down a little. This is not the fist time that you're giving a presentation. You should be more confident in yourself.

M: I don't know. I can't help being uptight before any presentation.

M: Rose, 내 자동차 열쇠를 못 찾겠어요. 혹시 본 적 있어요?

W: 아니요. 화장대 위에 봤어요?

M: 네, 그런데 거기에는 없어요. 가방 안에도 다 찾아봤어요.

W: 탁자 서랍들도 확인했어요?

M: 아니요. 볼게요.

W: 있나요? 지폐를 꺼내면서 거기다 놔뒀을지도 몰라요.

M: 당신 말이 맞아요. 열쇠가 바로 여기 있네요!

W: 여보, 당신은 좀 침착할 필요가 있어요. 프레젠테이션을 하는 게 이번

이 처음은 아니잖아요. 당신 자신에 대해서 좀 더 자신감을 가지세요.

M: 모르겠어요. 프레젠테이션 전에 긴장되는 것은 어쩔 수가 없어요.

Q Which is correct about the man?

(a) The man is not prepared for the presentation.

(b) The man has lost his keys many times.

(c) The man is nervous about the presentation.

(d) The man found the keys on the dresser.

남자에 대해서 옳은 것은?

(a) 프레젠테이션을 준비하지 못했다.

(b) 열쇠를 여러 번 잃어버렸다.

(c) 프레젠테이션에 대해 긴장하고 있다.

(d) 화장대 위에서 열쇠를 찾았다.

해설 남자가 자동차 열쇠를 어디다 두었는지 몰라서 여자에게 묻고 있는 장면이다. 여기저기 찾다가 결국 탁자 서랍에서 열쇠를 찾았다. 이어지는 대화에서 여자는 남자에게 프레젠테이션이 있는 날마다 불안해하지 말고 자신감을 가지라고 말하고 있다. 그러므로 남자에 관해 옳은 것은 (c)이다.

함정 (a) 남자가 프레젠테이션 때문에 긴장하기는 하지만, 준비하지 못했는지에 대한 언급은 없다. (b) 남자가 열쇠를 여러 번 잃어버렸는지는 알 수 없다.

어휘 dear 친애하는 사람, 애인, 연인, (주로 부르는 말로) 여보 ┃ dresser 화장대, 옷장 ┃ search for ~을 찾다 ┃ drawer 서랍 ┃ might have p.p. ~했을지도 모른다 ┃ bill 계산서, 지폐, 법안 ┃ calm down 침착하다, 진정하다 ┃ confident 자신이 있는, 확신하는 ┃ can't help -ing 어쩔 수 없이 ~하다 ┃ uptight 초조한, 불안한

7 Inference II

(Telephone rings.)

M: Hi, Jenny. This is Tom here.

W: Hi, Tom. How are you?

M: Well, I'm good. I can hear a cat in the background. When did you get a cat?

W: That's my aunt's. She's gone on vacation, so I'm looking after him.

M: But didn't you tell me that you're allergic to cats? Or was it dogs?

W: Cats. Yeah, I used to be.

M: I remember when we were in college you had to look after someone's cat and you had to go to the hospital for a few days.

W: Exactly. But after I graduated, for some reason, I can get along with any pets.

M: Good for you. I hope you're having a good time with him.

(전화벨이 울린다.)

M: 안녕, Jenny. 나 Tom이야.

W: 안녕, Tom. 잘 지내지?

M: 응, 좋아. 어딘가 뒤에서 고양이 소리가 들리는데. 고양이는 언제 샀니?

W: 우리 숙모 거야. 휴가 가셔서 내가 돌보고 있어.

M: 근데 너 고양이 알레르기 있다고 말하지 않았니? 아니, 개였던가?

W: 고양이야. 맞아, 그랬었어.

M: 우리가 대학 다닐 때, 네가 누군가의 고양이를 돌봐 주었다가 며칠 동안 병원에 있었던 게 기억나.

W: 맞아. 하지만 졸업 후, 어떤 이유에서인지, 어느 애완동물하고도 잘 지낼 수 있게 되었어.

M: 잘됐구나. 고양이랑 잘 지내길 바래.

Q What can be inferred from the conversation?

(a) The man is worried about the woman looking after his pet.

(b) This is the second time the woman has looked after her aunt's cat.

(c) Cats cause more health problems than dogs for many people.

(d) They have known each other for many years.

이 대화에서 추론할 수 있는 것은?

(a) 남자는 자기 애완동물을 돌보고 있는 여자를 걱정하고 있다.

(b) 여자가 숙모의 고양이를 돌본 것이 이번이 두 번째이다.

(c) 많은 사람들에게 고양이는 개보다 건강상의 문제를 더 많이 일으킨다.

(d) 그들은 몇 년 동안 알고 지내는 사이이다.

해설 숙모가 휴가 동안 맡긴 고양이 한 마리를 여자가 돌보고 있다. 남자가 기억하기로는 여자가 대학 때 고양이 알레르기가 있었는데 어찌 된 일이냐고 묻자, 이제는 괜찮다고 대답하고 있다. 여기서 알 수 있는 것은 두 사람이 서로 알고 지낸 지 꽤 오래되었다는 사실일 것이다.

함정 (a) 남자의 고양이가 아니라, 숙모의 고양이이다. (b) 예전에 누군가의 고양이를 돌봤다고 했지, 숙모의 고양이를 두 번째 돌보고 있는지는 알 수 없다. (c)에 대한 내용은 언급되지 않았다.

어휘 look after ~을 돌보다, 보살피다 ┃ allergic to ~에 대해 알레르기가 있는, ~을 몹시 싫어하는 ┃ used to 이전에는 ~이었다 ┃ get along with ~와 잘 지내다

8

W: As I said last class, early humans had no records of

either history or science that could help them understand their world. They also lacked a system of reasoning or logic that they could use to comprehend the physical and biological phenomena that they observed — from the birth of a baby to the falling of a leaf, the flow of a river or the rise of the sun. So they created myths to explain the things that they could not understand. For example, the Biblical story of Babel is a myth to explain the existence of different languages in the world. All human societies, right from primitive times, have displayed this tendency to create wondrous stories for real-world events beyond their understanding.

W: 지난 강의에서 말씀드렸다시피, 초기 인간은 그들의 세계를 이해하는 데 도움이 될 만한 역사나 과학에 대한 기록을 갖고 있지 않았습니다. 그들은 또한 자신들이 관찰한 물리적, 생물학적 현상 — 아기의 탄생으로부터 나뭇잎이 떨어지거나, 강물이 흘러간다든가, 태양이 솟아오르는 것 — 을 이해하는 데 이용할 수 있는 어떤 논리적, 추리 체계를 갖고 있지 않았습니다. 그래서 그들은 자신들이 이해할 수 없는 이런 현상을 설명하기 위해 신화를 창조해냈습니다. 예를 들어, 바벨에 대한 성서 이야기는 세상에 다른 언어들이 존재한다는 것을 설명하기 위해 만들어낸 신화입니다. 원시 시대로부터 모든 인간 사회는 실제 세계에서 일어나고는 있지만 자신들은 이해할 수 없는 일들을 설명하기 위해 불가사의한 이야기를 만들어 내는 경향을 보였습니다.

Q Which is correct according to the lecture?

(a) All humans once spoke a single language.

(b) Ancient myths are usually based on truth.

(c) Myth-making has long been a part of human culture.

(d) Diverse primitive societies have often invented similar myths.

강의에 따르면 사실인 것은?

(a) 모든 인간은 일찍이 하나의 언어를 사용했다.

(b) 고대의 신화는 일반적으로 사실에 근거한다.

(c) 신화를 만드는 일은 오래전부터 인류 문화의 한 부분이었다.

(d) 다양한 원시 사회에서 종종 유사한 신화를 만들어냈다.

해설 신화가 생겨나게 된 배경을 설명하는 강의이다. 원시 시대부터 오늘날에 이르기까지 인간은 자신들이 이해하지 못하는 상황들을 신화를 통해 이해하고자 했다는 내용의 강의이므로 정답은 (c)이다. 나머지는 언급되지 않은 것들이다.

어휘 reasoning 추리, 이론 logic 논리, 논법 phenomenon 현상 (pl. phenomena) observe 관찰하다, 목격하다 myth 신화 Biblical 성서의, 성서에 나오는 primitive 원시의, 미개발의

tendency 경향, 추세 wondrous 불가사의한, 놀랄 만한

9 Inference II

W: Today I'll be talking about the heroines in Shakespeare's plays. Although women's rights were unheard of in his time, Shakespeare depicted women's issues with great insight. His heroines showed a complex range of emotions and abilities, and were not simply "weak women" needing protection from men. He showed his heroines coping against a society established by sexism for instance, one of his heroines had to wear a man's disguise so that men would take her seriously. Other women, such as those in *King Lear*, devised sophisticated social and political strategies. It could even be argued that he was intensely skeptical of the sexist social values of his time.

W: 오늘 저는 셰익스피어 연극의 여주인공에 대해 얘기할 것입니다. 그 시대에는 여성의 권리라는 것이 잘 알려지지 않았던 때임에도 불구하고, 셰익스피어는 심오한 통찰력으로 여성 문제들을 묘사했습니다. 그의 작품의 여주인공들은 복잡한 감정 상태와 능력들을 보여 주고 있으며, 단순히 남성들의 보호가 필요한 "나약한 여성들"도 아니었습니다. 셰익스피어는 성차별적 사회에 맞서 싸우는 여주인공들을 보여 주었습니다. 예를 들어 그의 여주인공 중 한 명은 남장을 하여 남성들이 자신을 진지하게 받아들일 수 있도록 했습니다. '리어왕'에 등장하는 여자들처럼, (셰익스피어 작품의) 또 다른 여자들은 정교한 사회 정치적 전략을 고안해냈습니다. 심지어 그는 그 시대의 성차별적 사회 가치 체제에 대단히 회의적이었다는 주장도 있습니다.

Q What can be inferred from the lecture?

(a) Shakespeare's progressive vision contributed to feminism.

(b) Shakespeare was cynical about women in power.

(c) Shakespeare's heroines succeed because of innate strength.

(d) Shakespeare was critically aware of discrimination against women.

이 강의에서 추론할 수 있는 것은?

(a) 셰익스피어의 진보적인 시각이 페미니즘에 기여했다.

(b) 셰익스피어는 힘 있는 여성들에 대해 냉소적이었다.

(c) 셰익스피어 작품의 여주인공들은 타고난 능력으로 인해 성공한 것이다.

(d) 셰익스피어는 여성 차별을 비판적으로 인식하고 있었다.

superstitious thought.

(b) Abstract thinking was first introduced by the Pythagoreans.

(c) Philosophy emerged in ancient cultures around the world in 600 B.C.

(d) Some philosophers saw mathematical relationships reflected in reality.

이 강의에 따르면 사실인 것은?

(a) 고대 철학은 미신적 사고 원리를 강화했다.

(b) 추상적 사고는 피타고라스 추종자들에 의해 처음 도입되었다.

(c) 철학은 기원전 600년경 전 세계적으로 고대 문화에서 출현했다.

(d) 일부 철학자들은 현실 세계에 투영된 수학적 관련성을 파악했다.

해설 처음 추상적 사고의 도입은 당시 급진적인 사상가들에 의해 주도되었는데, 이 그룹이 수학적 사고방식을 접목한 피타고라스 추종자들이었다고 했으므로 정답은 (d)이다.

함정 (a) 자연을 논리적으로 설명한 급진적 사상가들 가운데 피타고라스 추종자들이 선두에 있다고 했지 그들이 처음 추상적 사고를 도입했는지는 알 수 없다.

어휘 emergence 출현, 발생 abstract 추상적인
ultimate 근원적인, 최고의 nature 자연, 자연 현상(법칙)
superstition 미신 explanation 해설, 설명
prior to ~에 앞서, ~보다 전에 radical 급진적인
departure (방침 등의) 새 발전, 출발, 떠남 thinker 사상가
Pythagoreans 피타고라스 학설 신봉자 mathematic 수학적인
ratio 비, 비율 discernible 보고 알 수 있는, 식별할 수 있는
adhere to ~를 견지하다, ~을 신봉하다

해설 셰익스피어 작품 속 여주인공들에 대한 강의이다. 그 당시 시대적 흐름과 달리 셰익스피어 작품 속 여주인공들은 여성 차별에 대항하는 나름의 능력과 자세를 지니고 있었는데, 이는 작가의 비판적인 시각에서 비롯되었다는 내용이다. 따라서 정답은 (d)이다.

함정 셰익스피어의 시각이 오늘날 입장에서 볼 때 페미니즘적일 수 있으나 그의 행보가 페미니즘 발전에 기여했다는 (a)의 내용은 지나친 억측이다.

어휘 heroine 여주인공
unheard 알아주지 않는, 귀담아 들어 주지 않는 insight 통찰력
protection 보호 cope against ~에 맞서 대처하다
sexism 성차별(주의) disguise 가면, 가장복
devise 궁리하다, 고안하다 sophisticated 기교적인, 세련된
strategy 전략 intensely 강렬하게, 심하게 skeptical 회의적인
sexist 성차별주의자(의) progressive 진보적인
innate 타고난 discrimination 차별, 구별

10

W: I'd like to introduce you to Western philosophy by going back to the 6th century B.C. This saw <u>the emergence of abstract</u> thought relating to the ultimate nature of the world and human life. This significant move from <u>superstition to explanation</u> characterizes ancient Greek philosophy. Prior to that time, most people felt that "gods" or other supernatural forces were at work in all the things around them. The idea that nature could be logically explained was <u>a radical departure from the past</u>, led by a group of what were then radical thinkers. Such a group of men were the Pythagoreans. They followed Pythagoras's view that all features of the world reflected <u>mathematic ratios and a discernible system</u>. They also believed that human life should <u>adhere to a system</u> as well.

W: 기원전 6세기로 거슬러 올라가 서양 철학에 대해 소개해드리겠습니다. 이 시기에는 세계와 인류 삶의 근본적인 자연 법칙과 관련된 추상적인 사고가 출현합니다. 이처럼 미신에서 설명의 단계로의 중대한 이동이 고대 그리스 철학의 특징입니다. 그 시대 이전에는 대부분의 사람들이 주변의 모든 사물로부터 신이나 다른 초자연적 힘들이 작용하고 있다고 느꼈습니다. 자연이 논리적으로 설명될 수 있다는 개념은 과거로부터의 급진적인 발전으로, (이런 생각은) 당시로서는 급진적인 사상가 그룹에 의해 주도되었습니다. 이들 그룹의 사람들은 피타고라스 학설 신봉자들이었습니다. 그들은 세상의 모든 것들이 수학적 비율과 식별 가능한 시스템을 반영하고 있다는 피타고라스의 견해를 따랐습니다. 그들은 또한 인류의 삶 역시 마찬가지로 시스템을 따라야 한다고 믿었습니다.

Q Which is correct according to the lecture?

(a) Ancient philosophy reinforced the doctrines of

LISTENING REVIEW

A

1. sophisticated	2. disguise
3. discrimination	4. tendency
5. primitive	6. allergic
7. uptight	8. incoherent
9. incapacitate	10. emergence
11. discernible	12. adhere
13. superstition	14. abstract
15. skeptical	16. innate

1. very complex or complicated

2. unusual clothes or altered appearance

3. the practice of treating one person or group of people less fairly or less well than other people or groups

4. an inclination to do something

5. belonging to a society in which people live in a very simple way, usually without industries or a writing system

6. becoming ill or get a rash when you eat, smell, or touch something

7. tense, nervous, or annoyed about something

8. talking in a confused and unclear way

9. to weaken someone in some way, so that they cannot do certain things

10. the process or event of coming into existence

11. It is used to explain that you can see something or recognize that it exists.

12. to act in the way that a rule or agreement says you should

13. belief in things that are not real or possible, for example, magic

14. It is used to describe an idea or way of thinking that is based on general ideas rather than on real things and events.

15. doubtful, cynical, dubious or unconvinced

16. It is used to describe a quality or ability that a person is born with.

B

| 1. a | 2. b | 3. a | 4. b | 5. b |

1. 너희 둘이서 어딘가에서 만나기로 했던 것 같은데.

(a) I guess you both were supposed to meet somewhere.

(b) I thought you both had to make an appointment somewhere.

2. 당신이 그녀를 Lee's 카페에서 한 시간 이상 기다리게 만들었다.

(a) You had waited for her more than an hour at Lee's cafe.

(b) You made her wait for more than an hour at Lee's cafe.

3. Nevada 대학의 모든 사람들이 그가 한 일을 듣고서 놀라워했어요.

(a) Everybody at Nevada University was surprised to hear what he's done.

(b) It was surprising that everyone heard what he has done to Nevada University.

4. 우리가 요청하지 않아도 그는 언제나 우리에게 기부할 거라고 생각했어요.

(a) We thought he'd already donated to us even before we asked him.

(b) We thought he'd always donate to us even if we didn't ask.

5. 우리는 10대들이 우리 제품에 대해 알게 하는 데에 집중해야 한다.

(a) We should have teenagers notice we are focusing on our product.

(b) We should focus on getting teenagers to notice our product.

C

1. Threats are likely to make the target country fearful.

2. Women over 35 years of age seldom drink our product.

3. I'm not sure if he would like to see me.

4. Purchase any item worth over $50.

5. I became very caught up in the situation.

1. threats are likely / fearful / to make the target country

2. over 35 years of age / women / seldom drink our product

3. to see me / if he would like / I'm not sure

4. any item / purchase / worth over $50

5. very caught up / in the situation / I became

D

| 1. a | 2. b | 3. a | 4. b | 5. b |

1. Fever is the body's way of trying to fight sickness.

(a) You can get a fever when your body is trying to fight against illness.

(b) You get a fever when your body is strong enough to fight sickness.

2. You might have left them while you were taking out some bills.

(a) You took out some bills before you left them.

(b) They might have been left when the bills were taken out.

3. I can't help being uptight before any presentation.

   (a) Every time I have a presentation, I get nervous.

   (b) I get so nervous when I'm stuck in a presentation.

4. Didn't you tell me that you're allergic to cats?

   (a) I didn't know you are allergic to cats.

   (b) I thought you are allergic to cats.

5. They created myths to explain the things that they could not understand.

   (a) They couldn't explain or understand myths they had created.

   (b) Myths were created to explain what they couldn't understand.

CHAPTER 08 STANCE / FUNCTION

VOCABULARY PREVIEW

01. resign 사임하다, 사직하다

02. dean 학장

03. overhear 어쩌다 듣게 되다, 엿듣다

04. qualified 자격 있는, 실력 있는

05. disciplinary 규율의, 징계의

06. liable 책임을 져야 할

07. obesity 비만

08. resort to ~에 의지하다, 도움을 청하다

09. shed 벗어 버리다, 없애다

10. lean 여윈, 마른

11. prevalent 널리 보급된, 만연한

12. in this respect 이 점에서

13. intervention 간섭, 중재

14. excuse 변명, 구실, 핑계

15. genuine 진짜의

16. aggravate 악화시키다

17. mitigate 누그러뜨리다, 완화하다

18. severity 가혹, 격렬함

19. binding 의무적인, 구속력 있는

20. be in jeopardy 위험에 빠지다, 위태롭다

21. strike 파업, 쟁의

22. demolish 부수다, 폭파하다

23. be doomed to (나쁘게) ~될 운명이다

24. prevailing 널리 보급되어 있는, 유행하고 있는

GUIDED LISTENING

1	1. c	2. b	2	1. d	2. b
3	1. a	2. b	4	1. c	2. c

1 Conversation

M: Is it true that Professor Stanley <u>has resigned from his post</u> as dean of the university?

W: I guess so. But <u>there's something more to it</u>.

M: What?

W: Well, I believe he's been fired. I overheard some professors discussing it.

M: That can't be true. How could someone as qualified as him be fired?

W: Actually, the board members didn't like <u>his administration methods</u>. And you know that Professor Stanley <u>never paid attention to the board members</u> and their <u>disciplinary measures</u>. So, ultimately he lost his job.

M: That's really a loss for the school. He was a good administrator.

W: Yeah, I agree.

M: Stanley 교수님이 대학 학장 자리에서 사임한다는 것이 사실이니?

W: 그런 것 같아. 하지만 그게 다가 아니야.

M: 뭔데?

W: 음. 교수님은 해고되신 것 같아. 몇몇 교수님들이 얘기하는 것을 엿듣게 되었거든.

M: 그럴 리가 없어. 교수님만큼 실력 있는 분이 어떻게 해고될 수가 있겠어?

W: 사실, 위원회에서 교수님의 행정 스타일을 좋아하지 않았나봐. 너도 알잖아, Stanley 교수님은 위원회나 그들의 징계 조처들에 대해 전혀 신경 쓰지 않으셨어. 그래서 결국 직장을 잃게 된 거지.

M: 학교로서는 정말 손해. 교수님은 정말 훌륭한 관리자였는데.

W: 그래, 나도 동감이야.

Stance

1 Which best describes the speakers' feeling?

(a) They are worrying about upcoming exams.

(b) They are distrustful of the board members.

(c) They are concerned about a professor's resignation.

(d) They are optimistic about the next administration.

화자들의 감정을 가장 잘 묘사한 것은?

(a) 다가오는 시험에 대해 걱정하고 있다.

(b) 위원회를 불신한다.

(c) 교수의 사임에 대해 걱정한다.

(d) 다음 행정부에 대해 낙관적이다.

해설 학장의 사임에 대한 남녀의 대화이다. 학교로서는 손해라는 남자의 말에 동의한다는 여자의 대답으로 보아 (c)가 정답임을 알 수 있다.

함정 학교 위원회가 교수를 좋아하지 않았다는 내용은 있지만, 그들이 위원회를 불신하는지에 대해서는 알 수 없으므로 (b)는 오답이다.

Detail

2   Why was Professor Stanley fired?

(a) He administered the school as he liked and ignored others.

(b) The board members didn't like the way he administered.

(c) The board members have found a better qualified person.

(d) He was neglecting his work while he was administering.

Stanley 교수는 왜 해고되었는가?

(a) 그는 다른 사람들을 무시하면서 자기 좋은 대로 학교를 운영했다.

(b) 위원회가 그의 관리 방법을 좋아하지 않았다.

(c) 위원회가 더 자질을 갖춘 사람을 찾아냈다.

(d) 운영하는 동안 그는 자신의 일에 소홀했다.

해설 Actually, the board members didn't like his administration methods.(사실, 위원회에서 교수님의 행정 스타일을 좋아하지 않았나 봐.)에서 정답을 찾아볼 수 있다.

함정 교수가 위원회나 그들의 징계조치들에 대해 신경 쓰지 않았다는 말은 있지만, 두 사람의 대화는 부정적인 접근이 아니라는 데에 유의한다. 따라서 두 사람은 (a)의 이유로 교수님이 해고되었다고는 생각하지 않는다.

어휘 resign 사임하다, 사직하다 | post 지위, 직장 | dean 학장 | be fired 해고되다 | overhear 어쩌다 듣게 되다, 엿듣다 | qualified 자격 있는, 실력 있는 | board 위원회 | administration 행정, 관리 | method 수단, 방법 | pay attention to ~에 주의하다 | disciplinary 규율의, 징계의 | ultimately 결국, 마침내 | upcoming 다가오고 있는 | be concerned about ~에 대해 걱정하다 | resignation 사직, 사임

2   Conversation

W: Excuse me, I purchased this CD here.

M: I see...

W: May I exchange it now?

M: Is there any problem with it?

W: Actually my friend bought this for me. I dropped it by mistake and now it's not playing.

M: So the CD was damaged through your mistake, right?

W: But I haven't used it even once. I feel you should exchange it.

M: Well, I will have to talk to my manager about this.

W: 실례지만, 여기서 이 CD를 구입했는데요.

M: 네, 그렇군요….

W: 지금 교환할 수 있을까요?

M: CD에 무슨 문제라도 있습니까?

W: 사실, 친구가 이걸 저에게 사주었어요. 실수로 떨어뜨렸는데, 돌아가지가 않아요.

M: 그러니까 이 CD가 손님의 실수로 망가졌다는 거군요, 그렇죠?

W: 하지만 한번도 사용한 적이 없어요. 바꿔 주셔야 한다고 생각하는데요.

M: 음, 이것에 관해 저희 매니저에게 이야기해야 할 것 같네요.

Stance

1   What can be inferred about the man?

(a) He thinks that the company can fix it in no time.

(b) He thinks he will have to exchange it with a new one.

(c) He feels that the woman will have to pay for a new CD.

(d) He is not sure if the company is liable for its replacement.

남자에 대해 추론할 수 있는 것은?

(a) 회사가 그것을 즉시 고칠 수 있다고 생각한다.

(b) 그것을 새 CD로 교환해 주어야 한다고 생각한다.

(c) 여자가 새 CD에 대해 돈을 내야 할 것이라고 생각한다.

(d) 회사가 교환해 줘야 할 책임이 있는지 확신하지 못한다.

해설 친구에게 선물로 받은 CD가 고장이 나서 교환하러 간 내용이다. CD는 여자가 떨어뜨려서 망가졌기 때문에, 남자는 교환해 줘도 되는지 매니저에게 확인해 봐야 한다고 말하고 있다. 그러므로 정답은 (d)이다.

Detail

2 Why isn't the CD playing?

(a) Because the woman put it into a wrong player.

(b) Because the woman accidentally let it fall.

(c) Because the woman has torn its cover by mistake.

(d) Because the woman bent it to pull it out.

CD는 왜 작동하지 않는가?

(a) 여자가 잘못된 플레이어에 넣었기 때문이다.

(b) 여자가 실수로 떨어뜨렸기 때문이다.

(c) 여자가 실수로 포장을 뜯었기 때문이다.

(d) 여자가 꺼내다가 구부러지게 했기 때문이다.

해설 I dropped it by mistake and now it's not playing.(실수로 떨어뜨렸는데, 돌아가지가 않아요.)라는 여자의 말에 남자가 So the CD was damaged through your mistake, right?라고 다시 확인하고 있는 내용으로 보아 CD는 여자가 떨어뜨려서 망가졌다는 것을 알 수 있다.

어휘 purchase 구입하다 exchange 교환하다
by mistake 실수로 liable 책임을 져야 할
replacement 교환, 대치

3 Monologue

M: Obesity is a serious problem in America. Recent statistics reveal that roughly 33 percent of American adults between the ages of 25 and 74 are overweight. Most obese Americans resort to dieting to shed extra pounds from their bodies; however, that rarely works. Despite that, dieting has become so common that nearly half of American women and a quarter of American men are on diets, estimates a study. Yet, because dieting rarely works, Americans are not getting leaner but fatter. Today, on average, Americans are six pounds heavier than they were in 1960.

M: 비만은 미국에서 심각한 문제입니다. 최근의 통계에 따르면, 25세에서 74세의 연령층 사이의 대략 33퍼센트의 미국 성인들이 과체중이라고 합니다. 대부분의 뚱뚱한 미국 사람들이 몸에 붙어 있는 여분의 살을 없애기 위해 식이요법에 의존하고 있지만, 그것은 거의 효과가 없습니다. 그럼에도 불구하고, 식이요법은 매우 보편화되어 미국 여성의 거의 절반과 미국 남성의 4분의 1이 다이어트를 하고 있다고 한 연구는 추산하고 있습니다. 그러나 식이요법이 거의 효과가 없기 때문에, 미국인들은 점점 마르는게 아니라 점점 뚱뚱해지고 있습니다. 오늘날 미국인들은 몸무게가 1960년보다 평균 6파운드 정도 더 나갑니다.

Function

1 Why does the speaker mention the pounds comparison?

(a) to emphasize that many Americans are fatter now

(b) to show how much weight Americans should lose

(c) to illustrate that their lifestyle has changed a lot

(d) to imply that the average American will gain more weight

화자가 파운드를 비교한 이유는 무엇인가?

(a) 많은 미국 사람들이 지금 더 뚱뚱하다는 것을 강조하기 위해서

(b) 미국 사람들이 몸무게를 얼마나 줄여야 하는지 보여 주기 위해서

(c) 그들의 생활양식이 많이 변했다는 것을 설명하기 위해서

(d) 보통의 미국인이 체중이 더 늘 것이라는 것을 암시하기 위해서

해설 미국 성인의 33%가 과체중인데, 거의 대부분 식이요법에 의존하고 있으나 별로 효과가 없어서 점점 더 뚱뚱해지고 있다는 내용이다. 마지막에 1960년보다 평균 6파운드가 더 나간다고 말한 것은 미국 사람들이 뚱뚱해지고 있다는 것을 다시 한번 강조하기 위한 것이다.

Comprehension

2 Which is correct according to the talk?

(a) Most Americans are on diets.

(b) Almost one third of American adults are overweight.

(c) American children gained 6 pounds last year.

(d) Dieting is helpful to lose weight.

이 이야기에 따르면 옳은 것은 무엇인가?

(a) 대부분의 미국 사람들이 다이어트 중이다.

(b) 미국 성인의 거의 3분의 1이 과체중이다.

(c) 미국 아이들은 지난해보다 6파운드 더 나간다.

(d) 식이요법은 몸무게를 줄이는 데에 도움이 된다.

해설 미국 성인의 비만에 대한 이야기이다. 33%가 과체중이며, 여성의 절반, 남성의 3분이 1이 식이요법을 하고 있으나 별로 효과가 없다는 내용이다. 그러므로 (b)의 내용이 옳다는 것을 알 수 있다.

함정 (a) 대부분의 미국인들이 다이어트 중이라는 언급은 없다. 미국 아이들이 아니라 미국인들이, 지난해가 아니라 1960년보다 6파운드 더 나간다고 되어 있으므로 (c)도 틀린 내용이다.

어휘 obesity 비만 statistics 통계 reveal 드러내다, 나타내다
roughly 대략 overweight 과체중의 obese 살찐, 뚱뚱한
resort to ~에 의지하다, 도움을 청하다 shed 벗어 버리다, 없애다
rarely 거의 ~가 아닌 despite ~에도 불구하고
estimate 추정하다, 어림잡다 work 효과가 있다 lean 여읜, 마른

4 Monologue

M: I am going to put forward my views about the income gap prevalent in our society. There is a large gap between the incomes of the upper and the lower classes, and there is no indication that this gap may be narrowed. <u>Inequality in income</u> is largely due to capitalism, <u>making the rich richer and the poor poorer</u>. Capitalism is responsible <u>for the further widening of the income gap</u> with each growing year. It also <u>gives rise to an unhealthy competition</u> where everybody wants to succeed. The growing global economy has done nothing favorable in this respect. We have to rethink whether the "economic freedom" of capitalism might be better replaced by more <u>government controls and intervention</u>.

M: 우리 사회에 만연되어 있는 소득 격차에 대한 저의 의견을 발표하려 합니다. 상위층과 하위 계층의 소득에는 커다란 차이가 있고, 이러한 격차가 좁혀질 것 같은 기미는 없습니다. 소득에 있어서의 불균형은 주로 자본주의에 기인한 것인데, 부자는 더 부자로 가난한 사람은 더 가난하게 만듭니다. 해가 거듭될수록 소득의 격차가 점점 더 커지는 것은 자본주의 때문입니다. 자본주의는 또한 모든 사람이 성공하기를 원하는 불건전한 경쟁심을 유발합니다. 커져가고 있는 세계 경제는 이런 점에 대해서 아무런 도움이 되지 않았습니다. 우리는 자본주의라는 "경제적인 자유"가 더 많은 정부의 통제와 간섭으로 대체되는 것이 더 좋지 않을지 다시 생각해 봐야 합니다.

Stance

1 What can be inferred about the speaker?

(a) He is concerned about government intervention.

(b) He is doubtful of the indication of income gap.

(c) He is negative about the current capitalism.

(d) He is positive about the global economy.

화자에 대해 추론할 수 있는 것은?

(a) 정부 개입에 대해 걱정하고 있다.

(b) 소득 격차의 징후에 대해 의심스러워한다.

(c) 현재 자본주의에 대해 부정적이다.

(d) 세계 경제에 대해 긍정적이다.

해설 소득의 격차가 날로 커져가고 있고, 그 원인을 자본주의에 두고 있으므로 화자는 현재 자본주의에 대해 부정적이라는 것을 알 수 있다.

Main Idea

2 Which best explains the speaker's opinion?

(a) Globalization has a positive impact on underdeveloped countries.

(b) Government must not intervene in the market.

(c) Capitalism should be changed for a better system.

(d) Income inequality only exists in capitalist societies.

화자의 의견을 가장 잘 설명한 것은?

(a) 세계화는 재개발국들에 긍정적인 영향을 미친다.

(b) 정부는 시장에 개입해서는 안 된다.

(c) 자본주의는 더 나은 체제로 변화되어야 한다.

(d) 소득 불균형은 자본주의 사회에만 존재한다.

해설 소득 격차의 원인을 현재 자본주의라고 보는 화자는 정부의 개입으로 상황을 호전시킬 수 있을 것이라고 제안하고 있다. 그러므로 화자가 말하고자 하는 것은 자본주의가 더 나아져야 한다는 (c)이다.

함정 소득 불균형의 원인이 자본주의이기는 하지만, 자본주의 사회에서만 소득의 불균형이 생긴다는 언급은 없으므로 (d)는 오답이다.

어휘 put forward 제안하다, 제출하다 view 의견, 관점 income gap 소득 격차   prevalent 널리 보급된, 만연한 indication 징조, 징후 inequality 불평등 capitalism 자본주의 give rise to ~을 일으키다, 생기게 하다   competition 경쟁 favorable 호의적인, 적절한 in this respect 이 점에서 intervention 간섭, 중재 underdeveloped country 재개발국, 후진국

PRACTICAL LISTENING

1. d	2. d	3. c	4. a	5. d
6. d	7. d	8. a	9. b	10. d

1 Stance

M: Rita, why didn't you <u>turn in your chemistry assignment</u>?

W: I'm sorry, Mr. Taylor. My computer is <u>out of order</u>.

M: You didn't save your assignment and the computer crashed, right?

W: Yes, and I didn't have any backup.

M: You've been giving the same excuse <u>for all your late submissions</u>.

W: Well, Mr. Taylor, this time <u>it's genuine</u>.

M: I hope this is the last time I hear that excuse.

W: <u>I will never let you down</u> again.

M: I've also heard that before.

M: Rita, 화학숙제를 왜 제출하지 않았니?

W: 죄송합니다, Taylor 선생님. 제 컴퓨터가 고장 나서요.

M: 숙제를 저장하지도 않았는데, 갑자기 컴퓨터가 멈춰버렸다, 이거니?

W: 네, 그리고 백업 받아 놓은 것도 없어요.

M: 제출이 늦어질 때마다 계속 똑같은 변명을 하는구나.

W: Taylor 선생님. 이번에는 진짜예요.

M: 이제 그런 변명을 듣는 게 마지막이면 좋겠구나.

W: 다시는 실망시키지 않을 게요.

M: 그것도 전에 들어본 이야기구나.

Q Which of the following best describes the man's feeling?

(a) satisfied

(b) sad

(c) worried

(d) disappointed

남자의 심정을 가장 잘 묘사한 것은?

(a) 만족스러운

(b) 슬픈

(c) 걱정되는

(d) 실망스러운

해설 화학숙제를 제출하지 않은 여자에게 남자 선생님이 그 이유를 묻고 있는 대화이다. 여자는 숙제를 하다가 컴퓨터가 갑자기 고장이 나서 제출하지 못했다고 그 이유를 설명하지만, 선생님은 숙제가 늦어질 때마다 계속해서 똑같은 변명을 하고 있는 여자의 말을 믿지 못한다. 이런 상황에서 선생님은 실망스러운 심정일 것이다.

함정 슬프다거나 걱정스러운 마음은 아니다.

어휘 turn in 건네다, 제출하다 | chemistry 화학 | assignment 숙제, 과제, 임무 | out of order 고장 난 | save 저장하다, 보관하다 | crash 작동하지 않다, 갑자기 기능을 멈추다 | backup 백업, 여벌, 지원 | excuse 변명, 구실, 핑계 | submission 제출(물), 복종, 굴복 | genuine 진짜의

2

M: In today's talk on geriatrics, we will learn about osteoarthritis. This condition commonly affects the weight-bearing joints, hands, knees and lower back. It is prevalent in some form among most adults above 40, especially in joints that are used repeatedly or stressed during physical activity. While obesity is known to aggravate osteoarthritis, particularly in the weight-bearing joints, it is possible for individuals to develop it even if they are not overweight. Currently there is no known method of prevention or cure for osteoarthritis although there are many simple ways to mitigate its severity.

M: 오늘 이야기할 노인병학에서 골관절염에 대해 배울 겁니다. 이 병은 일반적으로 몸무게를 지탱해 주는 관절, 손, 무릎, 허리 아래쪽에 영향을 줍니다. 40세 이상 대부분의 성인들에게 어떤 형태로든 만연해 있는데, 특히 신체 활동 중 반복적으로 쓰거나 힘이 가해지는 관절에 생깁니다. 비만이 골관절염 중에서도 특히 무게를 지탱하는 관절을 악화시키는 것으로 알려져 있고, 과체중이 아니더라도 그런 증상이 나타날 수 있습니다. 현재로는 알려져 있는 골관절염 예방책이나 치료제는 없지만, 고통을 완화해 주는 간단한 방법은 여러 가지 있습니다.

Q Which is correct about osteoarthritis according to the lecture?

(a) It is primarily caused by obesity.

(b) Its effects cannot be minimized.

(c) It can be prevented only by regular exercise.

(d) It is common among people over 40.

이 강의에 따르면 골관절염에 관해 옳은 것은?

(a) 주로 비만 때문에 생긴다.

(b) 증상을 줄일 수 없다.

(c) 규칙적인 운동만으로도 예방할 수 있다.

(d) 40세 이상인 사람들에게 흔한 병이다.

해설 중년 이후 흔히 걸리는 골관절염의 증상과 치료에 대한 설명이다. It is prevalent in some form among most adults above 40(40세 이상 대부분의 성인들에게 널리 퍼져 있다)라는 표현을 들었다면 쉽게 풀 수 있는 문제이다. prevalent를 common으로 바꾼 (d)가 정답이다.

함정 (a) 비만이 이 병을 악화시킬 수는 있으나 비만으로 인한 질병은 아니다. (b) 증상을 줄일 수 있는 방법이 많다고 했다. (c)는 언급된 바가 없다.

어휘 geriatrics 노인병학 | osteoarthritis 골관절염 | weight-bearing 체중을 지탱하는 | lower back 허리 아래쪽 | prevalent 널리 퍼져 있는, 보급된 | physical activity 신체 활동 | obesity 비만 | aggravate 악화시키다 | cure 치료법 | mitigate 누그러뜨리다, 완화하다 | severity 가혹, 격렬함

3 Function

W: Can you have a look at my computer?

M: Why? Is there a problem?

W: I'm unable to get online.

M: How long have you had that problem?

W: Well, it was working fine until last night. This

morning when <u>I switched it on</u>, though, I couldn't <u>access the web</u>.

M: Oh, I see. I think I see what's wrong.

W: What is it?

M: Do you remember what was wrong with Susan's computer?

W: Oh, no.

M: Yes. She took it to the service center, but <u>it was in vain</u>. She had to buy a new one.

W: I still want to try to take it to the service center.

W: 내 컴퓨터 좀 한번 봐줄래?

M: 왜? 문제 있니?

W: 온라인이 안 되네.

M: 얼마 동안 그랬어?

W: 어젯밤까지는 괜찮았는데, 오늘 아침에 컴퓨터를 켜니까 웹에 접속이 안 돼.

M: 어, 알겠다. 뭐가 잘못됐는지 알 것 같아.

W: 뭔데?

M: Susan의 컴퓨터에 뭐가 잘못되었었는지 기억나?

W: 아, 안 돼.

M: 맞아. 그녀도 서비스 센터에 가져가 봤지만 허사였잖아. 새로운 것으로 하나 사야 했어.

W: 나는 그래도 서비스 센터에 가져가 볼래.

Q Why does the man mention Susan's computer?

(a) to tell the woman to take the computer to the service center

(b) to explain that the man has fixed her computer

(c) to suggest the woman buy another computer

(d) to imply that the problem is not very serious

남자가 Susan의 컴퓨터를 언급한 이유는?

(a) 여자에게 컴퓨터를 서비스 센터에 가져가라고 말하려고

(b) 남자가 그녀의 컴퓨터를 고쳤다고 설명하려고

(c) 여자에게 다른 컴퓨터를 사라고 제안하려고

(d) 문제가 심각하지 않다는 것을 암시하려고

해설 여자의 컴퓨터가 온라인 연결이 안 돼서 웹 접속이 불가능한 상태이다. 컴퓨터를 살펴본 남자는 Susan의 컴퓨터가 그랬던 것처럼, 새로운 것으로 하나 사야 할 것이라고 말하고 있다. 그러므로 정답은 (c)이다.

어휘 **have a look at** ~을 한번 보다
switch on ~의 스위치를 틀다 ｜ **access** ~에 접근하다, 도달하다
in vain 무익하게, 헛되이

4

W: Ken, what's the time?

M: It's 3:30 p.m.

W: Oh God. I'll be fired! <u>I need to rush</u>!

M: What happened? Why are you <u>in such a hurry</u>?

W: I have <u>an appointment with a client</u> at 4 o'clock. That client is very important to my boss.

M: You still have some time. Don't worry. Where's your meeting?

W: It's on Middleton Avenue. <u>The thing is that I have to pick up some packages</u> at the office first.

M: I see why you don't have much time.

W: Hey! Could you drive me there?

M: I can't. I've got something to do at 4:00 p.m. <u>Why don't you call a cab</u>? It will be the fastest way to get there.

W: Maybe I should call my boss.

W: Ken, 몇 시야?

M: 오후 3시 30분.

W: 어, 이런. 잘리겠다. 서둘러야 해.

M: 무슨 일이야? 왜 그렇게 서두르는데?

W: 4시에 고객과 약속이 있어. 우리 사장님한테 매우 중요한 고객이야.

M: 아직 시간이 좀 있어. 걱정하지 마. 어디서 만나기로 했는데?

W: 미들턴 가에서. 그런데 먼저 사무실에서 물건들을 좀 가져가야 하는데.

M: 시간이 왜 충분하지 않은지 알겠다.

W: 저기! 거기까지 태워다 줄 수 있어?

M: 안 돼. 4시에 해야 할 일이 있어. 택시를 부르지 그래? 그게 거기로 가는 가장 빠른 길일 거야.

W: 사장님한테 전화하는 것이 좋겠어.

Q Which is correct according to the conversation?

(a) The woman will be late for an appointment.

(b) The man has a date with someone at 4:00 p.m.

(c) The woman forgot the location of Middleton Avenue.

(d) The man wants to accompany the woman.

이 대화에 따르면 옳은 것은?

(a) 여자는 약속에 늦을 것이다.

(b) 남자는 오후 4시에 어떤 사람과 데이트가 있다.

(c) 여자는 미들턴 가의 위치를 잊었다.

(d) 남자는 여자와 동행하기를 원한다.

해설 여자는 오후 4시에 중요한 고객과 약속이 있는데, 지금 시각이 3시 30분이다. 서두르는 여자에게 시간이 좀 있지 않느냐는 남자의 말에 사무실에서 물건을 좀 가져가야 한다고 하고 있으므로 여자는 약속에 늦을 것이라고 한 (a)가 정답이다.

함정 남자는 오후 4시에 할 일이 있다고 했으며, 데이트가 있는지는 알 수 없으므로 (b)는 오답이다.

어휘 fire 해고하다 │ rush 돌진하다, 서두르다 │
in a hurry 급히, 서둘러 │ location 위치, 소재, 장소 │
accompany ~와 동행하다, 함께 하다, ~을 동반하다

5 Function

M: In local news, recent figures show that almost 50% of people with teaching degrees from this state do not teach at local schools. <u>Upon graduation</u>, they often instead move to larger states <u>where the starting pay for teachers is much higher</u>. Worse, only a very small percentage of new teachers <u>elect to teach in the state's rural areas</u>, where the need for teachers is greatest. Of the teachers who do begin their careers in local schools, one-quarter reportedly leave within two years. Among the reasons for <u>this attrition</u> are poor pay and <u>inadequate administrative backing</u>. The Council for Education has responded to these findings by announcing immediate steps to resolve the situation.

M: 지역 뉴스입니다. 최근 수치로 볼 때 우리 주(州)에서 교직 학위를 받은 사람의 50%가 우리 지역 학교에서 가르치고 있지 않은 것으로 나타났습니다. 졸업을 하면서 이들은 교사 초봉이 훨씬 높은 더 큰 주(州)로 이주합니다. 더 심각한 것은 신입 교사들 중 아주 적은 퍼센트만이 시골 지역에서 가르치기를 선택하는데, 사실 이곳에서의 교사 수요는 매우 큽니다. 지역 학교에서 교직 생활을 시작한 교사들 가운데 1/4이 2년 내에 그곳을 떠난다는 보고가 있습니다. 이런 이직 원인 가운데에는 적은 월급과 불충분한 행정 지원이 있습니다. 교육위원회는 이 같은 상황을 해결하기 위해 즉각적인 조치를 취할 것이라고 발표하는 것으로 이 결과에 대응했습니다.

Q Why does the speaker mention poor pay?

(a) to emphasize that it is the consequence of administrative failure

(b) to indicate that it is the first thing teachers should consider

(c) to imply that teachers are getting poorly paid

(d) to suggest that it is one of the first things to be mended

화자가 적은 월급을 언급한 이유는?

(a) 그것이 행정 실패의 결과임을 강조하기 위해서

(b) 그것이 교사들이 고려해야 하는 첫 번째 것이라고 암시하기 위해서

(c) 교사들이 불충분한 보수를 받는다는 것을 암시하기 위해서

(d) 그것이 개선되어야 할 첫 번째 일임을 제시하기 위해서

해설 지역 학교 교사들 상당 부분이 보다 큰 도시에서 교직 생활을 시작하고, 지역 학교에서 시작하는 교사들도 2년 내에 1/4이 적은 봉급이나 불충분한 처우에 대한 불만으로 그곳을 떠난다고 했다. 화자가 적은 월급에 대해 언급한 이유는 월급이 개선되어야 한다는 의견을 개진하기 위해서 이므로 (d)가 정답이다.

어휘 figure 수치 │ teaching degree 교직 학위 │
elect 고르다, 결정하다 │ rural 지방의, 시골의 (↔ urban) │
reportedly 보도에 따르면 │ attrition 마찰, 마모, (수의) 감소, 축소 │
inadequate 불충분한, 부적절한 │
administrative 관리상의, 행정상의

6

M: Hi, what's that book?

W: It's a Sherlock Holmes novel.

M: What's the title?

W: *The Criminal*.

M: Oh! *The Criminal*? Have you seen the movie <u>based on it</u>?

W: No, <u>I guess you have, though</u>.

M: Yes, <u>the story is excellent</u>. Can I <u>borrow the book</u>?

W: But you already know the story.

M: Yeah, but <u>I want to compare it with the movie</u>.

M: 안녕, 그 책은 뭐야?

W: 셜록 홈즈의 소설이야.

M: 제목이 뭔데?

W: 『범죄자』.

M: 『범죄자』? 이걸로 만든 영화 봤니?

W: 아니, 근데 너는 봤을 것 같은데.

M: 그래, 스토리가 훌륭하지. 이 책 좀 빌려줄래?

W: 그런데 너는 스토리를 이미 다 알고 있잖아.

M: 그래, 하지만 영화랑 비교해 보고 싶어.

Q What can be inferred about the man?

(a) He has seen many Sherlock Holmes movies.

(b) He wants to see the movie based on the book.

(c) He does not like the story of the book.

(d) He has never read the novel before.

대화에 근거하여 남자에 대해 추론할 수 있는 것은?

(a) 남자는 셜록 홈즈의 영화를 많이 보았다.

(b) 남자는 책을 토대로 한 영화를 보고 싶어 한다.

(c) 남자는 그 책의 스토리를 좋아하지 않는다.

(d) 남자는 전에 그 소설을 읽어 본 적이 없다.

해설 여자가 가지고 있는 셜록 홈즈의 소설책 『범죄자』에 관한 두 사람의 대화이다. 남자는 그 소설을 원작으로 한 영화를 본 적이 있어서, 책의 스토리를 이미 다 알고 있지만, 영화와 비교해서 보고 싶다며 그 책을 빌려달라고 하고 있다. 따라서 정답은 (d)이다.

오답 (a) 셜록 홈즈의 영화를 많이 보았는지는 알 수 없다. 남자는 이미 그 영화를 봤고, 또 스토리가 훌륭하다고 했기 때문에 (b)와 (c)는 틀린 설명이다.

어휘 novel 소설   criminal 범인, 범죄자
based on ~에 기초한, ~에 근거한
compare (with) 비교하다, 견주다

7   Stance

M: My first duty is to remind everyone here that the proceedings of this union meeting are <u>strictly confidential</u>. This binding confidentiality was a part of the legal rules you agreed to when you joined the union. This is also important to our strategy. <u>Our position would be in jeopardy</u> if the press came to know of it. Now, as you all know the contract negotiations have failed and the company management is <u>being unhelpful as usual</u>. They refuse to increase our wages despite the fact that the company <u>earned record profits</u> this year and gave the board of directors over $30 million in stock options. In this situation I propose that we should <u>vote on a strike</u>. Those in favor of this plan please raise your hands.

M: 저의 첫 번째 임무는 여기 계신 여러분 모두에게 이번 조합 회담의 모든 사항들이 철저히 비밀에 붙여진다는 것을 상기시켜 드리는 일입니다. 이 비밀 유지의 의무는 여러분이 조합에 참여하실 때 이미 동의한 법적 조항의 일부입니다. 그리고 또한 우리의 전략에도 중요합니다. 만약 언론에서 이 일을 알게 된다면 우리의 입장은 위기에 봉착될 것입니다. 자 이제 모두들 계약 협상이 실패했고 회사 경영진 또한 언제나처럼 도움이 되지 않는다는 것을 아실 겁니다. 그들은 올해 사상 최대 이익을 올렸으며, 이사진들에게는 스톡옵션으로 3천만 달러를 지급했으면서도 우리의 임금 인상은 거부했습니다. 이런 상황에서 저는 파업 찬반 투표를 실시해야 한다고 제안하는 바입니다. 이 계획에 찬성하시는 분은 손을 들어주시기 바랍니다.

Q   Which best describes the attitude of the speaker?

(a) astonished

(b) relieved

(c) supportive

(d) furious

화자의 태도를 가장 잘 묘사한 것은?

(a) 놀란

(b) 안도하는

(c) 지지하는

(d) 격노한

해설 노동조합의 비밀 회담에서 대표가 연설하고 있다. 노동조합이 원하는 협상안이 경영진에 의해 부결되었기 때문에 파업 찬반 투표를 하자는 내용이므로 화자는 회사의 부당함에 대해 격노해 있음을 알 수 있다. 그러므로 정답은 (d)이다.

어휘 duty 임무   proceeding 진행, 처리, 의사(록)
union 연합, (노동) 조합   strictly 엄격하게
confidential 기밀의, 내밀한   binding 의무적인, 구속력 있는
confidentiality 기밀성, 비밀성
be in jeopardy 위험에 빠지다, 위태롭다
company management 회사 경영진
board of directors 이사진
stock option 스톡옵션, 주식 매입 선택권   strike 파업, 쟁의
in favor of ~에 찬성하는

8

W: One more hospital has been demolished <u>to enhance the cost efficiency</u> of our provincial healthcare system. A look at <u>the long waiting lists</u> for treatment and the serious shortage of medical facilities currently in place will show that this was a reckless decision. It has become normal to <u>pull down</u> old hospitals without waiting for new ones to come up. Even where efforts at rebuilding them are underway, work has been delayed <u>due to lack of funds</u>. If these are the so-called efficiency measures being followed, we can be sure that the bid to improve the healthcare system is <u>doomed to failure</u> and that the prevailing lack of healthcare professionals in this area will continue.

W: 우리 지방 의료 체계의 비용 효율성을 높이기 위해 병원 한 곳이 또 문을 닫았습니다. 최근 벌어지고 있는 긴 치료 대기자 명단들과 심각한 의료 시설 부족 사태를 보면 이는 무모한 결정이었다고 볼 수 있습니다. 새 병원이 다 지어지기 전에 오래된 병원을 허무는 것은 일반적인 일이 되었습니다. 재건축하려는 노력이 추진 중이지만, 자금 부족으로 연기되었습니다. 이러한 것이 소위 효율적인 방안이라면 의료 체계를 향상시키기 위한 시도는 결국 실패하게 되어 있으며, 만성적인 전문 의료진의 부족 현상도 계속될 것이 확실합니다.

Q Which statement would the speaker likely agree with?

(a) Cost efficiency measures in healthcare have been too extreme.

(b) Old hospitals must be torn down to make way for new ones.

(c) Better training for healthcare professionals is absolutely essential.

(d) Good hospitals will attract more healthcare workers to the province.

다음 중 화자가 가장 동의할 것 같은 내용은 무엇인가?

(a) 의료계의 비용 효율 정책은 너무 지나치다.

(b) 오래된 병원은 새 병원에 자리를 내줘야 한다.

(c) 전문 의료진의 보다 나은 훈련이 절대적으로 필요하다.

(d) 좋은 병원은 의료 종사자들을 그 지역으로 오게 할 것이다.

해설 의료 체계의 문제를 제기하는 지문이다. 비용 효율성만을 추구하다 보니 의료 서비스 여건이 현저히 떨어지고 있음을 지적하고 있다. 두 번째 문장에서 화자가 비용 효율 정책을 reckless decision이라고 한 데서 이 정책에 대한 화자의 태도를 분명히 알 수 있다.

함정 본문에 healthcare professionals가 언급되었으나, 인력이 부족하다는 얘기이지 훈련이 필요하다는 내용은 없으므로 (c)는 오답이다.

어휘 demolish 부수다, 폭파하다 enhance 향상시키다
shortage 부족 underway 진행 중인
bid to do ~하려는 시도, 노력
be doomed to (나쁘게) ~될 운명이다
prevailing 널리 보급되어 있는, 유행하고 있는
tear down 헐다, 부수다
make way for ~에게 길을 비키다, 양보하다

9

M: Have you been to the new bookstore in Jongno?

W: Yes, I went there just last week.

M: <u>Did you like the place</u>?

W: Well, there's <u>not much space inside</u>, but the collection of books they have is unique.

M: That's true. I found many books on Dokdo <u>which you can rarely find in other stores</u>.

W: Exactly, and <u>the lack of space hardly matters</u> since it has so many good books there.

M: Yeah, <u>I really feel like going there again</u>.

M: 종로에 새로 생긴 서점에 가봤니?

W: 응. 바로 지난주에 갔었어.

M: 좋았어?

W: 음, 내부 공간은 그다지 넓지 않지만, 거기 있는 책들은 정말 진기해.

M: 사실이야. 다른 서점에서는 좀처럼 찾을 수 없는 독도에 관한 책들이 많이 있었거든.

W: 맞아, 그리고 좋은 책들이 아주 많기 때문에 공간이 부족한 건 거의 문제가 되질 않아.

M: 응, 거기 정말 다시 가고 싶다.

Q What is mainly being discussed about the bookstore?

(a) its small size and location

(b) how the man and woman feel about it

(c) its unique collection of books

(d) its shortage of books on Dokdo

서점에 대한 무엇이 주로 이야기되고 있는가?

(a) 그 서점의 작은 규모와 위치

(b) 남자와 여자가 그 서점을 어떻게 생각하는지

(c) 그 서점의 진기한 책들

(d) 독도에 관한 책 부족

해설 종로에 새로 생긴 서점에 관한 두 사람의 대화이다. 내부는 그리 크지 않지만, 진기한 책들이 아주 많기 때문에, 공간이 작은 것은 별로 문제가 되지 않는다고 대화이다. 즉 두 사람은 그 서점을 각자 어떻게 생각하고 있는지를 이야기하고 있기 때문에 정답은 (b)이다.

함정 두 사람은 지금 서점의 작은 규모만을 이야기하거나, 그곳의 진기한 책들만을 이야기하는 것이 아니라, 그것들을 다 포함한 서점에 관한 전반적인 느낌을 이야기하고 있는 것이므로, (a)와 (c) 자체가 정답이 되지는 못한다. (d) 또한 독도에 관한 책이 부족하다는 내용의 대화는 아니다.

어휘 have been to ~에 가본 적이 있다 space 공간, 장소, 여지
collection 수집(물), 더미 unique 독특한, 특이한, 진기한, 훌륭한
rarely 좀처럼 ~하지 않는 lack of ~의 부족, ~이 없음
hardly 거의 ~않는 matter 문제가 되다, 중요하다
feel like -ing ~하고 싶다 shortage 부족, 결핍

10

M: Old English <u>went through multiple changes</u> before it became Middle and then Modern English — the language we use widely today. While some of the changes were in grammar, <u>the most significant ones</u> were in vocabulary. There has not been <u>a linear progression</u> from Old to Modern English, with some words simply changing in spelling or pronunciation. Rather, during its development English has borrowed very heavily from other languages. It might surprise you to know that only about 20% of the words in the Modern English vocabulary originated in Old English.

The remaining 80% comes largely from foreign sources, notably Latin, Greek and Old Norse. <u>In any event</u>, a person speaking Old English would be <u>incomprehensible</u> to one speaking Modern English.

M: 고대 영어는 중기 영어를 거쳐 오늘날 우리가 폭넓게 사용하고 있는 언어인 현대 영어가 되기까지 다양한 변화를 겪었습니다. 일부 변화는 문법에 해당되지만 가장 중요한 변화는 어휘에서 나타납니다. 고대 영어에서 현대 영어로 발전해 오면서 단순히 철자나 발음상의 변화 같은 직선적인(1차원적) 변화만 있었던 것은 아닙니다. 오히려 그간의 발달 과정에서 영어는 외래어에서 상당 부분을 차용해왔습니다. 현대 영어의 어휘 가운데 고작 20%만이 고대 영어에 기원을 두고 있다는 사실을 알면 아마 놀라실 것입니다. 나머지 80%는 대부분 다른 나라의 언어, 특히 라틴어나 그리스어, 그리고 고대 노르웨이 말에서 온 것입니다. 어하튼 고대 영어를 하는 사람의 말이 현대 영어를 하는 사람에게는 무슨 말인지 이해하기 어려울 것입니다.

Q What is the main topic of the lecture?

(a) the cause of changes in Old English

(b) the borrowed words used commonly in English

(c) the evolution of vocabulary in Old English

(d) the history of Modern English vocabulary

강의의 주요 화제는?

(a) 고대 영어의 변화 원인

(b) 영어에서 일반적으로 사용되는 외래어(차용어)들

(c) 고대 영어에서의 어휘 발달

(d) 현대 영어 어휘의 역사

[해설] 현대 영어 어휘의 대부분은 고대 영어의 어휘와 상당 부분 다르다는 내용의 강의이다. 여기서 고대와 현대 영어 어휘가 어떻게 다른지 설명하고 있으므로 정답은 (d)이다.

[함정] 현대 영어의 80%가 외래어일 정도로 고대 영어가 많이 남아 있지 않다고 했다. 그러나 강의의 초점은 '외래어'가 아니라 현대 영어, 그 중에서도 어휘의 '변화'에 있다는 점에 주목하자.

[어휘] go through ~을 겪다, 경험하다 multiple 다양한, 복잡한 widely 넓게, 광범위하게 linear 선의, 직선의, 1차원의 progression 진행, 경과, 발달 originate 기원하다, 유래하다 Norse (고대) 노르웨이 사람, 노르웨이 말 incomprehensible 이해할 수 없는 borrowed word 차용어 evolution 발달, 진보, 진화

A

1. linear	2. originate
3. collection	4. demolish
5. enhance	6. prevailing
7. bid	8. jeopardy
9. strike	10. inadequate
11. rush	12. accompany
13. access	14. obese
15. excuse	16. genuine

1. straight from one stage to another

2. to begin to happen or exist

3. a group of similar things that you have deliberately acquired, usually over a period of time

4. to destroy a building completely

5. to improve the value, quality, or attractiveness of something

6. widespread, general, popular or common

7. an attempt to obtain something or do it

8. If someone or something is in this, they are in a dangerous situation where they might fail, be lost, or be destroyed.

9. stopping work for a period of time, usually in order to try to get better pay or conditions

10. not enough of something or it is not good enough

11. to go somewhere quickly or to do something as soon as you can, because you are very eager to do it

12. to go somewhere with someone

13. to have the opportunity or right to see information or equipment or use it

14. extremely fat

15. a reason which you give in order to explain why something has been done or has not been done

16. It refers to things such as emotions that are real and not pretended.

B

1. b	2. b	3. a	4. a	5. a

1. Stanley 교수님이 학장 자리에서 사임했다.

   (a) Professor Stanley has taken over his post as dean.

   (b) **Professor Stanley has resigned from his post as dean.**

2. 대부분의 뚱뚱한 미국 사람들이 여분의 살을 없애기 위해 식이요법에 의존한다.

   (a) Most obese Americans shed extra pounds through a diet.

   (b) **Most obese Americans resort to dieting to shed extra pounds.**

3. 미국 사람들은 몸무게가 1960년보다 6파운드 정도 더 나갑니다.

   (a) **Americans are six pounds heavier than they were in 1960.**

   (b) Americans in 1960 weighed 6 pounds more than they are now.

4. 이러한 격차가 좁혀질 것 같은 기미는 없습니다.

   (a) **There is no indication that this gap may be narrowed.**

   (b) This gap will not be narrowed without any indication.

5. 제출이 늦어질 때마다 계속 똑같은 변명을 하는구나.

   (a) **You've been giving the same excuse for all your late submissions.**

   (b) You've been excused all the time for all your late submissions.

C

1. **This condition commonly affects the weight-bearing joints.**

2. **There are many simple ways to mitigate its severity.**

3. **Do you remember what was wrong with Susan's computer?**

4. **I have to pick up some packages at the office first.**

5. **The starting pay for teachers is much higher.**

1. the weight-bearing joints / commonly affects / this condition

2. many simple ways / there are / to mitigate its severity

3. what was wrong / do you remember / with Susan's computer

4. I have to pick up / at the office first / some packages

5. is much higher / the starting pay / for teachers

D

1. a   2. a   3. b   4. a   5. a

1. Only a very small percentage of new teachers elect to teach in rural areas.

   (a) **Only a few teachers choose rural areas for their first position.**

   (b) Only a few new teachers stay in rural areas to teach.

2. Our position would be in jeopardy if the press came to know of it.

   (a) **We will be in trouble if the press finds out about it.**

   (b) We might put the press in danger if they come to know of it.

3. I propose that we should vote on a strike.

   (a) I suggest that we should go on strike.

   (b) **I propose that we decide whether to go on strike or not.**

4. The bid to improve the healthcare system is doomed to failure.

   (a) **The effort to improve the healthcare system will eventually fail.**

   (b) The attempts to improve the healthcare system will overcome failure.

5. Only about 20% of the words in the Modern English vocabulary originated in Old English.

   (a) **Only 20% of Old English words survived in Modern English.**

   (b) Most of Modern English words can be found in Old English.

AIM HIGH LISTENING

청취의 8가지 핵심 Question Types

토플, 텝스 등 각종 청취 테스트의 핵심적인 문제 유형을 면밀히 분석하여 세분하였다. 모든 유형의 청취 시험에 완벽하게 대비할 수 있도록 다양하고도 근본적인 listening skill들을 연습하도록 구성하였다.

다양한 형태 및 주제에 대한 청취

여러 유형의 테스트에서 접할 수 있는 강의, 연구 결과, 방송, 연설 등의 다양한 담화문과, 일상생활에서 일어날 수 있는 실질적인 대화를 청취함으로써 다양한 청취 형태와 주제에 익숙해지도록 하였다.

소리로 익히는 청취 훈련

청취 훈련을 위해서는 눈으로 읽고 손으로 쓰는 훈련보다는 소리를 듣고 익히며 그 표현을 소리로 인식하고, 같은 뜻이나 비슷한 표현 또한 소리로 인식하는 것이 중요하다. 따라서 읽거나 쓰는 것이 아닌, sound로 익히고 sound로 확인하는 다양한 청취 훈련을 하도록 구성하였다.

Guided Listening 훈련

Listening Notes를 통해 청취하는 내용의 핵심 정보를 메모하는 것은 물론 내용의 전체적인 흐름을 머리로 이해하는 훈련이 되도록 하였다. 청취 지문의 전형적인 구조에 익숙해짐으로써 '예측 청취'를 가능케 하여 전반적인 청해 실력을 향상시킬 수 있다.

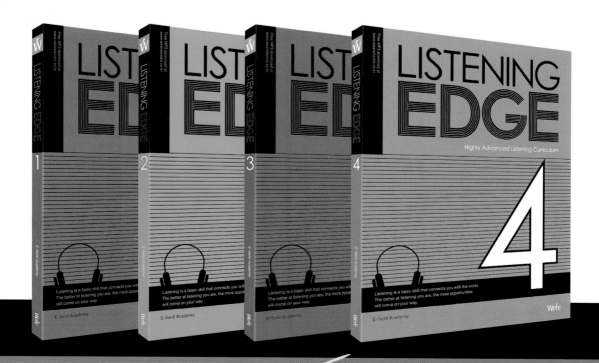